The Professor's Table

The Intelligent Woman's Guide to Good Cooking

The Professor's Table

The Intelligent Woman's Guide to Good Cooking

Evelyn Adams

Illustrations by H. Peter Kahn

South Brunswick and New York: **A. S. Barnes and Company**
London: **Thomas Yoseloff Ltd**

A. S. Barnes and Company, Inc.
Cranbury, New Jersey 08512

Thomas Yoseloff Ltd
108 New Bond Street
London W1Y OQX, England

ISBN 0-498-07606-7
Printed in the United States of America

CONTENTS

Acknowledgments   7

PART I   The Making of a Cook   11

SECTION A   15
Teaching Grandmother to Suck Eggs   15
(*An examination of basic cooking techniques*)
1. The Egg   16
2. Baking   41
3. Sauces   69
4. Meat and Potatoes   86

SECTION B   108
Move Over, Escoffier   108
(*The three techniques of preparation*)
5. Hash   109
6. Stuffing and Boning   129

PART II   The Cook's Repertoire   145

SECTION A   147
Windfalls and Emergencies   147
(*Cooking and preparation techniques applied to
general problems that every cook must face*)
7. Something for Nothing   148
8. By-products   172
9. The Sudden Guest   184

SECTION B   202
Guest List   202
(*Application of the techniques to the well-tempered menu*)
10. Of Feasts   203
11. Picnics   225
12. Feeding the Lions   248
13. From Ice-Breaker to Jaw-Breaker   268

Index   275

ACKNOWLEDGMENTS

For individual recipes, used as received, that appear in the text, I wish to thank Eleanor Malott, Helen Bristol, Mina Ross, Sarah Neblett, Chiyoko Ichikawa, Victor Lange, Maud Brown, Hermie-Frances Kinkeldy, and Hasmig Trittau.

Many others of the recipes here used started life out as the special creations of other people, but have been so altered that their creators would not perhaps wish to acknowledge them. By now they are anonymous or at least as much my own as anyone's. To all cooks near and far from whom I have drawn, my warmest thanks.

Special mention must be made of the excellent work done by Marcia Haney in organizing and typing the original material. I am also grateful to Lisa Robinson and Piquette Cushing.

The Professor's Table
The Intelligent Woman's Guide to Good Cooking

MEASURES

	American	English
1 cup of breadcrumbs (fresh)	1½ oz.	3 oz.
1 cup of flour or other powdered grains	4 oz.	5 oz.
1 cup of sugar	7 oz.	8 oz.
1 cup of icing sugar	4½ oz.	5 oz.
1 cup of butter or other fats	8 oz.	8 oz.
1 cup of raisins, etc.	5 oz.	6 oz.
1 cup of grated cheese	4 oz.	4 oz.
1 cup of syrup, etc.	12 oz.	14 oz.

1 English pint	20 fluid ounces
1 American pint	16 fluid ounces
1 American cup	8 fluid ounces
8 American tablespoons	4 fluid ounces
1 American tablespoon	½ fluid ounce
3 American teaspoons	½ fluid ounce
1 English tablespoon	⅔ to 1 fluid ounce (approx.)
1 English tablespoon	4 teaspoons

The American measuring tablespoon holds ¼-oz. flour

Part I

The Making of a Cook, like the making of a sculptor or a lawyer, starts with a strong interest. That interest, directed and disciplined by the intelligence, develops an expert. When talent is present as well, an artist evolves. But anyone, given interest in a subject and normal intelligence, can master any field he chooses to the point at least of adequate performance.

The born cook and the made cook are more alike than superficial observation might suggest. Whereas the born cook might put together a dish without benefit of recipe and the made cook would use one, each of them perceives the relationship of the ingredients to each other and understands the reasons for the particular technique of cooking employed. The made cook also may dispense with recipes after a certain amount of experience.

Recipes themselves are a kind of shorthand and guarantee very little until one knows the meaning of their cryptic injunctions: "cream the butter," "beat until light," "fold in," "stir until thick," "bake until set" and many others. They are in great part a collection of clichés which must be critically re-examined to be understood.

This sort of problem was demonstrated vividly to me when I came to deal with a group of women, all experienced cooks, who wanted to explore the empyrean of the *haute cuisine* and asked me to take them in charge. For an early session I had had prepared a copy of the Pound Cake recipe for each person, and after reading it each one of the five started to work around the large table in the dining room. Immediately questions arose and differences began to appear in the creaming of the butter. So the recipes were annotated. When the flour had been added and beaten in, more notes were made to indicate what the texture of the mixture should be at the time the eggs were added. Meanwhile individuals were making notes in the margins about what muscles to use while beating, how to hold the hand, speed, rhythm, etc. "How do we know when the eggs are beaten enough?" was the next question. And so it went. By the time the two-and-a-half-hour session was over, and the cakes were cooling gloriously on the racks, I was exhausted, and the recipes were so interlined and overwritten as to be almost unrecognizable. Even today, after several years of working with this group, now fourteen in strength, by which time I have learned to anticipate most of the gaps in the original recipe, I still find members of the group adding notes that presumably they find indispensable for the production of a perfect result. What these people were interested in was not merely creating an edible of even superlative version of a dish; it was in something more fundamental: an anatomy of cookery from fingers to forks.

So a general approach to the whole subject began to take form. We started with an ingredient, the egg for example, in its simplest aspect and followed its "complication" through the addition of first liquids then solids until we had reached the point where the egg was no longer the prime ingredient but merely auxiliary. We did much the same thing for flour, starting with the simple combinations and going on to the more elaborate. With each added ingredient not only flavor was changed but texture as well, and the actual cooking times and temperatures had to be altered. The handling of the material had to be different when proportions were changed. Most staggering of all, we discovered that the walls between certain sections of the menu crumbled when we viewed the whole from our new vantage point. The treatment of the egg either as prime ingredient, auxiliary, or merely supplementary took us into appetizers, main dishes, sauces, desserts, vegetable dishes and soups. Concentrating on flour, we ranged through breads, pastry, cakes, sauces, soups, supplementary dishes for the main course, and so on. One could not learn how to make a soufflé without automatically having his knowledge of cake-making increased.

Meanwhile something else was happening. We were discovering that the multitude of dishes in the many culinary cultures of the world are not so strange and unrelated as they seem at first glance. Hungarian noodles, Italian ravioli and Chinese egg rolls are all just variations on a theme. If you can make one you can make all; the dough is the thing. We reached the same kind of conclusion by studying manual techniques. Rolling out the thin sheets of noodle dough for Chinese egg rolls is similar though not identical to the rolling of the dough for Near Eastern puff pastry. So we came upon the principle of unity in diversity, as characteristic of cookery as of the world of nature or the mind of man.

Besides discovering these towering scientific and philosophical principles at work in our kitchens, we found ourselves involved in a sort of gastronomical semantics. When we were making köfte, someone noticed a similarity to a recipe for Swedish meat balls, so we researched and discussed until we had decided, to our own satisfaction at least, what made the one Turkish and the other Swedish. Such a detour leads inevitably to fascinating explorations, here via Italian meat balls, through leber knödl to soups in general and special.

What follows, then, is in part really an *un*recipe book. Where the beginner has his eye glued to each ingredient of a recipe in its printed amount and each instruction, the accomplished cook looks to techniques and relationships. Where the apprentice aims at imitating "the" dish created by Carême or Escoffier, the master cook uses materials according to principles that are organized in one great interrelated development. In order to achieve this the cook analyzes and dissects recipes to discover the common denominators, the variations on a theme, the progression of complexity in a series, until he has his material organized according to his liking.

Although the matter in the succeeding chapters has been accumulated over more than thirty years, it would never have been set down in black and white had it not been for the impetus provided by the members of the Food Interest Group of the Campus Club of Cornell University. To them my warmest thanks for their patience in the face of repetition, their enthusiasm for innovation and experiment, their intelligent criticism and, like King Henry VIII, their "unbounded stomach."

Here is nothing that is new, but all is newly examined in the light of hundreds of books read, cooks watched at their cooking, failures equally with successes assessed and annotated, and finally a one-man audience perpetually responsive beyond the wildest dreams of any would-be cook.

Section A

Teaching Grandmother To Suck Eggs is always more illuminating for the one who teaches than for Grandmother. All would-be Grandmothers please note that cooks' repertoires deal with foods in categories from soup to nuts, but an examination of the whole from the view of cooking techniques reduces them to four general areas: techniques for dealing with eggs; baking techniques; sauce techniques; and meat-and-potatoes techniques.

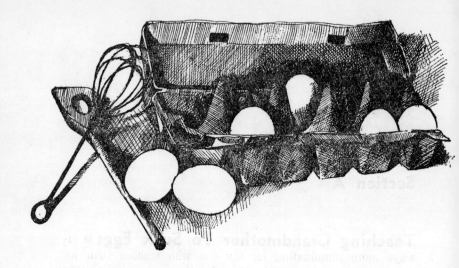

1. The Egg is probably the most versatile of all the food stuffs known to the cook, though the eggplant and the chicken are serious contenders. Myself, I've never been a partisan of the raw egg unadorned, but I'll remember as long as life lasts the picture of a friend eating—or drinking—raw eggs. This was many years ago in Albania, on the shores of Lake Ohrid, where we had stopped in the still early morning for a belated breakfast. After a late night we had made a hurried departure at dawn in the postal van, thereby missing the hotel breakfast. Everyone in the party was sleepy, and several of us were less than sunny, especially one of us who had replied too enthusiastically to the toasts of the hospitable Albanians on the previous evening. While the rest of us had coffee and bread with our scrambled eggs cooked on a tiny alcohol stove, he, with every sign of relish for returning life, concentrated on the raw eggs, puncturing them neatly and pouring the contents down his parched throat.

But once the egg is broken, it seems to me that there are more delightful ways of using it. In order to explore the protean aspects of the egg, let's start with the simplest dishes and proceed to the more complex.

Even the utterly simple poached egg is attractive and delicious; the way it was given to me as a child still seems little short of ambrosia. This we called simply

POACHED EGG AND MILK

1) Break an egg which has come to room temperature gently into a small pan of barely warm milk.
2) Let the milk heat gradually to scalding, by which time the egg is poached to perfection.
3) With a slotted spoon, lift the egg carefully onto a piece of crisp buttered toast in a soup bowl; pour over it the milk; season with salt and pepper and a sprinkle of fresh chopped parsley.

A scrambled egg is nothing more than an egg broken into a hot pan and forked until the white and yolk are inter-mingled. Calorie-conscious folk do the scrambling in a double boiler, substituting a modicum of milk for the butter or bacon fat in a skillet. But once milk is mixed with egg the result is a bit different from the true scrambled egg; it is really a kind of custard.

The difference between a scrambled egg and an omelet consists in the stage at which the egg white and yolk are mixed. Scrambled egg is mixed in the pan over heat; omelet is mixed cold before it is set on the fire, and no mixing occurs once the heat is applied. Omelets are susceptible of dozens of variations, and the results may be used in different parts of the menu: either as the central dish of a simple meal, as a bland introduction to a highly seasoned main course, or as dessert. They may be low-calorie main dishes, enriched with milk, sauced with meat, sea food or vegetables, or they may embody particles of meat, rice, cheese, herbs, or sweets.

The arguments about the constitution and cooking of omelets are many and fierce, and each Passionate Cook has his own immutable version. I prefer to reduce omelets to their lowest common denominator—eggs beaten before cooking—then qualify any dish based on that principle as water omelet, milk omelet, baked omelet, jam omelet, and so on.

For the most part, omelets are fried, though in my mother's kitchen an omelet was always baked; no other kind existed for her. Frying means cooking in lots of fat at a high temperature. (Sautéing, on the other hand, means cooking in a small amount of fat at high temperature; the small amount of fat in a hot pan makes the cooking food jump—*sauter*.) So to cook an omelet properly there must be plenty of fat, preferably butter in our culture, and it should be bubbling hot, but not smoking, when the egg is poured into it.

It would be convenient if we had in our small modern kitchens the space to store all of the pots and pans and utensils that are recommended to us from the pages of every cookbook, magazine and newspaper as being indispensable to the creation of this savory dish or that. But even though storage space is lacking, let's not forego the omelet. It can be made in a frying pan or skillet or shallow casserole. The hinged omelet pan is a pleasant gadget and ensures the fine-grained "skin" that is so rightly prized in excellent omelets, but the same effect can be created in at least two other ways. If you are using the good all-purpose frying pan, you may wish to develop the simple skill of "folding" your omelet. Make an indentation—not a complete cut—across the center of the cooked omelet with cake turner, spatula or knife, then slide under half of the omelet mass a spatula (for a small omelet) or a pancake turner (for a large one) and flip it over onto the other half. This is done when the omelet is cooked and ready to be slid onto a warm plate—not too hot a plate or the omelet will go on cooking and become dry or tough. Or you may wish to use the salamander technique. A salamander was originally a shallow pan filled with hot coals. To get the effect of a salamander in a modern kitchen, heat any smooth-bottomed pan very hot, grease the bottom on the outside, and press gently onto the surface of the omelet—again, just before you slide it out of its pan onto the warm serving plate.

A rolled omelet requires more skill than a plain or folded omelet but is far more fun to do. There are at least two ways to get this effect, one of them the classical French way of shoving and jerking the tilted pan roughly forward then backward so that the omelet rolls itself up against the far and lower rim of the pan. The second way is really cheating, but on the serving plate it looks exactly the same and is incomparably easier. Holding the pan tilted with the handle higher than the opposite side, use the spatula at the high side of the pan to lift the edge of the omelet. With a narrow rolling flip of the spatula the edge of the omelet will curl over on itself. All you have to do after that is keep it turning over on itself until it reaches the lower, far side of the pan.

We are told over and over by specialists in cooking that high temperatures toughen eggs. The exception to this rule is the omelet. It is put into a hot pan in which the fat is bubbling, and it cooks very quickly at a high temperature. An omelet slowly cooked is more than likely inedible because it's either too tough or too dry. The quick cooking ensures the sealing of the skin of the omelet, imprisoning the air beaten into it earlier, and it is the air expanding as it heats that inflates the whole mass. Slow cooking allows the air to escape before a skin forms. A beautiful omelet then should be toast-golden, hot, tender, light, and creamy but not wet inside.

Water tends to make a tender omelet; milk makes a sturdier one and a richer. Milk is used in a

BAKED OMELET (4 servings)

1) Beat the whites of 4 eggs with ½ tsp. of salt until quite dry.

2) Beat the 4 yolks until pale in color and thick in texture.

3) Add ½ cup of milk to the yolks and beat smooth.

4) Fold in the stiffly beaten whites, not too thoroughly.

5) Slide the omelet into a skillet in which you have melted about 2 tbsp. of butter. The skillet will of course be hot and the butter bubbling.

6) Put into a hot oven (450°) for about 15 minutes.

7) Slide the omelet onto a large warm plate with a pancake turner. Or if the skillet is one of the handsome modern ones, you may bring the omelet to table in it.

This sort of omelet makes a good supper dish served in conjunction with a platter of creamed spinach surrounded with crisp bacon curls. It is also an excellent omelet to serve with a sauce, perhaps one made of tomatoes, onions, and green pepper.

Dessert omelets are nearly always rolled. They are generally small, one to a person, and they may be served much as are French crêpes. It's a good idea to add a teaspoon of sugar for each egg used. The dressings for these omelets may be plain confectioner's sugar, jam or jelly, sweetened fruit with or without a liqueur or brandy, wine sauces, or plain good rum, warmed, set alight and poured over the omelet, then carried blazing to the salivating guests.

Omelets, when they use liquid at all, use relatively little, but when liquid is added to eggs in a quantity that approaches or exceeds the volume of the egg mass, the result is quite different. Custard, either boiled or baked, has a texture utterly unlike omelet. A great many English and American desserts call for a custard sauce. This is a so-called "boiled" custard, though it never really boils, for it is cooked over hot water which does not touch the bowl or pan containing the custard. In order then, to make

BOILED CUSTARD (6 small custards)

1) Beat 3 whole eggs only until the whites and yolks are mixed. (I like a pinch of salt added here.)
2) Add 2 cups of milk and mix well.
3) Add ⅓ cup of sugar and mix in well.
4) Put the bowl or pan over hot water, but do not permit the water to touch the bottom of the upper container, and stir constantly until the mixture thickens. Too much heat against the bowl will cook that part of the egg that touches it before the sauce is uniformly heated through. This part of the process is slow, so call upon your reserves of patience.
5) Cool somewhat before adding any flavoring reinforced with alcohol, such as vanilla or almond extract.
6) Serve either warm or cold.

This is a fairly rich custard. It's perfectly possible to achieve a respectable dish with only two eggs to two cups of milk. Using only yolks makes a yellower custard, hence richer looking. If this is what you prefer, remember that for one whole egg you will need to substitute two yolks.

One of the more elegant custards, used either as a sauce for, say, an exquisite sponge cake, or alone as a dessert is

ZABAGLIONE (SABAYON)

1) Put into the top container of a double boiler:

     2 egg yolks (one per person)
     2 tbsp. of sugar
     Pinch of salt
     2 tbsp. of Marsala wine; or you may prefer or have on hand Malaga, Madeira or sherry.
     ½ tsp. of other flavoring, such as vanilla or almond, if you like.

2) Place over hot water and beat briskly and constantly until thick, pale and frothy.
3) Serve either hot or cold.

You may of course serve boiled custard as a dessert. Old-fashioned Floating Island is such a one, using egg yolks, sugar and milk for the custard proper. The whites are beaten to a froth, sugar added, and the uncooked sweetened meringue, often topped with bits of tart jelly, set afloat upon the rich yellow base.

But dessert custards are more often the baked variety, and these go particularly well with brown, or browned, sugar trimmings. For a Crème Caramel, make a sauce of caramelized sugar and put it in the bottom of a greased pan or greased custard cups and proceed as for

BAKED CUSTARD (6 small servings)

1) Beat 3 whole eggs only until mixed. (Too much air added to the eggs causes the slow-baked custard to shrink.)
2) Add 2 cups of milk and mix. It is totally unnecessary to heat the milk.
3) Add ⅓ cup of sugar and a bit of salt, and mix.
4) Set the cups or pan in another pan containing warm water which comes about halfway up the outside of the custard container, and bake at about 350° for a half hour or longer, depending on the size of the container.

The custard is done when a smooth blade inserted in the center of the pudding comes out clean, as if oiled. Too rapid cooking makes a watery custard and one with large pores in the texture, and too long baking makes a dry, curdled-looking product.

When the Crème Caramel is inverted onto a serving dish, the caramelized sugar makes a sauce like a rather thin syrup, which gives an appetizing brown look to this bland but good dessert.

If cream is substituted for milk, and yolks used instead of whole eggs, the much richer result can make the very elegant

CRÈME BRÛLÉE (8 servings)

1) Beat 4 or 5 egg yolks with 1 tbsp. of sugar.
2) Add 1 tsp. of vanilla, or use vanilla sugar in place of plain.
3) Pour over the egg yolks 1 pt. (2 cups) of cream. This may be either hot or cold. Add a few minutes to the baking time if the cream is cold.
4) Bake in a shallow, buttered pan set in a pan of warm water, in a moderate oven (325°–350°) until cooked—about ½ hour.
5) Cool, then chill in the refrigerator, and do not take the next step for several hours.
6) Now, still several hours before you wish to serve the dessert, cover the top of the cold custard fairly thickly —about ¼ inch deep—with a smooth, even layer of light brown sugar. Dark sugar won't do as well here as it is still moister than the light.
7) Place the custard under the broiler and watch steadily until the sugar melts and runs smooth over the whole top surface. It will burn if you let either your eyes or your mind stray.
8) Chill again in the refrigerator before serving.
9) To serve, tap the glaze all over with the back of the serving spoon so that the candy will break and allow you to cut into the custard.

When egg whites are used without the yolks, the first addition in the development toward complexity is sugar. Loading the egg white with sugar changes the texture radically. Try, for example,

MERINGUES

(This recipe makes about 1½ dozen meringues 3″–4″ in diameter.)

1) Beat 4 egg whites (½ cup) with ½ tsp. of salt until very stiff.
2) Add, in 4 or 5 goes, 1 cup of sifted sugar, beating thoroughly after each addition. If using confectioner's sugar, use 1¼ cups.
3) Drop onto a baking sheet filmed with beeswax or paraffin. I heat the baking sheet and rub over it quickly a lump of paraffin.
4) Bake—or rather, dry out—in a very slow oven not over 275° for ½ hour to an hour, depending on the size of the meringues. Too high a temperature will make the meringues hard or tough. Too fast or too slow baking makes for shrinkage and sometimes for the deplored golden "dew drops."

Made very small, these may be used as candies, or as decorative units set in frosting on a cake.

However, when you want a meringue topping on a pie, use only one or two egg whites and cut the amount of sugar in proportion or to even less. A meringue topping, also, is baked in a hotter oven and for a short time; ten minutes at 350° is generally enough. It is not meant to be as dry as a dessert meringue.

When my mother served strawberry shortcake as a dessert, it always was sheet cake covered with the sweetened berries and topped with an uncooked meringue instead of the more usual whipped cream. It certainly made a lighter dessert and always seemed the ultimate in elegance. I use uncooked meringue on certain pies rich in nuts and eggs. Whipped cream on top of pecan pie or chocolate pie is just too much of a good thing for middle-aged gall bladders.

Returning to the whole egg, we're now ready to complicate matters further. We've already added liquid, sometimes sweetened; now let's see what happens when we add solids to a custard mixture. A small amount of flour added makes a batter, which can be baked on a griddle or in the oven. A large amount of solid in the form of flour makes a pudding. Somewhere in between batters and puddings lie—or should one say rise?—the soufflés.

The simple dipping batters can be enriched with more eggs and with fat; they can be lightened with baking powder, or with soda used in conjunction with an acid liquid like buttermilk or sour cream; they can have fat added and more flour until they develop into waffles. One of the ways to use batter that has mostly gone out of fashion is to bake it with meat. The English still serve

TOAD-IN-THE-HOLE (4 large servings)

1) Beat 4 egg yolks with 1 cup of milk and ¼ cup of flour until smooth and thick.
2) Let this stand for an hour or longer. This softens the flour particles and makes for tenderness.
3) Brown sausages or strips of steak, and arrange these in a shallow greased pan or casserole.
4) Beat the 4 egg whites with ½ tsp. of salt until stiff.
5) Fold the whites into the flour, egg yolk and milk mixture.
6) Pour the batter around the meat in the casserole and bake in a quick oven (about 450°) until the batter has risen and browned. This will take about 20–30 minutes for a dish roughly 8″ x 11″ x 2″.

Another interesting use of batters is for a superlative pancake, very light and tender. When the first snow falls have a dessert of

SNOW PANCAKES (4 servings)

1) Make a batter of:
    - 2 whole eggs, beaten with
    - 2 tbsp. of flour
    - 1 tsp. of sugar
    - a pinch of salt
    - ½ cup of milk
2) Let this stand for about an hour.
3) When ready to bake the cakes, and with the griddle already hot, dash outdoors and scoop up 1 tbsp. of fresh-fallen snow; dash back to the batter, and stir in the snow loosely, leaving bits of it unincorporated in the batter.
4) Bake immediately all at once on a large griddle, so that all the cakes are baked before the snow entirely melts in the batter.
5) Serve these like French crêpes with a sauce or jelly.

The melting snow leaves pores in the finished cakes. You'll hate to see the winter pass once you've gotten into the habit of thinking of snow pancakes for desserts.

When a little more flour is used than for batters and the mixture is fried in fat that bubbles at least halfway up the depth of the dropped batter, the results are fritters. They may be served plain as a hot "bread," dusted with sugar or topped with syrup, fruit, jam or jelly for a dessert, or they may have solids other than flour added to the batter and be served as a side dish to the main course. Strictly American are

CORN OYSTERS (8-10 fritters, depending on size)

1) Grate fresh sweet corn to the amount of 2 cups.
2) Beat 2 whole eggs with ¼ tsp. of salt.

3) Add the corn, black pepper, 1 tsp. of baking powder, ¼ cup (4 tbsp.) of flour, and 2 tbsp. of cream.
4) Drop into deep fat and cook until golden and puffed.

When eggs in a large amount are beaten separately and combined with a sauce of fat, flour and liquid, the baked result is one of the glories of cookery, the soufflé. This is a very short step in complexity beyond the custard, and is therefore treated like one in the baking. It is put into a buttered dish which is quite often set in a pan of hot water and baked at 375°, a somewhat hotter oven than custard requires because of the added solids. Using an extra egg white gives you a better chance at a beautiful soufflé, but any recipe will do if the temperature at which you bake the dish is right and *if you have beaten the eggs to their maximum volume.* If you can spare the time and eggs for an experiment, make two soufflés by the same recipe, in the one case beating the egg whites by electric or Dover beater, and in the other by hand. A whisk or wire beater and the wide circular hand motion, though slower, seem to incorporate far more air into the egg mass than the faster narrower motion of the mechanical beaters. Just to get the feel of this splendid dish, try first a plain

BASIC SOUFFLÉ (6 servings)
1) Make a medium to thick béchamel sauce using
    2-3 tbsp. of butter
    2-3 tbsp. of flour
    1 cup of hot milk
    salt and pepper
2) Cool the sauce.
3) Beat 4 egg yolks until pale and thick, and mix with the tepid or cool sauce.
4) Beat the 4 or 5 egg whites very stiff.

5) Fold the egg whites gently and loosely into the yolk and sauce mixture. Do not try for a homogeneous texture; the egg whites should not be too perfectly incorporated into the mixture.

6) Bake for about ½ hour in a buttered dish set in a pan of hot water in the middle of the oven which is at 375°.

More sauce (solids) to less egg makes a firmer texture, so that the soufflé will not fall as readily; but also the result will be less delicate. More solids in the soufflé require a hotter oven to start with, say 400°, so that the solids suspended in the egg mass may be immediately fixed. After 3 to 5 minutes the oven heat should be turned down to the standard 375°.

Be careful not to open the oven door while the soufflé is rising. But at the end of 20 to 25 minutes you may want to check on it. Make sure that the guests are ready for the dish, napkins spread and eyes alight, before bringing it to table, for it won't survive a sharp drop of 300° for more than a few minutes. You may find that you have on your hands not a soufflé but what a friend of mine calls a "soufflop." To a basic soufflé you may add all sorts of flavors to serve the particular purpose of the dish. Cheese, grated and added to the sauce, and sometimes sprinkled in the buttered dish, is probably the best known. Puréed vegetable, meat, or fish can transform a basic soufflé from a light entrée into the *pièce de résistance* of a meal. Sugar, syrups, puréed fruit, chocolate, or liqueurs can make it into an ineffable dessert. But eventually, if you keep on increasing the solids until the balance of solid and egg is completely changed, you will create not a soufflé but a pudding. The overbalance of solids forces us to retreat from the peak of the soufflè, where much air has been incorporated into the egg mass, back to the lower ground of custards.

Starting again with custard and increasing solids rather

than egg, we develop a pudding. One of the simplest of puddings, and such a humble dish that it rarely appears on a restaurant menu, but one that I find susceptible of elegance, is the Portuguese

AÇORDA (8 servings)

1) Cut crusts away from a one-pound loaf of good strong white bread.
2) Crumble the bread into a bowl and cover with enough milk to moisten the crumb thoroughly, but not enough to lie free around the bread.
3) Beat 2 whole eggs until mixed but not light with ½ tsp. of sugar and add to the moistened crumb.
4) Add salt and pepper to taste.
5) Put the bowl of mush and eggs over hot water on the stove and cook, stirring steadily until the custard and bread are melded and the mush thickens.

This, like the Italian panada, may be served in place of potatoes or rice, or it may be used as the base of a dish of sautéed shrimps, for example. Or it may be used like polenta, topping a casserole dish of meat and vegetables.

The spoon breads of the American South are technically puddings, and the Yankees who know real spoon bread are comparatively few, for real Southern spoon bread is made with fresh water-ground corn meal untreated with the chemicals that preserve it against weevils for its possibly long shelf life. Real Johnny Cake also requires freshly ground meal, and my husband's mother on the Pacific coast used to send across the continent for water-ground meal which she used exclusively for

RHODE ISLAND JOHNNY CAKE (8 servings)

1) Mix 1 cup of white, water-ground Rhode Island corn meal with 1 qt. of milk (4 cups).

2) Beat 2 whole eggs and add to the meal and milk.
3) Add salt and 2 to 4 tbsp. of melted butter.
4) Bake in a shallow, greased pan in a slow oven (300°) for about one hour.

Served at breakfast with butter and syrup before an open fire, this dish makes even the coldest, grimmest day begin well.

The spoon, or batter, breads of the South are much the same as Rhode Island Johnny Cake. Recipes vary in the proportion of liquid to solid, in the number of eggs used, in the amount and kind of fat, and in the kind of liquid used. Buttermilk is found in a number of recipes, in which case soda is added in the proportion of 1 tsp. to 2 cups of buttermilk. The more eggs, the lighter the result, until finally, when the liquid is reduced in proportion to the increased egg content, you get a result very like a soufflé.

Corn and meal seem to us to be typically American, though in Italy corn meal is used for a number of dishes, one of which is a form of corn bread, using corn-meal mush enriched with eggs, sprinkled with Parmesan cheese, and baked. This Gnocchi is good, but the one that I first tasted I like even better, and it is made with wheat rather than corn, and is called simply

SEMOLINA GNOCCHI

1) Scald 1 qt. (4 cups) of milk to which is added 1 tsp. of salt.
2) Pour in slowly, stirring with a wooden spoon or paddle, ¾ cup of farina (Cream of Wheat cereal) and continue cooking and stirring frequently for 20-30 minutes. By this time it will have thickened to the point where it will no longer pour, although it can still be stirred.
3) Add ¼ lb. (½ cup) of butter and stir until it is absorbed evenly.

4) Add 2 egg yolks, mixed but not beaten light, and stir in smoothly.
5) Spread on a flat plate or platter to the depth of about ½"-¾" thick and allow to cool completely.
6) Cut into lozenge or diamond shapes, and lay these on a greased baking sheet or in a shallow pan.
7) Sprinkle with Parmesan cheese and dot with butter. These may be built up in layers or kept separate.
8) Place in a hot oven to brown.
9) Serve hot.

Six hungry people will demolish this amount of Gnocchi in all too short a time.

Soft breads and puddings using eggs for the leavening agent may be further complicated by incorporating other solids for flavor. One of the most interesting is the kind that makes use of the blender to refine texture to the point almost of custard. Here is one that is half custard, half mousse, called simply.

CORN PUDDING (8 servings)

1) Mix in the blender until perfectly smooth
   1 cup (or more, if you like) of fresh corn cut or grated off the cob.
   1 tbsp. of flour
   1 tsp. of chopped onion
   2 tbsp. of cut-up parsley
   ½ cup of cream
   salt and pepper to taste
2) Add to the blended mixture 4 whole eggs well beaten.
3) Add 1 pt. (2 cups) of milk.
4) Put in a greased casserole or ring mold.
5) Set casserole in a pan of hot water and bake like custard.

By now we find that what is happening in this exploration of developing complexity is that the egg is becoming the chief enriching and leavening factor of the dish; we're really beginning to subordinate the egg proper to the position of handmaiden to some other ingredient or ingredients. But let's pretend anyway that it's still the egg itself that is of prime interest.

We've added liquids and solids and fats in small quantity to eggs to get the foregoing dishes. Let's now increase the fat content and investigate a different technique to make the pastry used in éclairs and cream puffs. This technique starts with the liquid, adds the solids, then beats in each egg separately. The chief danger point in the making of cream puff shells is one that is sometimes overlooked because it is outside the operations of mixing and baking. After the shells are baked and reposing proudly on a cooling rack, a small slit made near the base of each one allows the steam to escape. If this is done, the puffs will remain crisp and appetizing. Otherwise, it's a quick and simple matter to make

CREAM PUFF or CHOUX PASTE

1) Using a 2 qt. saucepan, so that there will be plenty of room for maneuver, bring a cup of water to boiling point.

2) Stir in ½ cup (¼ lb.) of butter and a bit of salt, and heat until the butter is completely melted, about the time the mixture again comes to the boil.

3) Add 1 cup of flour all at once and reduce the heat to medium while you stir the flour smoothly into the liquid. Continue the stirring until the paste makes a smooth ball and follows the spoon in a mass, leaving the rest of the pan clean. This will take about 3 minutes. BEWARE of cooking the paste so long that globules of fat are ejected onto the surface of the ball of paste. This would prevent the puffing during baking by hardening—really frying—the flour. But an undercooked paste is

just as bad. What is wanted is to cook the paste so that it will be hot all through and the flour will have absorbed the liquid and fat evenly and can then exert its binding and expanding powers.

4) Remove the pan from the heat and break into it one by one, beating thoroughly after each addition, 4, 5, or 6 eggs. The first one is easy enough to beat in; each successive one calls for more exertion. Four eggs make a good cream puff; but do experiment with more as you become more familiar with the technique. By the time that you've beaten in the fourth egg, the paste will have changed in texture and be very yellow, smooth and glossy, reflecting the light like satin.

5) Drop by spoonfuls onto an ungreased baking sheet. The fat in the paste is sufficient, as with good pastry of any sort, to lubricate the surface of the baking tin. To shape the shells more easily, I use a spoon in each hand: one to dip up; one to scrape off and shape the mound of paste.

6) Bake large puffs for about 40 minutes, starting them at 425°-450° and turning down the heat to 375° after 20 minutes. Small puffs will bake faster, in about 20 minutes at 400°-425°.

7) Remove the puffs to a rack and immediately make a small slit near the base of each to allow any remaining steam to escape.

Cream puffs when cold may be filled with innumerable things: custards, salads, creamed meat or vegetable fillings, or ice cream. A very effective dessert is the French

PROFITEROLES

1) Fill tiny cream puffs (dropped onto the baking sheet from a coffee spoon) when completely cool with custard filling flavored with vanilla, coffee or almond.

2) Arrange the puffs in a pyramid on a serving dish and cover with a

CHOCOLATE SAUCE

1) Melt 4 squares of semisweet chocolate in a bowl over hot water.
2) Add 1 tbsp. of sugar and ½ cup of water from the hot-water faucet. Stir in well and cook until smooth and thick.
3) Add 1 tbsp. of Madeira or brandy, and stir in. Use the sauce either warm or cold, but if it's to be served cold there will have to be a higher proportion of liquid.

This sauce can wait for hours over hot water. If it is too thick when you're ready to use it, add a teaspoon of hot water—or as much as necessary to restore it to the desired consistency.

Another impressive way to use choux paste is to make fish dumplings, called by their French name,

QUENELLES de POISSON

1) Put through the meat grinder, using a fine blade, and more than once if necessary to get the meat thoroughly smooth, about 1 lb. of raw fish flesh—no skin or bones. I have found halibut the best fish to use as the meat is lean; too rich a fish like swordfish or shad softens the dumplings too much. You may also grind up with the fish dried or cooked mushrooms, but raw mushrooms contain too much liquid.
2) Add to this salt, pepper (white preferably) and, if you haven't already used mushrooms, a trace of nutmeg or mace.

3) Now make a choux paste using
    1 cup of water
    4 tbsp. of butter (¼ cup or ⅛ lb.)
    1 cup of flour
    salt
    2 eggs and 2 extra egg whites; or use 3 whole eggs
4) Mix the fish with the paste thoroughly, then chill in the refrigerator.
5) When the paste is cold, work in 1 or 2 tbsp. of heavy cream. Too much liquid will make the paste too soft.
6) Form the quenelles by using two wet teaspoons of the same size and shape, holding one in each hand. Dip up some paste on the left-hand spoon, and use the right-hand one to smooth the top. Loosen the paste by turning one spoon under then over the dumpling held in the other spoon.
7) Have a large pan at least 3″ deep of simmering salted water or fish stock on the stove. When the quenelles are formed, drop them one by one carefully into the liquid so as not to stop the simmering. You may have to turn up the heat when you drop in the dumplings so that the temperature of the liquid won't fall too far. Keep the liquid barely simmering and poach the quenelles uncovered while they cook for about 20 minutes. They will sink to the bottom of the pan at first, then rise as steam is built up inside them. They should expand to at least half again their original volume.
8) Remove with a slotted spoon to drain on a rack covered with a cloth.

These delicious morsels may be refrigerated and kept for some days if they are filmed over with melted butter to prevent their drying out.

To serve the quenelles as a hot dish, make a sauce of the béchamel type, perhaps with white wine for part of the liquid, pour some into the bottom of a casserole, pack in the dumplings, cover with the remaining sauce and heat in the oven. Cover with buttered crumbs if you want a crusty top. Or you may wish to serve them chilled and unsauced as an hors d'oeuvre.

Admittedly this is a lengthy process, but the quenelles are much tenderer and of finer texture made by this method than by starting with a panade of bread crumb.

Cooking is seductive. It leads by gentle becks and nods from a broad highway to a byway. One such byway, lately become better known, is

GOUGÈRE (6 large servings)

1) Bring to boil 1 cup of milk or water, 2 tbsp. of butter, and 1 tsp. of salt.
2) Dump in all at once 1 cup of flour and stir until smooth and thick. The mass will, as in regular choux paste, follow the spoon in one large ball.
3) Remove from the heat, and when cooled a bit break into it 4 eggs, beating in each one thoroughly before adding the next.
4) Add about 3 oz. of Gruyere cheese cut in tiny dice— ¼ inch is not too small—reserving about 1 tbsp. to sprinkle on top later.
5) Spoon the mixture onto a baking sheet so that it forms a ring as if it had been inverted from a ring mold. Spooning it onto the sheet ensures a not-too-solid pack.
6) Sprinkle the remaining cheese dice over the top.
7) Bake at about 375° for 50 minutes until firm and crisp.
8) Leave it in the oven with the heat turned off and the door open for about 5 minutes before transferring to a warm plate and taking to table.

Choux paste is but a step in complication below cakes, where eggs with other ingredients reach the apogee of their development and treatment in relationship to each other and in the fine gradations of balance of ingredients, that is, of eggs to fat, to flour, to sugar, to liquid; of fat to flour, sugar and liquid—and so on.

There are literally thousands of cakes, and in a discussion of this sort it would be only confusing as well as impossible to attempt anything like a comprehensive survey of this branch of cookery. Classifying cakes roughly in two categories, the sponge and the butter cakes, we notice that whichever kind we are analyzing there is a mathematically beautiful balance among the ingredients. Sponge cakes use half as much weight in flour as they do of either eggs or sugar. Therefore, taking a large egg to equal 2 oz., the required amount of sugar is 2 oz.; the required amount of flour is one ounce. In this country we generally measure flour by dry measure, so since one ounce of flour is a scant ¼ cupful, our basic recipe begins to go like this:

> 1 egg (2 oz. or ¼ cup)
> scant ¼ cup of flour (1 oz.)
> ¼ cup of sugar (2 oz.)

Promoted to cake size the basic recipe would go:

> 4 eggs (1 cup)
> scant 1 cup of flour
> 1 cup of sugar

What a beautifully symmetrical scheme this is! But, as we've seen demonstrated any number of times, there are wide variations in recipes, so you'll find that most sponge cake recipes call for more than four eggs to each cup of flour.

Angel food is of course a sponge cake using only egg whites —really a meringue with flour added—and it follows the same scheme as the sponges, but with a little extra sugar:

> 1 cup of egg whites
> scant cup of flour
> 1¼ cups of sugar

Almost all other cakes call for fat in addition to the eggs, sugar, and flour. Chief of these, and also schematically satisfying, is Pound Cake, for which a specific recipe is given in the following chapter. Here the proportions were originally

    1 lb. of eggs
    1 lb. of butter
    1 lb. of flour
    1 lb. of sugar

This cake is still made to this formula by cooks who prefer to weigh their ingredients rather than measure them by cupfuls.

A Pound Cake is a butter cake in which the fat is creamed. This technique is used for a large number of butter cakes beside Pound Cake. The proportions of ingredients in creamed butter cakes can vary in the amount of fat from ½ to equal the amount of flour. The same variation can apply to sugar, and the same to eggs. When melted fat is used, the amount is much less; it is half or less than half the amount of flour. The same proportions hold when the fat is rubbed into the flour.

If there is a voracious audience for your baking, you can create your own favorite cake recipe by varying first the proportions of the basic ingredients, then by substituting and adding ingredients. Quantities of recipes call for liquids, especially milk. Many call for syrups, from honey through the various kinds of molasses. Indeed, some even call for beer. Remember to alter sugar measurements when you add sweet liquids or semiliquids. Brown sugar, being less refined than white, has less sweetening power; also, being moister, it must be packed tight for measuring.

Cake techniques vary, but all have in common the purpose of lightening the mixture to hold air inside. In the fine sponge cakes and pound cakes, the beaten eggs are the leavening agent, but most other cakes, where the proportion of egg is smaller, add a second leavening agent in the form of yeast, baking powder, or baking soda in conjunction with an acid. In almost all cakes, however, the beating of the eggs is crucial. Properly beaten eggs will increase in volume six to eight times their original bulk. Egg whites whip to a higher volume than egg yolks. If a very light cake is wanted, beaten egg whites are folded in at the end of the mixing period. Warm eggs whip to a higher volume than cold ones—and much faster, which is why some recipes call for beating eggs in a bowl over hot water.

Now after all this exploration of the egg to its final glorification in cake, let's take a look at an exception. There are a number of eggless cake recipes, but few satisfy the real cake-craving. One that does, for me at least, is the old recipe, brought up to date, for

VINEGAR CAKE

1) Sift into a bowl
   2½ cups of flour
   1 tbsp. of baking powder
   ½ tsp. of salt
2) Rub in with the fingers ¾ cup of butter.
3) Add 1 cup of raisins, or raisins and currants, mixed with ¾ cup of sugar.
4) Stir 1 tsp. of baking soda into 2 tbsp. of cider vinegar and add this to 1 cup of milk.
5) Combine the liquid with the fat, flour, fruit and sugar mixture.
6) Put the batter into a greased and floured cake tin or loaf tin and bake for at least an hour (depending on the depth of the tin you are using) at 375°.

You may like nuts in this cake, but if so, cut down on the butter, for it is very rich.

Techniques for using the egg in cooking range all through the menu. In some dishes the egg itself is central; in hundreds of others it has only a supporting role; but wherever an egg is introduced into a recipe it is there because of its peculiar characteristics. A cook must understand the relation of the egg to the other ingredients of the dish in order to foresee her results. In addition, a general awareness of the functions of the egg, its reaction to heat, and its relation to liquid and solid, allows the cook to move beyond the pickets of a rule to the wider country of creative cookery.

2. Baking is in danger of becoming a lost art. Packaged mixes multiply; frozen products increase; and the calibrated and thermostated oven relieves the kitchen overseer—for cook she hardly is—from any chore more exacting than turning a switch or setting a timer. This would be all to the good if the products were as interesting and satisfying to the palate as to the eye. Unfortunately the reverse is true.

The human palate is imperious. If it is provided with a standard product and knows no other it is satisfied with the standard, but if it is once allowed a variation it demands not just that one variation but more and more changes and surprises. So the cook who ventures into the province of baking must be prepared to become an expert. And what rewards she will reap, for the satisfactions of successful baking outweigh even those of the gratified palate.

Mastery of baking will yield to a determined and inquisitive intelligence. Basically baking is the subjection of a mixture of liquid and dry ingredients to dry heat over a period of time which may vary from very brief to very extended. Early on in the history of cookery, the dry heat was an open fire, which as it acted on the mixture could be seen to change it from a wet blob of mush to a semi-dry mash, and later to a golden crusty cake, and finally perhaps to a black crumbly cinder; so the action of heat on the material to be baked is fundamental to competence in baking.

The baking of meal or flour with liquid, the simplest of all possible combinations, is easy enough in theory, but when fat or leavening agents are included and adjustments of baking time and temperature are required, those of us who can read are inclined to rely uncritically on the directions in one or another of the millions of recipes available to us. Even so, we sometimes have failures and we don't know why. Recipes, tested and retested, are unlikely to be wrong, and since our stoves are practically foolproof, the fault must lie, we conclude, in ourselves. This is the point at which a number of otherwise well adjusted cooks turn to the packaged mixes, rather than risk further disappointment.

Not so our inquisitive cook. "If primitive woman could do it," says she, "I, product of a thousand generations, and proud heiress of the cooks of Greece, Rome, and Fanny Farmer—I, too, can bake a perfect cherry pie."

But let's sing small at first and work up gradually to the high notes.

The simplest and oldest of combinations, meal and water, used and loved in every culture, is made by the Mexicans using fresh yellow corn meal into

TORTILLAS

1) Pour boiling water over an equal measure of yellow corn meal with a bit of salt added.
2) Stir or beat with the hand, spoon or paddle until the mixture is smooth and very thick. Keep on beating

longer than you think is necessary and you will find
that the mixture continues to thicken further.

3) Pat or roll into thin cakes. If you choose to pat the
dough, you'll need dry hands, so flour your hands well
and handle the dough lightly. The Mexicans are very
expert at tossing the dough from hand to hand until
it stretches to a large, flat, airy disc. This same technique
is used in the Near East with yeast dough to make large
flat loaves of bread. Tortilla dough is flimsier, however,
than yeast dough, unless you're lucky enough to get hold
of some *masa*, the freshly ground corn meal used in
Mexican communities; so I find it simpler to roll out
the dough on a floured board or cloth.

4) Transferring the tortillas to the fairly hot ungreased
griddle is a tricky business, so have the board as close
as possible to the stove.

5) Brown the tortillas very slightly, but do not allow them
to bake crisp, for they are probably only in their first
stage of use. They are very good served as a hot bread,
but in general they are used as wrappings, or they are
fried in deep fat or buttered and toasted for *tostados*,
or are used as layers between meat and vegetables in
a casserole.

6) Cool them on a rack if they are not to be eaten immediately, but if they are later to be fried they'll
turn out better if they are sweated under a cloth.

Our own American Indians made a loaf bread using corn
meal and boiling water, then baking it.

The oat cakes of Scotland started out as simple dried
cakes of oatmeal, water and salt, but fat of some sort is included in the modern recipes. Much the same development
has taken place in this country with the simple corn breads:
ash cake, hoe cake and corn pone. All were originally corn
meal, salt and water, the differences between them resulting

from the cooking techniques used. Ash cakes were baked, covered top and bottom with cabbage leaves, in hot wood ashes on the hearth. Hoe cake was baked on a griddle, pone in an oven. Hush-puppies, although the same mixture, were not baked but fried in deep fat.

Corn pone is nowadays considered fit for only homely meals; for dressy ones the more elaborate and richer breads are served: corn sticks, spoon bread, and others. Incidentally, "pone" comes from the Algonquin word for bread, and irresistibly calls to mind the Latin word *panis*. The original pone was an ash cake but soon went into the oven. By now, although it is enriched in its simplest form with fat, it still recalls its humble origin in its form: it must always show the print of the fingers that shaped it. If you'd like to try modern

CORN PONE or CORN DODGERS

1) Set the oven to heat at 450° or a little higher.
2) Put drippings of pork, bacon or ham fat into a dripping pan or shallow roaster, and heat to sizzling but not smoking, either in the oven or on top of the stove.
3) Have a bowl of cold water by you to dip your hands in, for you'll form the warm dough with your fingers.
4) Put white corn meal, the fresher the better, into a bowl with some salt, about ½ tsp. to ¾ cup of meal.
5) Pour boiling water into the meal, stirring vigorously the while, until the dough is moist but not flowing. The amount of water will vary according to the freshness of the corn meal.
6) Pick up in the left hand about 2 tbsp. of the dough. Pat it into an oval cake about a half inch thick and roughly the length of your palm. Press between the extended and closed fingers lightly but firmly. This automatically makes fingerprints on both top and bottom of the cake.
7) Put the cakes, as fast as you can shape them, into the sizzling hot fat.

8) Bake in the hot oven about 15 to 20 minutes. They should be golden with darker ridges on the outside and somewhat soft inside. Meal browns slowly, so if you think the dodgers are done and they're still not brown enough, slip them under the broiler for a moment rather than leave them in the slower heat of the oven where they may dry out too much.

Broken and buttered while hot, these are the perfect accompaniment to a simple meal: soup, salad, fried fish, or stew.

Corn pone may also be baked on a griddle and basted while cooking with the generous drippings you've used on the griddle. Either way they're excellent.

Once meal is ground sufficiently fine, flour is the result, and it is in the form of flour that the cereals are chiefly used in baking. Now behold a miracle: once fat is added to flour the baked result becomes pastry; for what could be more different than a damp fresh tortilla or crusty, grainy corn pone and, say, a flaky *vol-au-vent* case? But they are very close cousins. In the one case, meal, salt and liquid are put together and baked; in the other case, flour, salt, liquid and the new ingredient, fat, are combined. Try for yourself and prove that nothing is easier than

PIE

1) Take a double handful of flour, dump it into a bowl, and add about 1 tsp. of salt. (You may prefer more or less salt the second time.)

2) Work into the flour with the fingers of the right hand as much lard as the flour will absorb—about ¼ lb. for the double handful of flour.

3) Add a small lump of butter for that buttery flavor. By this time, the dough when squeezed lightly, should

hold together in big, almost greasy lumps. Don't aim at a perfectly homogeneous mass at this stage, however. It's the bits of undistributed fat that make the finished crust flaky.

4) Now add cold water from the faucet and work the dough into a ball. Use as little water as possible and work only until the mass of dough will stick to itself without bits dropping off. Amounts of water cannot be given, for different kinds of flour absorb quite different quantities of liquid. After a trial or two, you will be able to judge how much water is needed for the flour that you are using.

5) Roll out on a lightly floured board or cloth with a floured roller into a sheet as thick or thin as you like.

6) With a spatula or knife make sure that the dough is not sticking to the board, flip half of the sheet over onto the other half and lift quickly into the pie tin.

7) Unfold and adjust the sheet of dough, trim it with a knife or scissors, crimp with the fingers or fork-mark the edge, and the crust is ready to bake.

Probably the best advice to give to a novice pastry cook would be, "Relax!" Either tension or timidity makes for toughness in the end product. And certainly one doesn't need a ball-bearing rolling pin; a high-shouldered wine bottle will do just as well, and a smooth piece of broomstick or hoe handle even better. In general, the thinner the diameter of the roller, the sooner you achieve a thin sheet of pastry.

If you are fresh out of lard but have on hand some vegetable oil, you can still make an elegant pie. Just be sure that the flour has enough fat distributed throughout it to hold together in big lumps when you squeeze it gently just before adding the water.

An incorrigible "rich" cook will think that milk would be better than water as a liquid, in which case that dollop of butter should be omitted or the crust may not hold together when it is rolled out. But even if it does break up, it will "eat" very fine. And should it break when put in the pie tin, it can always be mended and patted smooth; the seam will disappear in the baking.

Freed from the bonds of measuring for pie crust, you will be rewarded by having bits of dough left, and there are a myriad of uses for those bits. Roll out the dough and spread half the sheet with sliced or grated cheese and dot with butter. Fold the unspread half over on top of the spread half and repeat the rolling, cheesing, buttering and rolling. Then cut the pastry into "fingers" and bake it. Or you may like to try the English

LARDY JACKS

1) Roll out a sheet of pastry and spread on it sugar, brown or white, a little cinnamon and/or other spice, and currants, and dot generously with small chips of cold lard.
2) Fold over and roll out gently twice more, repeating the spreading on of the filling.
3) Place in a tin or on a baking sheet and mark with a knife the places where you will break or cut it when it is baked. Completely cutting through the pastry allows the filling to run out and the layers to come apart, so don't try it. I did, and that's how I learned not to.

The baking of pastry requires a hot oven, say at 450°. Too low a heat makes the fat sweat out of the dough, and a greasy baked crust is unattractive.

I once watched a Brazilian cook make what she called a pie by a completely different technique. She mixed a dough of flour, salt and a little baking powder with a small amount of butter—about a quarter of the amount of fat that I use for pie crust—and milk as the liquid. When it held together but was still sticky, she turned it onto an unfloured board and kneaded it as one would knead bread. She continued kneading —and talking—for at least ten minutes, by which time the dough no longer stuck to the board or the hands and was a smooth satiny ball. Then, still without benefit of flour, she rolled out her sheet of pastry on the kneading board. The result was perfect and delicious though less rich than our pastry.

The arcana of puff paste are numerous, and in this age of prepackaging all but impenetrable. Reading recipes for puff paste that range from the cold scientific, with mechanical diagrams, to the homely accounts passed down in particular families, complete with lore and "hints" and personal or fanciful vagaries, is enough to confuse even a moderately expert cook. But since puff paste is merely an extension in complexity of plain pastry, a determined person of average ability ought to be able to master this skill.

Puff paste is richer than pie paste. Whereas pie dough is about 3 parts flour by weight to 2 parts of fat, puff paste is a 1-to-1 relationship. Loading the flour with that much fat requires something more complicated in technique than the simple business of rubbing the fat into the flour. Instead of the fat's being distributed through the flour vertically, we might say, it is laminated in horizontal layers and remains in a more or less unmixed state between layers of the unpermeated paste. When the pastry is baked, the melting fat enters the paste leaving spaces between the layers of paste. The air in these vacated spaces expands and raises the pastry —puffs it.

Here is how I make

PUFF PASTRY

1) Put a scant 2 cups of flour and 1 tsp. of salt into a bowl.

2) Divide 1 cup (½ lb.) of butter into quarters: 2 oz. each.

3) Work into the flour with the fingers the first 2 oz. of butter. The butter should not be too hard and cold, nor should it be creamed or melted.

4) Work about ¼ cup of liquid into this, using as part of the liquid the strained juice of half a lemon; the rest should be water.

5) When the paste is smooth and homogeneous from working it with the fingers, roll it out onto a lightly floured board to the thickness of about ¼″. The sheet of dough should be about 6″ wide by 18″ long, or three times as long as wide. Try to keep the corners square.

6) Using the second quarter of butter, put little dabs of it over ⅔ of the sheet of paste. Be sure to leave about half an inch of unbuttered margin near the edges.

7) With dampened fingers moisten all the edges of the sheet of pastry.

8) Fold the unbuttered third of the sheet of paste over the middle third, and the buttered end-third over that.

9) Press the dampened edges together with the fingers or with a firm blow of the rolling pin.

10) Let this rest for any length of time between 15 minutes and 1 hour to allow the dough to lose its elasticity after having been worked. It must not be allowed to get warm, so it's wise to put the package wrapped in cloth or foil in the refrigerator.

11) Repeat the rolling, dabbing with butter, sealing the edges, and the rest period until the remaining two lots of butter are used. Each time you roll the pastry after the first time place it so that the sealed edges are facing to and away from you, the folds being at the sides.

12) Repeat rolling and folding the dough three times more with 10-15-minute rests between the operations. Since you are not now adding more butter it is unnecessary to

seal the edges with moisture, but remember to give a quarter turn to the folded package of pastry each time.

Two points are crucial in the making of puff paste. First, the rest periods are essential. Kneading, rolling or otherwise handling dough develops the gluten and makes the dough elastic. Elastic dough cannot be rolled as successfully as quiescent dough. The second point has regard to temperature. Butter begins melting just above the freezing point. Warm butter will penetrate dough and thereby destroy the desired structure of the pastry. Keeping the paste cold is essential. I fought against this waste of time but finally had to capitulate to the laws of physics to the extent of chilling the dough between rollings. I no longer have any trouble to speak of in making puff paste.

Of the many uses for puff pastry patty shells are high on the list. To form them have two round cookie cutters of different diameters. Roll out the dough to $\frac{1}{4}''$ or $\frac{1}{2}''$ thickness and cut out the patties with the larger cutter. Pile up three rounds and, using the smaller cutter, cut partially through each complete stack. When the shells are baked the centers can be easily lifted out and any soft parts removed.

Once the shells are baked, they may be used with a variety of fillings. The way that we perhaps know them best is with a filling of chicken à la king, but sea food or mushrooms in a rich sauce do just as well, and for desserts the fruit creams or fruit with custard are delightful.

Baking powder biscuit bridges the gap in the development toward complexity between plain pastry and the yeast doughs, for biscuit dough is a combination of flour, fat, liquid and the easy and quick leavening agent, baking powder. The mixing technique described for pie crust is just as good for

BISCUIT

1) Put flour and salt and baking powder into a bowl in the proportions of

1 cup of flour

1 tsp. of salt

1 or more tsp. of baking powder

2) Lightly mix in the fat with the fingers until the dough, when squeezed gently, will hold together in lumps about the size of a walnut. There is not as much fat in biscuit dough as in pie crust, you see.

3) Add water and mix with hand, spoon, or paddle until the dough is the consistency you want, either fairly dry for rolled biscuit, or almost batterlike for those baked in biscuit tins, or midway between those two for dropped biscuit or for scones which are generally baked on a griddle.

4) Bake in a hot oven on a greased sheet or in greased biscuit tins. The larger the biscuit, the longer the baking time, but fifteen minutes should be roughly right for large biscuits baked at 425° to 450°.

The whole process from getting out the equipment to serving the biscuits takes a half hour or less, depending on how nippy you are with your fingers.

But when you come to make proper bread, plan to be at home most of the day. If you start right after breakfast you should be able to cut a slice off the just-cool loaf for that after-school snack.

Bread is basically flour and liquid with the addition of the leavening agent, yeast. The flour may be dark or white, or a mixture of both, or it may be partly meal. The liquid may be water or milk or potato water. If you use milk you are of course including some fat. If you want fat, but not butter fat, use water plus the desired fat. Most people prefer seasoned bread and therefore use some salt. Salt, in addition to seasoning, prevents too rapid fermentation of the yeast. But the variations of seasoning may be as infinite as the flavors known to mankind. The only constant in bread recipes is the yeast, and that must be alive. Live yeast grows quickly when fed with sugar, which develops naturally from the breaking down of the starch under the influence of the liquid. Most recipes for bread will include sugar, but even without the added sugar yeast will grow and bread can be made, though the process will take longer.

Since there are so many brief chores to be done of a morning, I prefer to use a sponge method, which gives me odd half hours to do dishes, make beds, or even read yesterday's newspaper. So here is my basic recipe for

WATER YEAST BREAD (sponge method)

1) Use tepid water. (Scald liquids that may contain bacteria harmful to yeast, notably milk, then cool to lukewarm.)

2) Dissolve yeast in the lukewarm liquid, or cover yeast with sugar and mash with a fork. Let it stand for a few minutes and it will be completely dissolved.

3) Combine water and yeast and add flour to make a sponge about the consistency of a thick waffle batter, but it isn't necessary to beat the batter to perfect smoothness.

4) Add salt—about ½ tsp. for each cup of flour—but this really depends on taste.

5) Cover the mixture with a lid and a cloth (wool is best), and let rise until bubbly and lively. This will take from half an hour to an hour.

6) Add enough flour now to make a soft dough. This will still "flow" somewhat and be very sticky.

7) Knead until the dough is smooth and homogeneous. If you use a large enough bowl, you need not bother

getting out a board on which to knead. The dough
will soon not stick to the hands or the bowl. If it *should*
still be sticky after ten minutes of kneading, you
haven't used enough flour, so add a little more. Different kinds of flour absorb different amounts of liquid.
The heavier, darker flours require less water and more
kneading than white flour.

8) Now cover the dough warmly and closely (I use a
lid atop a damp linen or cotton cloth and an old woolen
afghan over all), and set out of draughts to rise. If
the dough is well kneaded it does not have to rise in
a greased bowl. I use the same large stainless steel
bowl for the whole process up to the point of shaping
the loaves, but if the insulating covers are insufficient,
chilling may result in a metal or pottery bowl, and
chilling a yeast dough does far more injury to a loaf
than a low but even temperature. Wood is an excellent
insulation, so if there are doubts about draughts, grease
a wooden bowl for the raising of the dough.

9) Punch down the dough with spread fingers when it has
rested and risen for about ½ to ¾ of an hour, and
turn it over in the bowl.

10) When it has risen to double its bulk, cut it with a
sharp knife into pieces appropriate to the baking tins
you're using. The pans should be about ⅔ full.

11) With greased hands, lightly shape the loaves with a
downward pull on each side. Put the loaf into the
greased tin, rounded part down to grease what will be
the top, pick it up and flip over, and adjust the dough
in the tin.

12) Cover with a cloth and let rise until the loaves have
rounded somewhat above the sides of the tin.

13) Bake in a hot oven (450°) for the first 5-10 minutes,
depending on the size of the loaves. Turn down the
heat to 300° for the remainder of the baking time. A
loaf made in a small tin will take less time to bake

than one made in a large one. I count on 1¼ hours for a 2 lb. loaf. When well baked, a loaf will have shrunk from the sides of the pan and should sound dry and hollow when rapped on the bottom with the knuckles. If it gives a heavy thud instead, put it back in the oven for a while longer.

14) Turn the bread onto racks to cool.

For a soft crust, paint the hot baked loaves with fat or milk, or cover with a cloth to steam. A crisp crust is one that cools and dries quickly. A pan of water in the oven during the baking helps make a crisp crust.

The amount of yeast to use is up to the cook. The more yeast, the faster the process; consequently, since sugar makes yeast grow and divide and become more yeast, the more *sugar*, the faster the process. Temperature and humidity also have a bearing on the growth of yeast. An even, humid atmosphere is ideal. If there are draughts, there is chilling plus evaporation. Too much heat kills the yeast. You may need to turn the dough in the bowl several times during the rising period to prevent the drying out of the surface and the consequent formation of a hard crust on the unbaked dough. Low temperatures of themselves will not prevent yeast from growing and dough from rising. Put some dough in the refrigerator overnight and prove for yourself that yeast grows in a cold but even temperature.

The particular texture that you want in your loaf is a matter for you to decide, and there are many different ingredients and balances of ingredients that affect texture, but in general an even fine grain is desirable in bread. Large, irregular holes occur if the air in the dough is not redistributed during the rising process; therefore the kneading, the punching down, and the molding of the loaves.

Proper kneading is a knack which one acquires in handling dough. Using both hands, pick up the mass of dough at the

side farthest from you, pull it over on top of the part nearest
you, and with the heels of the hands press firmly down and
outward toward the sides. Turn the dough ¼ way around
and repeat, over and over again, until the dough is resistant
and fighting back under your hands rather than inert and
almost flowing as it was when you began.

When the bread is baked it will shrink from the sides of
the greased pans so that a shake, or a thump on the bottom
of the tin, will loosen it completely, and it will slide out onto
the rack. I dry tender-crust loaves on their sides or upright
so that the rack won't leave a pattern on the rounded top.

If you'd like to try your hand at another technique, make
6 to 8 flat loaves of

TURKISH PIDEH or SYRIAN BREAD

1) Dissolve one cake of compressed yeast in a little warm
   water.
2) Put about 5 lbs. of flour in a large bowl or dish pan
   with a little salt—about 1 tbsp.
3) Add dissolved yeast and gradually work in as much
   warm water as is needed to make a smooth elastic
   dough. You might as well measure out about 8 cups of
   water to start with, though you may not use it all
   with a hard wheat flour and you may need more with
   a soft wheat flour or with pre-sifted flour.
4) Knead the dough in the bowl until it is resistant and
   elastic. By this time it will stick to itself rather than
   to your hands or to the bowl.
5) Cover with a damp cotton or linen cloth, then a lid,
   and insulate warmly against draughts, and leave it to
   rise for about 3 hours. By this time it will have easily
   doubled in bulk and you may feel its warmth as you
   handle it.
6) Cover a large counter or table with a cloth on which
   flour has been sprinkled, and have a bowl or a mound
   of flour handy.

7) Cut off pieces of dough, rough spheres about 6″ in diameter. (The space between the extended thumb and index finger is just about the right diameter.)

8) Dip each piece in turn in flour and shape by pulling down the four sides of the loaf with the fingers to the underside, as if you were molding a loaf for a round baking tin. Turn over and drop gently onto the floured cloth with the rounded floured side up.

9) Cover and let rest for about 15 minutes before the next operation.

10) Heat the oven very hot as for pizza: 500°-600°.

11) With each loaf follow this procedure: flatten the dough with the palm of the hand and poke the circle with the tips of the spread fingers. This redistributes the air in the dough and somewhat stretches it. Now pick up the flat round and toss it from hand to hand, giving it a twist as you fling it and keeping the hands up at about eye level and at least 3 feet apart. Use the extended and spread fingers to catch the loaf and to spin it and stretch it. Soon it will be about 10″-12″ in diameter and falling over your wrist and halfway up your forearm with each toss.

12) Lay it now on a large wooden paddle or a large flat spade or snow shovel, clean and dry of course, and dusted with flour. Smear the top of the loaf quickly with egg and water forked smooth.

13) Slide the flat loaf with a jerk of the paddle forward then back onto the floor of a gas oven, or the foil-covered lower rack of an electric one. With a bit of practice, a quick light shove of the paddle gets the loaf nicely in the center of the oven and leaves the empty paddle, happily, in your hand.

14) Bake in the oven for 10-15 minutes. After 5 minutes move the loaf to an upper rack of the oven and slide a second loaf in on the bottom rack or the floor of the oven. If you can't get a high enough temperature in

your oven to brown the loaves sufficiently in the 10-15 minute period, remove the loaf from the oven and slide it under the broiler *very* briefly for the final finish.

15) Cool the loaves, now golden brown and bubbly looking, either on a rack or on a cloth over layers of newspaper. The steam in these loaves can very quickly ruin a formica counter top if there is no insulation.

Pizza is made by much the same technique, but the loaves are still thinner and must be baked faster at easily 600°.

Pideh is ideal bread to take on picnics, for it is broken when served rather than cut, so the knife you forgot to take along is unnecessary, and the loaves stack nicely in a basket. The same dough is often used for making meat turnovers, basted as they bake with olive oil, and these either hot or cold are a perfect picnic dish.

Once the basic bread techniques are understood a whole new realm of baking is opened up. Using mashed potato with the flour, and potato water for the liquid, and keeping the dough very soft, and finally baking the small rounds on a slow griddle for about a half hour, you achieve English muffins. These are superb freshly baked, and nearly as good split and toasted for breakfast the following morning. But homemade English muffins must always be forked open rather than cut, for they're so much fresher and tenderer than the bought ones that the crumb can be mashed by cutting with a knife.

If you've ever had Saffron Bread in Cornwall, you'll never rest until you lay your hands on some real Spanish saffron and make for yourself the aromatic

CORNISH SAFFRON BREAD (or CAKE)

1) Steep 1 tsp. of Spanish saffron stigmas, or ½ tsp. of powdered saffron, in a cup of boiling water, strain the liquid and use as part of the liquid for the bread.

2) Use more sugar than in straight bread, say ½ cup to one yeast cake and about 5 cups of flour.

3) Melt some lard or butter in the liquid—either water or milk, but water makes a lighter bread.

This is superb toasted, and either toasted or not takes to honey most happily.

Then there's the whole range of special French breads like brioche and croissants, enriched with quantities of butter or eggs or both, and there is the so-called French bread itself, a water bread, well kneaded, and baked in a long loaf on a baking sheet. To achieve the characteristic appearance of French bread, mold the bread into a long loaf, and slash the top diagonally before putting it into the oven. A glaze of egg and water further enhances the surface. To get the thick crust that is the hallmark of such a loaf, put the bread on the upper rack of the oven and place on the lower rack a pan of water.

Sourdough is bread that uses as leavening some dough left from a previous baking. The yeast is kept growing in an even temperature where it collects wild yeast from the air. This gives the characteristic sour taste that we relish in old-fashioned

RAISED BUCKWHEAT CAKES

1) Using 2 cups of lukewarm water, stir into it 1 cup of buckwheat flour and 1 cup of white flour, 1 tsp. of salt, and 1 yeast cake mashed with 1 tbsp. of sugar.

2) Let this stand, covered, overnight.

3) Bake in the morning on a griddle. You may like to add another tsp. of sugar when you stir up the batter before baking, as most of the original amount will have been "eaten" by the yeast. Save out some of the batter and keep it in the refrigerator.

These first cakes will be good, but wait! For the next baking you will need about ½ cup of the original batter instead of the yeast cake. Otherwise, proceed as before until just before you bake the cakes. At this point add ½ tsp. of baking soda dissolved in 1 tsp. of water. This counteracts extreme acidity but allows the characteristic sourdough flavor to come through. Bake as before. The cakes get better and better with each succeeding batch of batter over the winter, until finally you have an especially hungry horde to feed and have to use up the batter. Now you'll have to start all over again with a fresh yeast cake.

From yeast-raised buckwheat cakes to batters in general is an easy transition. Some ancient genius discovered the leavening power of eggs and opened the way for cooks to achieve artistry. Batters are made up of a small amount of flour and a large amount of liquid plus eggs which are themselves partly liquid and partly fat, among other things. A simple "dipping" batter is used for that delectable Chinese Phoenix-tail Shrimp or Japanese Tempura, in which the green shrimp are peeled, all but the tail, dipped in batter and fried in sesame or peanut oil or lard. For 2 lbs. of shrimp here is the

DIPPING BATTER

1) Beat 2 eggs only to smoothness with 2 tbsp. of water.
2) Add 4 tbsp. of flour and 1 tsp. of salt and beat smooth, so that there are no lumps.

liquid. The first stage used just enough liquid to hold the meal together. Then with pastry the binding was partly ac-
See what has happened to the original mixture of meal and complished by a new ingredient, the fat. In the yeast doughs the amount of flour holds more liquid than in pastry, and

there's a new ingredient, the yeast. With batters the balance of liquid to flour changes completely: there's much more liquid than solid matter, and now eggs are generally included. With so much more liquid to solid the heat has to be increased so that the batter doesn't spread to a mere film, so pancakes and griddle cakes are baked at high heat. Have you noticed how much better the last cakes of a batch are than the first ones? The major reason is that the griddle is by this time very hot. Although most pancakes are baked on a griddle, the large pancakes served in England for dessert are often baked in the oven, in which case they're called

OVEN-BAKED PANCAKES

1) Beat 2 eggs only until mixed.
2) Add ½ cup of flour and ½ tsp. of salt and mix well.
3) Add from 1 to 2 cups of liquid, depending on whether you prefer a "cake-y" or a more "custard-y" pancake. The liquid may be all milk or half milk and half water. Water makes a more tender cake.
4) Bake in a hot oven, 450°, in greased pie tins until brown.
5) Remove to a warm serving dish, spread with jelly or jam, roll up, and dust with sifted confectioner's sugar.

These are best served hot but are still good when cold. For a really sweet dessert add a tbsp. of sugar as the batter is mixed. Try to mix the batter at least an hour before baking; a pancake batter is always the better for standing. Certainly if you're making a crêpe in the French or Italian style you must let the batter rest, for these pancakes are very thin and light. The resting period allows for the expansion and softening of the flour particles in the liquid, and an even distribution of air throughout the mixture.

Batters are rewardingly versatile. Besides being used for dipping and for dessert pancakes, they may be used as hot-

bread accompaniments to main course dishes, as wrappings
for fillings of meat or vegetables or both, as layers in a casserole dish, or as layers in a molded dish.

One of the best known of all the batter breads is

YORKSHIRE PUDDING

1) Put 4 tbsp. of flour with 1 tsp. of salt into a bowl.
2) Break 2 eggs into a well in the flour.
3) Pour in ½ cup of milk and beat until fairly smooth.
   A rotary beater will do the job quickly and easily.
4) Add another generous ½ cup of milk and beat it in.
5) Let stand covered for an hour or longer.
6) Heat drippings in a large shallow pan until smoking
   hot, then pour the batter in.
7) Bake at a very high temperature, 450° or higher, for
   about 20-30 minutes.

This old English recipe makes a most delightful pudding,
half omelet, half hot-bread. It is extremely delicate and will
fall readily, so let it stand in the opened oven for a minute
or so until everyone is seated at table and served, then bring
it on in the dish in which it baked.

The modern form of Yorkshire pudding is like a popover
batter, and once thoroughly baked it does not fall, but it
hasn't at all the texture of the old recipe.

Pancakes serve wonderfully for luncheon dishes. The little
Italian spinach pancakes are one example. The finely chopped
and creamed spinach should be seasoned with olive oil rather
than butter. Make all the little 3″ pancakes; put a teaspoon
of spinach on each, and roll up so that it looks like a short,
fat cigar. Place all the little rolls on a lightly greased baking
sheet, sprinkle with freshly grated Parmesan cheese, and toast
lightly under the broiler. These with a glass of cold white
wine, followed by a green salad, make a memorable hot-
weather lunch.

By substituting other ingredients for the flour or the milk in pancake batter, innumerable variations can result, just as with the raised breads. There the yeast was the only constant; here the eggs are the constant. When cottage cheese replaces the milk, a much drier mass results, rather like dropped biscuit dough; and baked on a griddle, each cake flattened with the spatula after it is dropped, the end product is quite Russian in effect, especially if they're served with cold sour cream.

When potatoes replace the bulk of the flour you have

POTATO PANCAKES

1) Put through the fine knife of the ordinary meat grinder:
   a large peeled and roughly cut onion
   4 medium-sized potatoes, peeled and cut up.
2) Add about ½ to ¾ cup of flour, salt, and lots of pepper.
3) Beat in with a paddle or spoon 2 large eggs.
4) Drop onto a hot surface (skillet or griddle) well lubricated with lots of fat. Flatten with the spatula. Turn only once. They should be brown and crusty when served, with an indefinable inside texture—half cake, half mashed potato, but wholly delectable.

Served with a highly seasoned or smoky meat (sausage, bacon, ham, corned beef) they're a superb accompaniment to a meal. Or you might enjoy them as we do topped with sour cream, like blintzes, and served as the main attraction of a light supper or luncheon menu.

Batters may be further developed to include fat, and even an addition of baking powder for increased airiness. Waffles *must* include fat to achieve that exquisite glistening crust.

And waffles bring us very close indeed to cakes. The clue to cakes is the richness. They are rich either in eggs or fat, or both, and they are rich in sugar. The basic meal and liquid have by now been relegated to a secondary position in the hierarchy of ingredients. Of the genus cakes, the sponges achieve richness by increasing the egg content of basic batters, and the butter cakes increase the fat content. Sponge cakes use little or no liquid in addition to that provided by the eggs themselves. They are a combination, basically, of sugar, eggs, and flour. The eggs provide liquid, fat and leavening, so there is a large amount of egg in proportion to the amount of flour. Since the eggs are the leavening they must be beaten to the point at which they will hold the greatest amount of air, and they must be handled delicately thereafter so that the air will not be dispersed. The sugar used in sponge cakes must be added rather slowly so that it can be distributed throughout the batter without allowing its weight to squash out some of the air that you've been at such pains to incorporate. The slow addition of the sugar allows it also to dissolve somewhat. One sponge cake recipe calls for making a sugar syrup to ensure just that. The flour too must be added slowly and delicately. That's why most recipes for sponge cakes call for folding in the sugar and flour. The folding process is the lifting of a large amount of the beaten egg up and over the small amount of the added ingredient until the new ingredient is incorporated in the egg mass.

The baking of a sponge cake of any sort is generally at a moderate temperature so that the egg content of the cake won't be toughened, and so that the flour particles have a chance to expand in the warming batter rather than harden in a blast of high heat.

Bearing in mind these points, let's proceed to a simple specific

SPONGE CAKE

1) Grate the rind of a lemon onto 1 cup of sugar and mix.
2) Beat 6 egg yolks until very pale and much increased in bulk.

3) Add sugar and rind mixture very gradually, say in 4-5 goes, beating all the time.

4) Add seasoning in the form of about 2-3 tbsp. of lemon juice, or 1 tsp. of vanilla. You may thin the vanilla with a tsp. of water.

5) Add the egg whites, beaten stiff, but not too dry, with ½ tsp. of salt. It is best to beat the whites by hand (I use a large platter and a fork) as the volume will be greater than if an electric mixer is used. Fold in the whites—oh, so gently—until they are partly but not completely blended with the yolk mixture.

6) Add just under 1 cup of flour measured after sifting, folding it in about a heaping tablespoonful at a time. When the flour is blended into the batter, pour it into the cake tin. Some authorities suggest an ungreased tin, so that the batter may cling to the sides of the pan as it rises. You may want to put a greased paper lining on the bottom of the tin, in which case grease the bottom of the tin, even if you haven't greased the sides.

7) Bake in a rather slow oven (325°) for about one hour for a tube pan, or proportionately less for layer-cake tins.

8) Allow it to cool in the tin before you remove it.

With this background, you may now proceed to sponge cakes using water or milk or even a small amount of fat. In any case, the clue to an excellent sponge cake lies in achieving a homogeneous batter without crushing the air out of it by impatience when adding the denser ingredients to the beaten egg.

The same treatment of an Angel Food cake will assure success, given the proper baking temperature and time. In addition, the beating of the whites of the eggs to the point at which they are stiff but still shiny and moist-looking is most important.

In general, successful butter cakes are easier for the inexperienced cook to make than are the sponge cakes, with the exception of the pound cakes. These enormously rich cakes so sadly often exhibit a "solid streak" that one sometimes wonders why they're even attempted. But once the principles of butter cakes are understood, the veriest tyro can turn out an exquisite pound cake.

In pound cake the fat content is as high as possible; more fat would probably fry the batter. In the old recipes the proportions were one pound of butter, one pound of sugar, one pound of flour and one pound of eggs—hence the name. Modern so-called pound cakes are sometimes smaller, but the proportions are much the same though not invariably so.

Old cookbooks often present recipes in illuminating ways, and though I should be loath to forego the effort-and-time-saving of many of our appliances I have learned much from watching cooks who didn't hold with all these frivolous modern ways and used some of the techniques that are described in old books. Watching my grandmother and mother making pound cake taught me more about cake batters than the hundreds of books that I've consulted. In spite of that I'm going to try to tell you in print what to look for in a cake batter in general, and how to create a work of art in this particular

POUND CAKE

1) In a large bowl cream ¾ lb. of butter. Use the fingers of your right hand only; you'll need the left hand clean for opening the door to the cat or dog or the Fuller Brush man, any one of whom is sure to signal for you as soon as you get well into the creaming process. Now the creaming of butter means exactly that. It does not mean melting it. It *does* mean turning the butter into a substance like whipped cream. The human hand is the best instrument that I know for

this purpose. The warmth of the fingers softens the butter rather quickly. Then, with the fingers of the hand open and the whole hand loose and relaxed, start beating the soft mass, using the hand like a flexible paddle. Soon the butter will begin to pale and stand up in soft peaks. Use the muscles of the forearm rather than the shoulder muscles or you'll soon weaken. When you find that there is no perceptible further change in color (after about 10 minutes of beating) the butter is ready for the next step.

2) Add 2 cups of flour which has been sifted 3 times, and continue beating with your hand until the mixture is homogeneous and fluffy, rather like a hard sauce with beaten egg white in it. This takes another 7-10 minutes.

3) Meanwhile you've set 6 whole large eggs and a pinch of salt to being whipped by the electric mixer or a slavey with a Dover beater. (I was the slavey when Mother made Pound Cake.) These should increase in bulk 6-8 times during the beating.

4) Add to this lovely pale volume of beaten egg 2 cups of sugar, sifted once, and continue beating.

5) Add 1 tsp. of baking powder to the egg-sugar mixture.

6) Add 1 tbsp. of lemon juice to the egg mixture and beat it in. By this time the egg mixture will be just about the same color as the flour and butter mixture, and very nearly the same texture as well.

7) Now add the egg mixture all at once to the butter-flour mixture. Beat them together, still using your hand. Soon the batter will be smooth, but it will still look granular, so keep on with the hand beating. Finally you will achieve a perfectly homogeneous batter so fluffy and perfect that you are in danger of becoming lost in admiration.

8) Now it is ready for the flavoring: 1 tsp. of vanilla and 1 tsp. of almond extract. Beat this in, but don't yet wash that right hand.

9) Take the large tube pan or spring form (which you
   had the foresight to grease just before you began to
   cream the butter) and put the batter into it by hand-
   fuls. Use a finger to scrape out the last smidgin of
   batter and now wash your hand; you're through!

10) Bake in a moderate oven—about 350°. One large cake
    takes about 45-50 minutes; two smaller ones take
    about 30-35 minutes.

11) After it is baked, let the cake stand for a few minutes
    in the oven with the door open. At this point it should
    show signs of having shrunk a bit from the sides of
    the pan, and it should have an elastic spring when
    pressed ever so gently in the center of the mass be-
    tween the tube and the side of the pan.

12) Place the cake in its tin on a rack and let it cool for
    a few minutes. Then loosen it around the sides and
    around the tube with a knife or spatula and turn it
    out onto a rack. If it doesn't slip out easily, let it cool
    a bit longer. A tap on the bottom of the pan will often
    loosen it sufficiently to allow it to drop out.

This cake seems to me to be too good to frost, but you
may prefer a simple icing on it. One last point: margarine
cannot be substituted for the butter. It just won't whip as
light.

Once you've made this cake "by hand" you'll be aware of
the changes which occur in a batter when successive ingredients are added, and you'll be able to see how beating affects
batters at different stages. These changes are so rapid when
mechanical aids are used that they escape the untrained eye.

Most of the operations for this cake are performed sitting
down, working in your lap, so although the best part of an
hour has to be allowed for the preparation it is not a tiring
process.

When a cook "bakes" she deals primarily with flour. Flour,

like the egg, is used all through the menu, so the techniques for dealing with it must be understood. The application of heat to dishes using flour is crucial, but in addition, the manipulation of certain combinations using flour is what makes the dish specific. Further, analyzing the relation between flour and other materials can explain to us the reasons for much of the manipulation and for the baking times and temperatures required for a successful product.

3. Sauces are at once the admiration and the despair of the uninitiated, and yet sauces are essentially just accompaniments to a dish, either liquid or semiliquid, that enhance the basic flavor or texture of the food. The key word in this definition is "accompaniment." Sauces are supplementary in function, never so dominant as to reduce the major part of the dish to a mere base, with the notable exception of curry where the sauce *is* the dish.

Classification of the multitude of existing sauces is a problem. They may be classified by

1) texture: natural (*au jus*), thin or thick
2) temperature: hot or cold.
3) geographical source: Chinese, French, Greek, etc.
4) major ingredients: egg, garlic, wine, tomato, etc.
5) function: *for* meats, fish, poultry, game, vegetables, salad, or dessert.

But however they are classified, mastery of sauce making is achieved when texture is studied and the power of the ingredients to affect texture is understood. For our purposes then, the examination of sauces in their textural aspect may prove enlightening.

If we divide sauces into thick and thin, we find that the thin sauces are in general easier to make, but the thick sauces are far more widely used. Although it isn't just to say that the English know but one sauce,* there is an element of truth in that statement, and we Americans who inherit so largely from the British culinary culture share in their reputation. "The" sauce referred to is the ubiquitous white sauce which can cover meat, fish or vegetables with a sometimes anonymous gluey blanket of little or no flavor. The white sauce, however, is of ancient and proud lineage, since it is the practical application of an intellectual principle: the reduction of liquidity by the addition of blended solids.

Sauces may be thickened in several ways, but the most widespread method in our culture is by the use of flour. There are for the flour-thickened sauces two "genus" sauces which are the framework on which are constructed all the great basic species of flour-thickened sauces. The white sauces are built as follows:

Thin	Medium	Thick
1 tbsp. fat	2 tbsp. fat	3 tbsp. fat
1 tbsp. flour	2 tbsp. flour	3 tbsp. flour
1 cup liquid	1 cup liquid	1 cup liquid
seasoning	seasoning	seasoning

The brown sauces are similarly constructed, except that browned flour is used, and, since browned flour doesn't have the thickening power of unbrowned, something over 1 tbsp. of browned flour is needed to 1 tbsp. of fat. Also the cup of liquid should include the classic brown stock.

The fat used in sauce-making may be butter, margarine, oil, drippings, lard, or solid vegetable fats. The starch may be wheat, arrowroot, rye, oat, barley or corn, or crumbs. The

---

* *"Il y a en Angleterre soixante sectes religieuses differentes, et une seule sauce."*

Attributed to Francesco Caraccioli, 1752-1799.

liquid may be water, milk, cream, bouillon or broth made of fish, meat, game, fowl or vegetables, or it may be wholly or in part wine. The seasoning may range from the usual salt and pepper, through herbs and vegetables, meat, fish, fruit, all the way to seeds and nuts.

Having fixed the proportions of the genus sauces, we can now proceed to make a real sauce—a species sauce—which is a named sauce.

The basic white sauce, the type to which many species are related, is, as all cooks know,

BÉCHAMEL SAUCE

1) Melt 1 tbsp. of butter and let it heat until it foams.
2) Add 1 tbsp. of white flour and stir until smooth. Turn down the heat now, for too rapid cooking of the flour will actually prevent the expansion of the particles and the binding effect that you are striving for. During this stirring the flour cooks, expands, and absorbs the butter.
3) Add gradually, stirring constantly, 1 cup of hot milk. The milk being close to the temperature of the *roux* unites smoothly with it and the troublesome lumps of a bad sauce are avoided.
4) Add salt. When the sauce has thickened to a velvety smoothness, it is ready. It must be kept over the heat for long enough so that the particles of flour can exert their absorptive and thickening powers, which is why so many recipes use the direction, "Allow to come to a boil."
5) Strain and serve.

Ingredients probably added to béchamel sauce are onion and parsley. Ingredients possibly added are chopped or minced raw veal—added in the beginning to the butter—and nutmeg or thyme for seasoning.

Béchamel sauce as made by a good chef is always strained before serving. Even if no solids other than flour are used, straining seems to enhance the velvety texture. If solids are used, straining is obligatory.

The term *roux* used in recipes is merely the French word for the mixture of flour and fat. A white sauce uses a *roux blanc,* a mixture of fat with white flour just as it comes from the sack, and it is cooked only long enough for the flour particles to unite with the fat and expand in the heat. Some sauces demand a *roux blond,* in which case the flour and fat mixture is cooked until it becomes golden. This further cooking of the flour imparts a slight intensity of taste to the finished sauce. A *roux brun,* as the term implies, requires browned flour. Browning the flour may be accomplished by cooking the flour and fat still longer than in the case of a *roux blond,* or the flour may be browned before it is combined with the fat. This is done either in a dry skillet on top of the stove over low heat or in the oven. In either case it must be watched carefully so that it heats and browns evenly. Burnt flour will give a scorched taste to the finished sauce. If brown sauces are in great demand in your household, you may brown a large quantity of flour at once and store it in a jar or canister ready to hand, instead of browning the small amount needed for each sauce as the occasion arises. A brown gravy, by the way, is not necessarily a true brown sauce; for the brown color may come from the meat and meat juices which have browned in the pan, not from browned flour and brown stock.

The second great white sauce is all too seldom encountered in this country, for we do not often boil fish and meats and therefore do not have on hand the requisite white stock, but for certain dishes it is indispensable to serve

VELOUTÉ SAUCE
1) Melt 1 tbsp. of butter and let it foam.

2) Add 1 tbsp. of white flour. Stir, and let the paste cook over lower heat without browning.
3) Add 1 cup of white stock heated to boiling point, and stir until thick and smooth.
4) Add salt and pepper to taste and strain before serving.

Mushroom trimmings or peelings are often added to the butter, or are cooked in the stock. Lemon juice may also be added as part of the liquid.

You may now begin to play the variations on these two basic white sauces and make, perhaps,

THICKENED VELOUTÉ

1) Make 1 cup of velouté sauce and let it cool somewhat.
2) With a whisk (*wisp*, slotted spoon, etc.), beat into the warm sauce 1 egg yolk. It's a good idea to fork the egg smooth with a bit of water before adding it to the sauce.
3) 1 tsp. of lemon juice may be added as well, if you fancy it.
4) Strain before serving.

Or you may want a classic

CREAM SAUCE

1) Make 1 cup of béchamel sauce.
2) Add ¼ cup of heavy cream.
3) 1 tsp. of lemon juice may be added here, too.

Béchamel sauce may also be enriched with egg yolk and is still called just béchamel.

For easy sauce-making, I use a wide shallow pottery casserole with rounded sides over an asbestos mat; a square corner can trap the *roux* so that a spoon won't reach it. But if you have a Swedish *wisp*, a sort of little besom made of twigs, you can blend a smooth sauce in a pan of any shape or size. The only spoon I use for sauces is a thin wooden one, by now much worn on one side, but I prefer it to a metal one for it doesn't get as hot as metal and consequently doesn't allow the *roux* to cook on it and form potential lumps, and it is much quieter than a clattering metal spoon.

A flour-based sauce will develop a thick skin on its surface if it is allowed to cool. This is unsightly, texturally unpleasant, and unnecessary, and can be avoided by gently flooding the surface of the warm sauce with butter, oil or milk. If there isn't too much butter or milk used, it may be stirred into the sauce on reheating, but oil should be skimmed off. Or, if it is covered with butter, the sauce may be chilled and the thin cake of butter be lifted off and saved for future use.

A number of braised dishes are served with a sauce made from the liquid in which they are cooked. In this case it is convenient to thicken the sauce with tiny balls of a mixture of creamed butter and flour. This is called in many recipes by its French name, *beurre manié*, or in English "kneaded butter." If you keep in mind the proportions for a flour-thickened genus sauce, you can make your finished product the desired thickness by this method. It is only necessary to remember that for 1 cup of liquid you will need for a thin sauce 1 tbsp. of fat and 1 tbsp. of flour. The little balls of fat and flour must be stirred carefully into the hot liquid so that they unite evenly with it and thicken it to the desired smoothness. Straining the sauce prevents any fragments of meat, vegetable or herbs from disfiguring the appearance of the dish and enhances the gloss of the work of art.

All the named brown sauces, made with a *roux brun*, use the same techniques as the white sauces, and nearly all include the classic French

BROWN SAUCE

1) Melt ½ cup fat (not chicken) in a large heavy pot.
2) Add a carrot and 2 medium-sized onions roughly chopped. Cook until the onions begin to color.
3) Add ½ cup of flour and blend well, stirring until the flour takes on a brown color.
4) Now add about 1 qt. of good brown stock—of which you will need 2 qts. in all, a clove of garlic, a stalk or two of celery, parsley, thyme, and a bay leaf.
5) Simmer and let thicken, then add all but the last cup of the remaining qt. of stock. Turn down the heat and let cook slowly until the sauce is reduced to half its volume, skimming off fat or scum as it rises. This sauce gives up its fat as a white sauce does not; therefore it is a little less rich in calories.
6) Add ¼ cup of tomato sauce, or ½ cup of tomato purée, or somewhat more of tomato juice. Cook until these are thoroughly blended. Add salt and pepper at this time, if you wish to include them. If the stock was well seasoned, they won't be necessary.
7) Strain the sauce and add the last cup of stock and let the cooking continue slowly until the sauce is reduced again to about 4 cups and has been skimmed completely free of fat.
8) Strain and use, or store in the refrigerator.

Brown sauce is hardly a sauce in its own right but is required for the making of Demi-glace or Espagnole sauce, itself one of the basic ingredients in the many species of brown sauces. Espagnole sauce is brown sauce plus mushrooms, sherry and concentrated beef broth.

In the ordinary kitchen the classic brown sauces are a trouble to make, for they require stock made in exacting ways. But once the basic brown sauce is understood, approximations of it and the sauces depending on it may be made with whatever good stock you can muster and the results will be just as good as the classic ones but with the added attraction of your individual stamp upon them.

The basic hot sauce thickened with egg is Hollandaise. If you understand what makes Hollandaise tick you can make any egg-thickened sauce. Timid cooks don't dare cook it long enough for fear that it may curdle. Impatient cooks try to make it too quickly by using too high a heat. Either course is fatal. Make up your mind to spending time and care on this great sauce, and insist on a perfect consistency. A low heat is the first and major requirement. Use a double boiler and do not let the upper part come into direct contact with the hot water beneath. It is wise to start with a very little water in the lower compartment and add a little cold water to it from time to time in order to keep the water from boiling. I find that a heavy pottery bowl, which heats slowly, is better than metal over the hot water. A little bit of water with the egg in the beginning also helps prevent too rapid initial cooking.

The second requirement is the proper beating of the eggs. Use a Swedish *wisp* if you can get one, or any tool that will touch all parts of the container and keep the egg moving. The beating must be brisk and consistent. No part of the egg mixture must be allowed to get hotter than the rest.

The third point has to do with the addition of the butter. Even if the butter is creamed, it is considerably cooler than the egg in the warm bowl over the hot water. It has to be united with the egg, and the smaller the amount of butter added at a time, the sooner it will be melted and blended with the egg. However, don't carry this principle too far or you'll never want to tackle the sauce a second time; adding the butter in three or four goes is about right.

Recipes for Hollandaise vary from cook to cook and from book to book, depending on the degree of thickness desired or the degree of sharpness. For about two cups of fairly standard

HOLLANDAISE SAUCE

1) Put 3 egg yolks and 1 tbsp. of water into a heavy bowl that will fit closely over a pan containing about 1″ of hot, not boiling water. Keep the heat of the water in the lower compartment just under boiling point. Check from time to time, and, if necessary to bring the water below boiling point, add a tbsp. of cold water.

2) Beat the egg yolks with a *wisp*, or whisk, with an even stroke, making sure that no area of the bowl is left untouched for any length of time. Continue the beating until the eggs are light in color and texture.

3) Now add the first ¼ lb. of butter. (You will use ¾ lb. in all.) Have the butter at room temperature and cut up into pieces, or have it creamed. Continue beating until the butter is completely absorbed and the sauce begins to thicken.

4) Repeat until all the butter is used and the sauce is thick.

5) Add 1 tsp. of lemon juice or vinegar and beat in thoroughly. Add salt here if you like, and possibly some white pepper.

6) For a still more elegant finish strain the sauce through a fine sieve.

Unsalted butter makes a better Hollandaise and in less time for it holds less water than salted butter.

For a very thick sauce increase the number of eggs. A thinner sauce will result when fewer egg yolks are used, or when a little water is added toward the end of the process. For a sharper sauce increase the amount of lemon juice or vinegar.

Having made Hollandaise, you will be able to make any sauce based on it, or you may make the similar but more elaborate

BÉARNAISE SAUCE

1) Cook until reduced to ½ its volume:

> ¼ cup white wine
> ¼ cup vinegar
> 1 tsp. of chopped fresh tarragon (¼ tsp. dried)
> 1 tsp. of chopped fresh parsley or chervil (½ tsp. dried)
> 1 tsp. of chopped shallots
> salt and pepper if desired.

2) Strain this through a fine sieve into the bowl in which you will make the sauce.

3) Add 3 or 4 egg yolks and beat over hot water until light in color and texture.

4) Add softened butter in thirds or quarters of the total amount, using about ½ to ¾ lb. in all.

5) When thick, strain again and serve.

If you wish to use the chopped herbs as an eye-catching finish for the sauce, reserve them and add them after the sauce has been strained into the sauce dish or over the food.

One of the great sauces of the Near East is the Greek sauce, Avgolimono. This is much sharper than Hollandaise and it uses a higher proportion of liquid and little or no fat. Similar to it is the sauce used in France to finish a Blanquette de Veau, for which some of the seasoned stock in which the meat has cooked is strained, cooled and mixed with egg yolks and lemon. This mixture is then beaten into the warm strained stock. When it is thick and smooth, heavy cream is added and the sauce is strained over the meat waiting in a hot dish.

In addition to flour and eggs, cornstarch is used to thicken sauces. The Anglo-Saxon culture confines the use of cornstarch almost exclusively to dessert sauces, but the Chinese use this starch for the beautifully clear sauces in their meat, vegetable or fish dishes. I prefer to use cornstarch in presenting a dish of cooked meat, sliced, covered with mushroom caps, and surrounded with my own version of

MADEIRA SAUCE

1) In a large, shallow pan or skillet sauté mushroom caps in a little butter. Remove the mushrooms and place on top of the cooked sliced meat in a casserole.
2) In the same skillet rub into the remaining fat a paste made of 1 tsp. of cornstarch and 2 tbsp. of water.
3) Add immediately about 1½ cups of the strained stock in which the meat has been cooked. Stir, so that the paste is dissolved in the liquid.
4) Add about ½ cup of Madeira wine. (I generally use Sercial.)
5) Add salt and pepper if necessary. Stir until viscid and very clear and smooth.

When the sauce is finished and poured over the meat, the dish can then be put in the oven for a final blending and heating. The oven heat reduces the volume of the sauce somewhat so that it is thicker than when first made.

Butter tilted ever so gently into a thin "natural" sauce is enough to thicken it to a very slight degree. Such a sauce must not be reheated or the butter will separate. Cream also, with its high butter-fat content will do much the same thing but imparts an opaque aspect which butter does not.

Sometimes a purée of vegetables, herbs and meat will reduce liquidity sufficiently for the purposes of special dishes.

Rice flour is used in certain curry sauces for thickening; and in the neighborhood of New Orleans, filé, which is powdered sassafras leaves, is used, when okra is not, to thicken gumbo.

A refinement of flour-thickening is the *panade* (*panada*) of the Mediterranean countries, where the fresh crumb of a loaf of bread, crumbled and soaked in milk, water or stock is the binder of a sauce. In England a version of this is served with roasted meats, game or poultry. A roasted pheasant there is unthinkable without

BREAD SAUCE

1) Put a peeled small onion stuck with a clove into 1 cup of milk and bring slowly to a boil. Remove the onion.
2) Add 2 heaping tbsp. of the crumbled crumb of fresh bread—no crusts.
3) Add salt and pepper and simmer very gently, stirring occasionally, for about 10-15 minutes.
4) Add a small piece of butter and 1 tbsp. of cream. Stir in and heat again.
5) Strain if not perfectly smooth.

Bread sauce is thicker than a béchamel and has a faintly grainy texture, which because it is expected is very pleasant.

Probably the most important cold sauce is mayonnaise. Nothing is better on a salad of home-grown vegetables than this sauce home-made with a good olive oil. But again the lore and legends cluster about it so that many otherwise excellent cooks don't attempt it. Out of sheer laziness I first discarded the rule that the oil must be dripped in, and discovered that the mayonnaise took much less time to make, didn't separate, and got quite as thick as by the weary dripping process. Since eggs beat up more quickly at room temperature, I start with a warm egg. If I have a blender at hand I use it, but a Dover beater used at fairly rapid rpm does the job just as well and in a very few minutes. Here then is how I make about two cups of

MAYONNAISE

1) Put a whole egg, which has been allowed to come to room temperature into a bowl with salt and pepper and about 2 tbsp. of cider vinegar, or a little more of lemon juice. When I use lemon juice I add a pinch of sugar.
2) Beat this mixture until light in color and texture.
3) Add about 1 tbsp. of oil and beat it in thoroughly. I prefer olive oil for the flavor, but a salad oil will make just as smooth and stable a sauce.

4) Add about ¼ cup of oil and beat.
5) Add all the rest of the oil. You'll use a total amount of about 1 to 1¼ cups. Beat until the sauce is thick and smooth. The faster you beat, the more readily the oil is incorporated into the egg mixture, and the more oil you can use—within limits.

The multitude of uses for mayonnaise need not be enumerated—I believe there is even a recipe for cake that calls for it. But sometimes individual dishes seem to want something special in the way of a mayonnaise-like dressing. A fish aspic for example, all pale topaz jelly and white flesh, can seem a bit pallid on anything but a black plate, so I make for it a version of

SAUCE VERTE

1) Mince finely the leaves of either fresh dill and parsley, or fresh tarragon and chervil, until you have about ¼ cup.
2) Blend thoroughly with 1 cup of mayonnaise.

A spoonful of white wine or brandy added to this does not thin it too much and adds that *je ne sais quoi* that makes your guests go mildly raving homeward. But if you've put wine in the aspic don't waste that spoonful on the sauce; it won't be detected.

There is one sauce I'd like to mention, and not simply because it is curious. The Spanish make a most delectable fish dish and serve it with a chocolate sauce, not however a sweet sauce. The steaks of fish (halibut is what I use) are sautéed with chopped onion and mushrooms in oil or butter. Then a teaspoonful of grated bitter chocolate is rubbed into the fat remaining in the pan along with a rounded teaspoonful of flour, and white wine and a little water are used for the liquid. The chocolate, as well as adding fat, provides a subtle unctuousness that is indefinable, mysterious and wholly exotic.

When we come to consider dessert sauces, we notice immediately that the principal characteristic is not development by thickening the texture, but development by enrichment in sugar or fat, or both. Textural change is secondary in importance. Crushed or blendered fruit is probably the simplest of all sweet sauces. When sugar is added to strawberries and served on cake or biscuit, the result is strawberry shortcake. When the fruit is cooked and sugar added, apples become applesauce. Reducing the fruit juice by cooking has the effect of increasing the proportion of sugar to liquid. (Melted jelly is a good fruit sauce, for example.) Wines or liqueurs added to fruit syrups also increase sugar content as well as making a flavor change.

The thickening of dessert sauces is more often achieved by the addition of egg than by the addition of starch, but when starch is used it is rarely flour that provides it, but cornstarch. Cornstarch needs no fat to make it combine smoothly with the liquid, and it makes a bright transparent sauce, very appealing to the eye. Mixed with a bit of cold liquid— water for convenience—to a thin paste and added to cold fruit juice, in the proportion of 1 tsp. of cornstarch to 1 cup of sweetened juice, then heated gradually to boiling point and kept moving constantly by stirring briskly, a lovely light bright sauce results. Infinite changes can be rung on this simple scheme. Brown sugar may be used for the sweetening. A bit of salt sparks almost any food, and sweet sauces are no exception. A stick of cinnamon or a few drops of vanilla extract will combine delightfully with certain fruits. Wine rarely if ever hurts a fruit sauce. It makes a superb addition quite often, especially Madeira with peaches, port with cherries or claret with figs. A little experimenting will provide you with your own list of flavor affinities.

Chocolate always makes a moderately thick sauce because of its fat content, and after fruit it is perhaps the greatest boon to dessert-sauce makers. Consider the superb dessert

MONT BLANC (MONTE BIANCO)

1) Make a purée of cooked chestnuts.
2) Add sugar, cream and wine (Marsala, cognac or rum for choice) in the proportion of 1 cup of purée to 2 tbsp. of sugar, ¼ cup of cream, 2 tbsp. of wine, and ½ tsp. of vanilla extract as well, if you like.
3) Mound this in a cone on the serving dish and chill in the refrigerator.
4) When it is cold and ready to serve, pour over it a sauce of semisweet chocolate melted in a double boiler with water or wine added to keep it liquid enough. Or use bitter chocolate and add sugar.
5) To gild the lily, top with whipped cream.

Chocolate, largely fat, needs little enrichment beyond sugar; even so, we proceed to make a fudge sauce by adding cream and/or butter, or we use it as the flavor of a hard sauce which is basically just butter and sugar, lightened in texture perhaps with beaten egg white or brandy or both.

The remaining dessert sauces are enriched and thickened with egg. They are, in other words, custard sauces, and are considered as custards in the chapter on the egg, but one such sauce I'll include here because it is a perfect example of the highest development from thin to thickened, and from simple to complex enrichment. To make

LEMON BUTTER (LEMON CHEESE or LEMON CURD)

1) Cream ⅛ lb. (¼ cup or 4 tbsp.) of butter.
2) Add 1 cup of sugar and blend well.

3) Add 2 whole eggs and a third yolk and beat until light in color and texture.

4) Add the strained juice of 1½ average-sized lemons and the grated rind of a whole lemon. Don't be alarmed if the mixture looks curdled at this point.

5) Put over hot water and stir steadily until the mixture is smooth and thick, the consistency of cornstarch pudding. This takes about 20 minutes to a half hour, so call on your supplementary fund of patience.

6) Put into jars and seal.

Lemon butter is said to keep indefinitely. I've never been able to verify that statement. It's a superb pudding, a delicious filling for a cold tart, a luscious spread on ginger-bread—or just plain bread, and it makes a delightful filling between layers of cake.

Expertise in sauce-making may tempt you to supply them with every dish. Don't; resist. A great many foods suffer from the detraction of sauces. I'll warrant that few people in our culture know the real flavor of good fresh spaghetti; it's so often served with tomato or meat sauce. Sometime, if you can grow your own basil, either sweet or purple, collect enough of it to fill ½ cup when finely chopped. Then proceed to serve

BASIL SPAGHETTI

1) Cook ½ lb. of fresh spaghetti or spaghettini (still thinner than spaghetti) in lots of rapidly boiling salted water until it is "just done." The color changes to a paler cream, and the pasta no longer looks so opaque as when it was dry. It is not mushy, but is soft enough to cut with a spoon. Drain it and put it into a heated dish.

2) While the pasta cooks, mash a cut clove of garlic in bowl with ½ tsp. of salt.

3) Add to it the chopped basil and 2 tbsp. grated Parmesan cheese and 1 tbsp. olive oil.
4) Add 1 tbsp. butter and ½ cup of the hot water in which the pasta has been cooking and blend well.
5) Pour over the pasta and bring to table. I like a generous sprinkle of freshly ground black pepper as well.

With either a white or red wine this is a lovely main dish for a hot summer night, especially if you've served a soup first, or if it's followed by a flavorsome dessert.

One last sauce I'd like to mention that doesn't seem to fit in anywhere, for instead of reducing liquidity in order to make it, a solid is brought to liquidity by the addition of water. It is the sauce used for Crême Caramel, a custard with a caramel sauce. For a custard made with one pint of milk, here is how to produce

CARAMEL SAUCE

1) Put 1 cup of sugar in a skillet over low heat until it melts and browns, caramelizes.
2) Add ½ cup of water, stir hard and fast to smooth out the candy-like bits, and let cook until the mixture is smooth and clear.

This caramel is then put into the greased pan in which the custard will be baked. Or you may caramelize the sugar directly in the pudding mold or pan—with the result of scorched fingers unless you have one of those pleasant French pudding molds that come equipped with a detachable handle.

Mere classification seems to make an approach to sauce-making easy. The only talents a sauce-cook needs are those required for any other branch of cookery: patience and interest. Given those the skills follow with experience.

4. Meat and Potatoes are the center of dinner menus in the Anglo-Saxon culture, and the "meat-and-potatoes man" admits no substitute for potatoes and limits "meat" to mean roasted or broiled beef with an occasional nod to lamb or ham. This would mean a sadly narrow repertoire for the cook, so if she's wise, she will begin early to train the palate of her private audience to a wider tolerance. To this cook, and eventually to her audience, meat will mean an infinite succession of dishes ranging from the justly prized roast beef, through lamb, veal, pork, fish, goat, venison, rabbit, squirrel, chicken, pheasant, Guinea hen, turtle, whale, shell fish and all the way to the so-called variety meats: tongue, sweetbreads, roes—indeed, eggs in all their fantasy—tripe, heart, kidneys, liver, brains, lungs and spleen. And this is not an exhaustive list. Potatoes *are* wonderfully useful, but what of rice and wild rice, all the splendid forms of pasta,

the breads of differing texture and flavor and use, the noodles, dumplings, fritters and pancakes, the rich crust of a meat pie? The cook can rejoice with Samuel Hoffenstein: "Oh, how various is the scene!"

The cook thinks in terms not of meat and potatoes as such, but of a balance of dishes heartily satisfying as the core of a dinner, and somehow this balance based on taste and satisfaction of the appetite comes out looking like an embodiment of the nutritionist's rule of protein and carbohydrate as the center of the meal. Our cook is not dismayed, or even much interested, that this should be so, for he—or more often she—has no prejudices for or against the rules of nutrition. He proceeds from different premises.

The basic premise for the cook is likely to be taste. "What will taste good?" she asks when she faces the meat counter with its files of roasts, steaks, ground meats, fowl, and variety meats. The second consideration is variety. If there has been a whole ham in the menu recently, one is hardly likely to want pork for a change—or corned beef. Something like chicken or fish has more allure. The third premise, or at least a modifying factor, is economy. A fine filet of beef at over two dollars a pound seems expensive compared to "ground beef," provenance unspecified, at 89 cents. The fourth condition to be satisfied is the one having to do with time of preparation and skill. A young mother will rarely consider Kievski cutlets, nor will a young working wife choose a beef tongue, except maybe for a weekend dinner.

Let us, however, serenely ignore these latter factors and consider merely the two that concern the cook as cook: taste and variety. Now a standing rib roast of beef surrounded with a golden, bosomy Yorkshire pudding resists competition fairly successfully, but there are other roastable cuts of meat that some people actually prefer. In countries where sheep are raised, beef is little used, and there the roast is either lamb or mutton. Unfortunately, we cannot get mutton in this country, so there's no point in discussing it, except briefly to regret the fact. But our lamb is good and deserves attention.

Probably the best way to roast any meat is over an open fire. This is the true roasting. What we call roasting in the twentieth century is really baking, done as it is in an oven where no occasional flame licks the surface, and where no smoke adds its savor to the meat. For that reason I like to sear a roast of any sort—not only to seal in the juices, but to get the smoky flavor in the crust.

In Turkey, the open fire for roasting is still in fairly general use, and here there is a superb roast called Döner Kebab. Even today, a walk down Istiklal Caddesi is sweet agony, for the savor of this roast comes from half a dozen small restaurants, and the sight of the upright spit in front of the glowing coals, smoking lightly and dripping fat and juice is all but unendurable. For this roast, slices of raw lamb are bound tightly around a metal spit so that the meat when ready to cook has almost the appearance of a natural leg of lamb. The meat is kept quite close to the charcoal fire, so that the outside cooks quickly. As the surface roasts, the attendant carves off thin, narrow slices. The inner uncooked meat is thereby exposed to the heat and in its turn cooks and is sliced off. No basting is necessary, for the inner juices and melting fat bathe each newly revealed surface. This is the acme of perfect roasting, but it isn't of practical interest for a cook in a modern kitchen—unless she happens to command a rotisserie grill, in which case it might be a possibility.

The French roast of lamb inserts thin slivers of garlic in horizontal slits under the skin, and this gives it its characteristic flavor. The same thing is done in Greece, where as well as the garlic, oregano is likely to be added and the whole leg smeared liberally with lemon juice and probably with olive oil.

One of our favorite lamb roasts is the Spanish

CORDERO ASADO À LA MANCHEGA

1) Trim a leg of lamb of the shank, so that the result is

a square cushion, and put it in a casserole into which it fits fairly closely. Set it in a hot oven or under the broiler for a few minutes, then turn down the heat to about 350°.

2) After the oven has cooled to the lower heat, baste the roast with dabs of butter and some dry white table wine. During the roasting, baste several times with more wine. You will need about a cupful altogether.

3) On top of the stove, stew in butter thin chips of garlic. I allow one small clove or ½ a large one per person.

4) When the garlic begins to color, add about 2 pimientos, chopped into small pieces, for 2 cloves of garlic. The canned pimientos are perfectly satisfactory. Heat this sauce thoroughly, then put aside until later.

5) Ten minutes or so before serving the meat, pour off the drippings from the roasting casserole into the pan of garlic and pimiento. Heat this to bubbling and serve as the sauce for the meat.

This sauce is gloriously rich and no help at all to liverish people, but once tasted it is unforgettable. The wine cuts the fatty texture, and the combination of pimiento and garlic is surprisingly subtle.

With this we like

PLAIN RICE

1) In a fine strainer measure out rice in the proportion of 1 cup for 4 people, and submerge the strainer in a bowl of cold water. Wash thoroughly by rubbing the grains between the fingers, changing the water frequently until no more loose starch remains to turn the water milky.

2) Put the rice into a large skillet or shallow casserole and cover with twice the amount of water that there is of rice: 1 cup of rice to 2 cups of water. Add ½ tsp.

to 1 tsp. of salt, depending on the seasoning of the dish to be served with it. With the Cordero Asado I use ½ tsp. of salt in the rice.

3) Put the skillet, covered closely, over a high heat until the water boils. Remove the cover; turn down the heat and let cook slowly until all the water has disappeared and little pits, like reversed bubbles, show in the surface of the rice mass.

4) Remove from the fire; invert a colander over the pan and cover with a dry cloth (linen is best). Let steam for about 10 minutes, then turn out into a bowl or onto a platter to serve.

Done this way the rice is dry with each kernel separate. It is easy to shape into a ring, if that is your pleasure, to hold a runny dish like curried eggs or creamed fish or meat. The Portuguese mold the hot rice then decorate it with black olives, a nice flavor and texture adjunct.

Veal is much in favor on the European continent and is presented there in delightful and inexhaustible variety. We see it here quite often in the form of veal scaloppini, cutlets sliced very thin, and stemming as the name suggests from the Italian cuisine. In Portugal one finds a superb roast of the loin, but because our American butchering is somewhat different from the continental I use a leg or rump for what is known in Portugal as

LOMBO DE VITELA

1) Marinate a leg or rump of veal for at least 2 hours in white wine into which you have sliced garlic. I use 2 cloves of garlic for about 6 to 8 lbs. of meat.

2) Dab the top of the roast with butter and roast on a rack in a hot oven for 5-10 minutes, then turn down the heat, allowing about 30 minutes per lb. at about 325°.

3) During the roasting period, baste frequently with the wine in which the meat has marinated, but be sure the garlic is strained out. The meat will have quite enough flavor from the long marinating period.

By the end of the cooking time the wine will have evaporated and cooked away almost completely and the sticky brown glaze remaining in the pan will make an ineffable gravy.

With this roast also we prefer plain rice to set off the flavorsome meat and gravy.

But not all good dishes are foreign. One peculiarly American roast is the Pennsylvania Dutch way of preparing a

ROAST LOIN OF PORK WITH BEANS

1) Soak marrowfat beans overnight. Pea beans will not do, as their skins are too firm.

2) The next morning bring the beans to the boil in fresh water; add salt, then simmer until the skins burst. Skim off the fluff as it rises.

3) Use a center cut of the loin of pork. It must not be too fat, so the better the quality of the meat, the better the dish. Put the meat in a commodious roaster and distribute the beans around it. They should be about 1½" deep in the pan.

4) Bury some onion at each end of the pan. I use one large or two small onions for about 1 lb. of beans and 4-6 lbs. of meat.

5) Sprinkle over the beans a pinch of dried thyme and one of marjoram or oregano. Or put a healthy sprig of the fresh herbs beside each piece of onion.

6) Spread on top of the beans and meat about ½ cup of brown sugar to 1 lb. of beans—more, if you have a sweet tooth.

7) Trickle over the beans and the meat about the same amount of golden syrup or dark corn syrup as you

have used of sugar. Then add the liquid in which the beans have boiled.

8) Set in the oven heated to 200°, and bake for 6–8 hours, depending on the size of the roast. Baste and stir the beans from time to time, turning under the top crusty part and exposing the damp underneath part. Do not stir during the last hour of baking. There should be a fluffy, lightly crusty topping of broken beans about the meat when it is ready to serve.

This dish is always accompanied in our household by Hot Cole Slaw, and if there are guests, by applesauce as well, though we find the sweet-sour of the Cole Slaw quite enough of flavor contrast.

Baked ham is often a disappointment to me, partly because good lean hams are hard to come by and those are the ones I prefer. But also, I do not fancy the sticky sweetness of a beautifully garnished ham; it's impossible to appreciate wine with meat of however good quality that has been covered with sugar and pineapple and such confections. So I've come to the point of ordering ham sight unseen from one of the several reliable places in the country where one can be moderately certain of getting lean ham, naturally smoked; and instead of baking it I steam it on a rack over ½" of water in a tightly covered roaster. For flavor enhancement, I drill a hole in the rind with a chisel and hammer and insert a twig or two of pine, the twig about ¼" thick and about 8" long from the cut wood to the end of the needle tuft. The resinous pine goes beautifully with the smoky flavor of the meat, and the aroma in the house is most seductive. With this meat we like to drink a light rosé. Since the meat is so plain, I rather let myself go in the matter of the "potatoes"—in this case a rice dish from Turkey, called

WEDDING PILAV

1) Wash the rice in a strainer submerged in a bowl of cold water, changing the water frequently until it no longer turns cloudy from the loose starch. Drain.

2) Stew some cut-up onion (1 small onion to 1 cup of rice) in butter until it is soft and beginning to color.

3) Add the rice, 2 tbsp. of pine nuts, and 2 tbsp. of currants, salt, pepper and a sweet herb like parsley, chervil or oregano. Stir well so that the butter penetrates the whole mass.

4) Add chicken broth in the proportion of 2 cups of broth to 1 cup of rice; cover and bring to the boil.

5) Turn down the heat and let cook very slowly until all the liquid is absorbed and dimples appear in the surface of the rice.

6) Remove from the heat, cover with an inverted colander and then a cloth, and let steam for 10 minutes before serving.

The only real fault in my private cooking audience is a tiresome tendency to prefer other carbohydrate dishes to rice. Theoretically, since I do the cooking, I have the final word in the matter, but I do enjoy once in a while the slow almost unbelieving delight that comes over his face when I serve instead of rice, perhaps, a

BATTER BREAD

1) Mix together 1 cup of fresh (preferably water-ground) corn meal and 1 tsp. of baking powder.

2) Beat 2 large eggs with 1 tsp. of salt and 1 tsp. of sugar until very light in color and thick in texture, then mix with the meal.

3) Melt 2 tbsp. of butter or lard in 1 cup of water brought to the boiling point. Add this and about 2 cups of milk

to the meal and egg mixture. If the meal is not too
fresh, be generous with the milk. You want a thin
batter.

4) Pour the batter into a deep, well-greased dish or pan
and bake in a hottish oven (375°) for ½ hour or longer,
depending on the shape and size of the dish.

Batter bread goes beautifully with ham and, like all corn
breads, with fish. If you're lucky enough to live near the
sea or to have a tame fisherman in the family you're lucky
indeed, for really fresh fish seems to me the most goodly meat
a kindly Providence devised for man. Living inland as we
do we sometimes don't recognize the fresh creature, being
used to the tired, much-traveled one. In England, not long
after the end of the last war, I stopped at a fishmonger's and
ordered some of "that fish" and asked what it was. It looked
like a tropical fish to me, all irridescent rose and blue with
a nacreous belly. My humiliation on being told that it was
mackerel at sixpence the pound was severe, but the English
fishmonger didn't really expect an American to know any
better. That mackerel, baked on a greased rack and dabbed
with butter, was the best of its kind that I've ever tasted. In
fact, for any fish my rule is: the fresher, the simpler. During
the shad season we do get quite good ones, and these I do
the same way as the notable mackerel: baked with dabs of
butter. Just once I tried the cooking-in-red-wine technique,
that method by which the bones are dissolved during long
slow cooking in the wine. The bones did disappear but so
did the flavor and the texture of the fish; it might have been
anything—animal, vegetable, or mineral. So never again!

During a ten-day stay on the island of Mytilene, alas! now
many years ago, I remember eating fish twice a day every
day and each time with gusto. I can't be sure at this remove
of time that I never ate the same kind of fish twice, but certainly there was an astounding variety. The methods were
baking, grilling and frying. The condiments were butter for

a dry fish, a squirt of lemon for a rich one. There were no herbs, no salt or pepper. These were provided in or with the salad; there were no other vegetables. There was always bread; there was rough wine of the island; there was cheese and sometimes fruit, and good Turkish coffee. No food was ever better, and not much has been as good since then.

Oddly enough, the chief objection made to fish is not on the basis of taste, but on the basis of the difficulty of eating it. Try eating fish twenty times in ten days and you will find that after two and a half days you can dismember a fish in very slippy fashion. And have you ever tried eating cold cooked fish? If it has been properly prepared it's just as good as hot, as long as it isn't greasy. One of the most elegant little suppers it has been my pleasure to attend followed a ballet performance in London. Our hostess, a young professional woman with little time to cook, served at ten at night baked fish as cold as the white wine, with a light salad to follow. Poached fish lends itself to cold service, and poaching is not difficult if your kettle is commodious or your fish not immoderately large. An old thin linen towel or cheesecloth to wrap the fish in so that it can be lifted whole from its bath, or for small fish a deep-frying basket, make poaching easy enough. Pallid as poached fish come out, they lend themselves to dramatic sauces, *verte* for cold, perhaps, and espagnole for hot, or just masses of very finely minced parsley in melted butter. If you'd like an Oriental effect, a sweet-sour sauce reinforced with soy, is attractive to both eye and palate.

Shellfish, unlike scaly ones, are enormously popular, partly perhaps because they retain their flavor and texture better when procesed by freezing or canning; but it's an observable fact that people who deplore the difficulty of getting bones out of a piece of shad don't a bit mind struggling with lobster or crab. And shrimps are a breeze—except for the cook. Even so, I'm perfectly willing to shell shrimps for a party of eight, for the result is so gratifying. This is how I make a dish that I often serve as a course by itself and call

SAUTÉED SHRIMP

1) Allowing ¼ lb. of shrimp per person, peel the raw shrimp. If you use just the fingers, slitting the underside with the thumbnail, you waste less time and motion than trying to use a knife. To get the shrimp tail out without breaking it off, spread the tail fins and pinch one of the two inner ones between the nails of the thumb and forefinger and gently pull on the body. The tail ought to come out attached to the body and quite often does, and the intestine is drawn out as well. All this can be done well ahead of the cooking which takes only a few minutes.

2) Stew chips of garlic or shallot in lots of butter until softened and cooked but not brown. Use a large pan so that later when the shrimps are added they won't be crowded.

3) Turn up the heat so that the butter bubbles and add the whole raw shrimps and stir about as they cook.

4) When the shrimps are pink (about 3 minutes), add 1 tbsp. of dry white table wine for each pound of shrimp, and cook for a minute or two longer. The wine should evaporate, and by this time there is practically no butter left either; it's inside the shrimp. You may add salt and pepper if you like.

I generally serve this on top of a mound of açorda. The fluffy somewhat sweet açorda sets off the crisp, clean sea flavor of the shrimp.

Another dish, tiresome enough to prepare in the early stage, but simplicity itself at the last minute, is what I call

SQUID SCALOPPINI

1) Cut off the head of the small squid and slit down the belly. Grasp the top of the "quill" and pull; all the innards come out attached to this transparent bone.

2) With the point of a small sharp knife—or your finger-nails—loosen the thin, purple-stippled skin at the top of the back and peel it off. Peel off all of it, for it toughens with heat.

3) Pound the snowy fillets between two sheets of paper toweling. I use a wooden potato masher. Do this with restraint, for the idea is to break the tough fibers without mashing or tearing the meat. You may wish to dip the fillets in seasoned flour; I don't, however.

4) In a large skillet in which butter is bubbling, drop the fillets and using a large pancake turner or meat lifter keep them flat for the half minute it takes to brown them on one side. Flip them over and brown the other side. Then release them and they'll roll up into enchanting little curly cylinders. Remove them to a warm serving plate immediately.

5) Turn off the heat and pour into the little remaining brown butter a wineglassful of one of the drier Madeira wines, Sercial, for example; stir it about for a second or two until it is sizzling hot. Pour over the squid rolls and serve.

The flavor of squid somewhat resembles abalone or frogs' legs, and even squeamish folk who shudder at the thought of tentacled monsters will annihilate this meat at table.

In the fall, when we find a giant puffball, I like to make an Oriental sort of dish that I call

SEPTEMBER SQUID (a two-pan dish)

1) In one skillet sauté puffball (1″ cubes) very quickly in butter (no substitute).

2) In the second skillet sauté in butter or olive oil cut-up scallions or perennial onion tops, dill, and either parsley or chervil, still all fresh from the garden, and cut into the pan with scissors.

3) Add the squid cut into small squares (¾") and the tentacles. It's simple to cut these with scissors.
4) Cook until the juice is somewhat reduced—just a very few minutes—and the meat is beginning to fry.
5) Push aside the meat and vegetable and make a sauce using the remaining butter, flour, white wine, cream, salt and white pepper.
6) Let simmer until the sauce is thoroughly cooked; add the puffball dice, and serve.

With a dish of this sort I serve the Chinese vermicelli, Fun Gee, made of mungo-bean starch and sometimes called Long Rice. These are put into boiling water, then with the heat turned low simmered for half an hour. They are very pretty, especially on a dark plate, and look like spun glass. Indeed, six young ladies in a family of our acquaintance call them "glass noodles."

Egg noodles are another matter and equally good, but they do still better as the accompaniment to stews, fricassees and braised meat dishes. Noodles are easy enough to make if you can fit the rolling, drying and cutting operations into your program for the day. And once you can handle noodle dough a whole new realm of dishes is available for experiment. For plain

NOODLES

1) Put 1 cup of flour into a bowl or on a pastry board.
2) Into a hole in the center put ½ tsp. of salt and a whole egg. At this point, if you want rich noodles, add a tsp. of olive oil or softened butter.
3) With the fingers work the egg and flour, bringing the flour in toward the well in the center and mixing lightly with the tips of the fingers, until finally all is smoothly amalgamated. Knead like bread until the paste is per-

fectly smooth and a bit elastic. With some flour you may find that you cannot get a proper dough without adding liquid. Use as little as possible or the noodles will take longer to dry.

4) Turn out the ball of paste and roll thin, less than ⅛″. A baton roller is a great help in this operation.

5) Let the sheet of dough dry for a while. It must not be brittle-dry, but dry enough so that it won't stick to itself.

6) Roll up into a fairly tight cylinder and cut across the roll into strips the desired width.

7) Separate the strands and straighten them and allow them to dry thoroughly before using or storing.

Plain homemade buttered noodles are not to be snubbed when served with, say,

BEEF TONGUE WITH DILL SAUCE

1) Bring the beef tongue to the boil then simmer it, allowing at least an hour for each pound, in water to cover to which have been added a large onion and any seasonings or vegetables your judgment dictates. Many people like a bay leaf and carrot added. I incline to less seasoning during the boiling and more in the sauce.

2) When the tongue is tender (after 3 to 5 hours, you'll see the tiny bones protruding from the root) remove it and skin it as soon as possible. The skin comes off more easily when the tongue is still hot.

3) Slice, arrange the slices on a warm platter, and pour over them the

DILL SAUCE

1) Make a béchamel or velouté sauce.

2) Stir into the sauce chopped fresh dill leaves and flowers or finely crushed dried ones.

A beef tongue is a sizable piece of meat for a small family, so I'm likely to keep back part of it for another dinner when I serve the sliced meat cold with

HORSERADISH SAUCE

1) Scrape or peel, then grind a fresh horseradish root in the meat grinder, using first the coarse, then a fine blade. A blender makes the chore simpler.
2) To ½ cup of ground root add
   1 tbsp. of cider vinegar
   1 heaping tsp. of sugar
   a pinch of salt
   ½ cup of heavy cream
3) Stir well and serve cold.

That sounds very simple, but I should warn you that it's not easy to come by a root of horseradish. We grow our own. It's a weedy plant and will take over as much ground as it's allowed, but we put up with it because the fresh root is so superior to that in bought sauces either wet or dehydrated. Without a blender the grinding process is unmitigated agony. The fumes start tears that onions wot not of, and when you've ground the root once, you almost can't bear the thought of putting it through the fine knife and enduring again that searing pain and the streaming eyes. And yet you do, for the result is matchless, especially with cold beef or hot sausages.

Plain boiled meats are not in great demand in our culture, but stews and fricassees are eminently acceptable. The difference between boiling meat or stewing it is that boiled meat is prepared in a large piece and stewed meat in small ones. Most of the dishes that we call stews are really fricassees, for the meat is first browned and a thickening agent like flour or meal is added before the liquid. In any case, boiling, stewing, and fricasseeing are all slow methods using a relatively large amount of liquid. Braising, similar in effect to fricasseeing, uses a small amount of liquid. The so-called red meats, beef and lamb, are almost always fricasseed—browned before the liquid is added. The "white" meats like poultry, fish and veal are often really just plain stewed or boiled.

Boiling and stewing, being very slow methods, can render to succulence even the toughest old muscle. Indeed, one can hardly find a chicken in the markets nowadays old enough to stew. But should you be lucky enough to get hold of an old hen, try making the simple but delicious Chilean dish called

CAZUELA DE AVE

1) Joint a chicken and bring to the boil then simmer until tender in just enough water to cover the meat.
2) Add in succession, according to the length of time it takes to cook each vegetable:
   small potatoes
   small onions
   green beans
   fresh peas
3) Add salt and pepper shortly before serving.
4) Put into a tureen and garnish with hard-boiled egg either sliced or coarsely chopped.
5) Ladle into large old-fashioned shallow soup plates, and let the diners spoon up the soup, then eat the meat and vegetables with a fork.

Veal, also a white meat, is another flesh that lends itself

superbly to stewing. The method that I prefer is the one called appropriately by the French

BLANQUETTE DE VEAU

1) Into a roomy kettle put pieces of breast of veal cut into small cubes about $1''$-$1\frac{1}{2}''$ square and cover with water.

2) Add an onion stuck with a clove or two, celery, and carrots cut into pieces, and such herbs as marjoram, chervil or rosemary—which has an affinity for veal, and a seasoning of salt and pepper.

3) Bring slowly to the boil, skimming off the fluff as it gathers.

4) Turn down to simmer and let cook until the veal is tender, about two hours or a little longer.

5) In another pan steam small onions in a very little water, and when they are nearly cooked add small whole mushrooms and cook them for about 5 minutes. Drain the minute amount of remaining liquid back into the stew pot.

6) Remove the meat from the kettle and set aside with the cooked onions and mushrooms on a deep platter or in a shallow bowl which should be kept warm while you prepare the sauce.

7) Strain the stew liquid and set 1 cup of it to cool to room temperature or below. Put another 2 cups of it in a saucepan and keep it hot over a low flame. You may use the pan in which the onions and mushrooms have cooked.

8) Beat 3 whole eggs until well mixed and stir into them the cupful of cold stock and the juice of a whole lemon and $\frac{1}{2}$ tsp. of sugar.

9) Now with a whisk beat the egg mixture into the 2 cups of hot stock.

10) Add $\frac{1}{2}$ cup of heavy cream and stir in well.

11) Pour the sauce over the meat and vegetables in the bowl.

If you present the dish on a platter it is prettier to arrange the vegetables around the edge after you've covered the meat with the sauce. Since this is a very blond dish, a sparkle of finely chopped parsley makes it more attractive.

Onions and carrots seem to be constants in stews and fricassees and tend to effect a sameness in the end result no matter what the meat. In the late winter I like to make a lamb fricassee using parsnips instead of carrots. Since parsnips are so very sweet, I add a bit of lemon juice when making the gravy. And with this humble dish we like

DUMPLINGS

1) Put into a bowl:
   1 scant cup of flour
   1 tsp. of baking powder (or more)
   ½ tsp. of salt
2) Mix into this with the fingers enough fat (lard, butter, suet or vegetable shortening) to make a crumbly mixture as for biscuit dough, which will amount to between ⅛ and ¼ cup, depending on the flour and your taste.
3) Add milk or water to make a rather soft dough. Mix well.
4) Either first pat out on a board and then cut into pieces, or drop directly from a spoon into the liquid which must be boiling when the dumplings go in. But the heat should then be lowered to barely simmering, so that the tender dumplings aren't torn apart by the vigorous action of the rapidly boiling water. Cover the kettle closely, for they cook in the steam. Resist the temptation to peek for you will thereby decrease the

pressure instantaneously, and before it builds again the dumplings will absorb too much moisture and end up sodden lumps of paste. Small dumplings about 1" in diameter will take about 12-15 minutes to cook; larger ones will take a little longer.

Instead of baking powder, beaten egg may be used, or both if you wish to make assurance doubly sure.

With a lamb or beef stew I sometimes serve a Bulgur pilav, which is made exactly like a pilav of rice but uses cracked wheat in place of rice. The Russian dish that is similar to it is made of cracked buckwheat—buckwheat groats—and with lamb is not too strong a flavor.

A fricassee or stew is kissing-kin to soup; indeed there's some doubt as to the classification of certain dishes like Cazuela. Soups are regarded in our culture chiefly as overtures to the main-dish opera. The hearty soups seem to me to be generally inappropriate introductions to a main course; I prefer to give them star billing and build the menu around them rather than up from them. This predilection dates from my childhood when Saturday-night dinners were frequently composed of rich homemade vegetable soup followed by a platter of spinach garnished with hard-boiled egg slices and bordered with crisp bacon curls. Pie was always the dessert. Nowadays I'm likely to plan soup for the evening meal on bread-baking days. A good ox-tail soup with fresh homemade bread is every whit as satisfying as ox-tail stew; there's little to choose between them, and one cook of my acquaintance calls either one indiscriminately "stewp," or maybe "stoup." Occasionally, when I find tripe in the market, we have either Philadelphia Pepper Pot or the much simpler

TRIPE AND ONIONS

1) With scissors cut the tripe into bite-size pieces and simmer 4 hours or longer in barely enough water to cover.

2) Add small whole onions which you have peeled and cut with a cross at the base. This prevents their coming apart in the cooking.

3) By now the liquid is much reduced, so add milk, or milk and cream, to bring up the proportion of liquid to soup consistency.

4) Add salt and pepper and a pinch of cloves or mace.

Serve this from a tureen with fresh bread and drink a mild beer with it. If you have room for dessert it will be for only fruit or cheese.

Chowders, too, are close to stews, the difference between them being that chowders are quick whereas stews are slow. Chowders are generally made of fish, a quick-cooking flesh, or vegetables like corn which are at their best when not overcooked.

A consideration of stews leads us gently but firmly to the meat pies and puddings. These are definitely in the Anglo-Saxon tradition. To make either a pudding or a pie of beef-steak and kidney you should have finely chopped or ground beef suet for the pastry. Strictly speaking, a boiled pudding is tied in a cloth and suspended in a deep kettle of simmering broth. Nowadays a mold is often used. This is set on a rack in a kettle, and the result is really a steamed rather than a boiled pudding. The pie, of course, is baked and less paste is used, for the dish of floured meat, onions, seasoning and liquid is usually merely covered with the rich crust. The baking of a meat pie is slow, to allow the meat to cook thoroughly, so the heat must be moderate to low to avoid burning of the crust.

Sometimes oysters are added to a beef pie; the flavor is delightful, but the texture of the oysters after the long cooking leaves much to be desired. Mushrooms, though, really enhance the dish, and a bit of red wine does no harm. The same technique can be used for chicken or any other meat, and we particularly like squirrel served in a pie.

One meat pie that doesn't conform to the general type and can hardly claim relation to stew is the Pennsylvania Dutch

CORN-VEAL PIE

1) Boil or steam separately and according to the time requirements of each:

> breast or tendrons of veal cut in small cubes
> whole small potatoes or potato balls
> corn on the cob,

and hardboil an egg for the garnish.

2) Cut the corn off the cob.

3) Make a velouté sauce using the meat and vegetable juices. Season it well.

4) Line a deep casserole with pie pastry and lay the cooked meat on the bottom, then the layer of potatoes, followed by the layer of onions and the layer of corn. Pour in the sauce and place on top the sliced hard-boiled egg; sprinkle all with minced parsley, and cover with the pastry top-crust.

5) Bake in a hot oven to blend the flavors and brown the crust.

During the last war when the cook in our family took an office job with the intention of aiding the war effort, our dinners were generally late and quite Spartan. All that remained at the meat counters at 5:30 p.m. were Spam and bones—literally bones, massive enough but with no shreds of meat attached. What to do with bones became a nearly diurnal problem. Cracked, they yielded marrow which beside adding bulk and flavor supplied a most velvety texture to the sauces of what were essentially vegetable stews.

Another of our stand-bys in those days turned out to be brains, for the prejudices against this meat are strong, and brains were available even when Spam was not. When I had the choice I inclined toward brains rather than bones, for to present the latter in attractive edible form took most of the evening. We repeated quite often the recipe that I evolved for

CALVES' BRAINS SYLVANER

1) Wash brains; remove arteries and membranes.
2) Blanch brains in boiling water for 2 minutes. Cool and cut into bite-size pieces.
3) Make a rich white sauce, using half cream, half Mountain Sylvaner wine for the liquid. Season with rosemary, salt and pepper.
4) To the sauce add chopped pimiento, chopped walnuts, and the cut-up brains.
5) Heat thoroughly and serve on crisp toast and drink with it the rest of the Sylvaner thoroughly chilled. (Any dry white wine may be used in place of Sylvaner.)

The soft texture of the brains is nicely piqued by the walnuts and the toast, and the bland color of the dish becomes attractive when jeweled with the bright red of the pimientos.

Using any one of the foregoing dishes and an appropriate starchy accompaniment a menu can easily be constructed by adding vegetables, salad, dessert, hors d'oeuvres or soup; for when the heart of the meal is interesting and good the impact of the whole is likely to be positive.

Familiarity with the meat-cooking techniques and a group of congenial carbohydrate dishes completes the cook's armory when added to an understanding of egg cookery, the uses of flour, and a knowledge of sauces. All the rest of cooking is manipulation, imagination and choice.

Section B

Move Over, Escoffier! How not to be a Plain Cook is a recurrent challenge to the housewife. This problem has very little or nothing to do with garnishing and decoration. It is almost entirely a matter of the preparation of food before cooking. The following preliminary techniques applied with care and imagination create a category of sometimes fabulous dishes.

5. Hash

5. Hash can be beautiful, though the connotations of clumsiness, drabness, the second-rate and stale cluster about the term. Basically the word means that which is chopped into small pieces, and from that standpoint a great many fine dishes can be classified as hash. Admittedly these are rarely made from leftovers, those perennial stepchildren of the kitchen. The characteristics of hash seem to me to be two: the ingredients are chopped, and there are several of them. Hash then is not a dish, but a technique of preparation.

Perhaps the most familiar dish of hash-from-scratch is chop suey, for which there is no recipe that I know of, and which is not even Chinese, though its Chinese name, which means "mixed bits," conveys the true hash technique. This dish includes meat and rice, plus other tidbits, fried in sesame, peanut or other vegetable oil. Chop suey, formless and generalized as it is, and scorned by the sophisticate, still has served as an introduction for countless curious palates to the techniques of Oriental cookery, a great many of which are based on quick cooking, which again implies small bits.

Hash dishes range from those in which the ingredients are chopped—merely cut up—to those in which the ingredients are chopped finer and finer until they become a paste. In the cut-up hash dishes the ingredients are loosely associated in a thin sauce; as the chopping becomes finer, the ingredients are bound together more closely by a thickening agent such as flour, eggs or gelatine.

The chopping technique gives a wide range indeed, and in the scope of a mere chapter we can hope to analyze only an occasional dish for each kind of hash. Let us start with one of the great Japanese dishes which is rapidly becoming more familiar to our Western palates. This dish is cooked at table over charcoal in a *hibachi,* in a chafing dish or in an electric frypan, and the cooking proceeds as the guests eat. Since everyone is watching what goes on with varying degrees of patience or greed, the ingredients should be attractively displayed: the appeal to the eye must be as inviting as the aroma and the savor of

SUKIYAKI

1) Assemble on a platter, arranging them in neat equal piles, and with an eye to color and texture variation, the following ingredients:

  10 or more medium-sized mushrooms, sliced vertically ¼" thick

  a small Chinese (Savoy) cabbage cut in strips ¾" wide

  ½ can bamboo shoots, washed and sliced ⅛" thick

  ¼ lb. of spinach leaves, washed and stems removed

  8 or 10 scallions cut into 1" lengths

  ¾ of a can of *shirataki,* a kind of vermicelli

2 lb. of sirloin or round of beef, sliced ⅛″ thick and
cut into strips about 2″ x ½″

2) Rub the hot pan (400° in an electric skillet) with a
piece of beef suet and put in some slices of meat.

3) Let the meat sizzle for a moment, then add some of
each vegetable, keeping the meat and vegetables bal-
anced in the same proportions as those on the platter,
and seeing to it that each is kept in its own part of the
pan.

4) Sprinkle over all the food as it cooks a sauce of
½ cup of Japanese soy sauce (shoyu)
¼ cup of Japanese sake or dry sherry
2 tbsp. of sugar
1 tsp. of Accent or monosodium glutamate.

5) Turn the vegetables and meat in the sauce and juices.
The best instruments for this operation are chopsticks.
The cooking will take about 10 minutes. The vegetables
still retain a semblance of crispness but are tender.

As soon as each person is served, another batch of meat
and vegetables goes into the pan. If the sauce gets too rich
in flavor or too thick because of evaporation during cooking,
add a bit of water.

This food is piping hot, so the Japanese serve with it
individual bowls of raw egg beaten smooth into which each
chopstickful is dipped before it is popped into the mouth.
The egg "cooks" on the hot food and tempers it to the tongue.
It also does what eggs are known in every culture to do:
smooths out sharp flavors and blends contrasting ones.

The Sukiyaki technique can be used for chicken or fish
as well as for beef, but then the resulting dishes have different
names.

When experimenting with frozen whale-meat, a group of
us applied to it the Sukiyaki technique and decided that it
was the most successful of the three we tried, the other two

being braising with vegetables and wine, and pot-roasting in the oven. We attributed the success to the quick cooking of the thin slices of meat, plus the relatively large amount of sugar in the sauce. There was in the finished dish none of the fish-oily taste that so many people find objectionable in whale-meat dishes. The pot roast also used a small amount of sugar and this was the next best of the three dishes. The braised dish, using wine, seemed actually to intensify the fish-oil flavor.

The English hash dish of Bubble-and-Squeak has a long history. In its original form it was made of fresh cabbage and "salted" beef, the original corned beef. Later it came to include potatoes, and now, so sadly far has it fallen from its high estate, it is often only potatoes and cabbage. Failing corned beef, an approximation of the original dish can be made with ham. This is how I make my own version and still call it

BUBBLE-AND-SQUEAK

1) Slice ham or corned beef as thin as possible and chop into narrow strips, ½" x 1½", and cut cabbage into strips of roughly the same dimensions. The cabbage should amount to nearly twice the bulk of the meat when heaped loosely on the chopping board.

2) Melt butter in a large skillet, and when it is bubbling put in the ham slices to sizzle for a moment, but don't let them cook to crispness.

3) Add the cabbage and shake the pan as the cabbage cooks, or move the bits about with a spatula or cake turner. The cabbage will take only a minute or so to cook. It should be hot through and still somewhat crisp, not limp.

4) Now either remove the meat and vegetable, or if the pan is large enough, just push the cooked bits aside

and make a simple milk gravy by adding flour to the
butter remaining in the pan, stirring it to a smooth
paste and adding milk. The large surface of a skillet
brings the sauce to the boil very quickly.

5) Add pepper and, if you like it, a sprinkle of coriander.

This dish must be served and eaten immediately, for if it
is allowed to stand the sauce becomes watery and the cabbage
tastes strong and feels overcooked and slimy. We like to
have it served on slices of crisp buttered toast.

Ground meat is simply a further refinement of chopped or
sliced meat, but what a difference the grinding makes to the
final dish. The smaller the mixed bits are, the closer they
pack together, and the finished dish has a texture quite other
than any of its ingredients. A molded ground-meat dish includes meat, seasonings and a binder. The finer the grinding,
the smoother the texture of the dish, so for the more elegant
forms of ground-meat dishes it may be necessary to grind
the meat with two or even three successively finer blades.
For a baked meat loaf, I consider two grindings sufficient.
What ruins most such loaves and reduces them to the status
of "mere" is the confusion of ingredients. If you start with
a bulk of good lean beef, plan to feature that flavor. Onion,
by all means; tomato, perhaps; veal for texture if you must;
but why, oh why, cover up these flavors with ham? If the
cook is sufficiently discriminating in the selection of ingredients, the lucky people who partake of the dish will be able
in their turn to detect individual flavors and their satisfaction
will be increased. But in the case of the meat loaf there is
room for the exercise of imagination to create something
unique. Here follows a skeleton recipe for a meat loaf to be
baked in a 2 lb. bread tin. If it must have a name, let us
call it

BEEF MEAT LOAF: Theme and Variations

1) Grind with the medium then the fine knife

    1½ lb. meat (round of beef); or

      1 lb. of beef and ½ lb. of veal; or

      1 lb. of beef, ¼ lb. of veal, and ¼ lb. of fresh or salt pork

      1 medium-sized onion; or 2 large shallots; or 2 scallions; or 1 clove of garlic

2) Add ½ cup of bread crumbs; or grind and add 1 medium-sized raw white potato.

3) Add seasonings:

    1 tsp. of salt; or less salt and 1 tsp. of Worcestershire or soy sauce

    ½ tsp. of pepper; or ¼ tsp. of pepper and 1 tsp. of prepared mustard

4) Add herbs:

    ¼ tsp. of dried thyme or a sprig of fresh thyme cut with scissors;

    large pinch of marjoram or oregano.

5) Add 2 eggs beaten, or 1 egg and ½ cup of broth—in which case increase the crumbs to ¾ cup.

6) If using only lean meat, add 1 tbsp. of melted butter or lard.

7) Mold and put in a greased loaf tin or on a greased sheet and bake for at least an hour in a moderate oven (350° or a little less).

8) To glaze, baste with liquid (milk, broth, wine, water or tomato juice). A pinch of sugar added to the liquid helps in the glazing.

9) Sprinkle minced parsley on the top just before serving.

If you'd like a veal loaf for a change, increase the fat content, cut down the onion flavor and change the herbs to chervil, basil or rosemary, and remember that the tomato has a natural affinity for veal. If you fancy lamb, you'll find that dill and tomato enhance the general effect, and garlic is really preferable to onion. A lamb loaf is improved by the addition of a sharp flavor: lemon or vinegar, or a bit of sharp pickle. Raw eggplant ground with the lamb gives a smoky flavor. If you use it cut down on the liquid content.

For meat balls, grind the meat still finer than for meat loaf. The best meat balls are very fine and close in texture and quite small, but the principle of their creation is the same as for meat loaf. They are a mixture of meat, seasonings and binding material. They can be grilled, baked, fried, braised or poached, but being small they must be subjected to quick cooking so that they do not dry and wither.

The meat balls of Turkey are most often grilled and served very hot—"sizzling," as their name, Cizbiz Köfte, implies. The Greeks are more likely to fry theirs, then serve them with Avgolimono sauce, but both are essentially one dish, being made of minced raw lamb, onion, bread soaked in milk or water, seasoned with salt and pepper and bound with egg. Before the Turkish köfte are grilled they are usually rolled in olive oil. The Greeks roll the tiny balls in flour and fry them or braise them before making the egg and lemon sauce. In Italy, meat balls are more often browned, then simmered in a tomato sauce and served frequently with spaghetti or other pasta; and here a combination of beef and pork is used in preference to lamb. By the time we have followed the meat ball to the chilly land of Sweden, the seasonings are reduced and the fat content is increased. Let's look at the Turkish and the Swedish meat balls in more detail. For

CIZBIZ KÖFTE

1) Grind three times with successively fine blades 1 lb. of lean lamb and 1 medium-sized onion.

2) Add the meat to a panada made of three slices of bread free of crust which have been soaked in water then squeezed dry.

3) Add salt and pepper and 1 egg, and mix all thoroughly.
4) With dampened hands roll bits of the mixture between the palms to form small balls.
5) Roll the balls in olive oil spread on a shallow plate.
6) Grill under moderate heat, and serve very hot.

For the Swedish

KÖTT BULAR

1) Grind three times with successively fine blades
    1 lb. of lean beef
    ¼ lb. of veal
    ⅛ lb. of fat pork
2) Add 1 tsp. of finely minced onion, salt and pepper, and a scant ½ cup of breadcrumbs soaked in ¾ cup of milk with ¼ cup of cream added.
3) Shape the meat balls by using two small spoons dipped in water, as for quenelles.
4) Brown the meat balls in butter, then cover with 1 cup of boiling broth or water and simmer for 15 minutes.
5) Serve in their gravy.

But meat balls need not be cooked at all. If you like your meat rare in the eating, try sometime as hors d'oeuvres

CANNIBAL MEAT BALLS

1) Grind three times with successively finer blades:
    1 lb. of lean beef (round or chuck) and 2 medium-sized onions.
2) Add and mix in thoroughly:
    ½ tsp. of freshly ground black pepper
    1 heaping tsp. of salt
    1 tsp. of prepared mustard

3) Shape into tiny balls—the size of a large marble.
4) Dip in the white of one egg beaten smooth with 1 tsp.
   of water, and roll in a plateful of something that will
   give a texturally different surface, e.g.:
   buttered and salted crumbs, with or without grated
     Parmesan cheese;
   chopped nuts—filberts for choice: or
   a mixture of minced parsley and grated lemon peel.
5) Chill and serve cold.

The justly prized *pâté de foie gras truffé* of France is a
true hash, but this must be left to the French, for the truffle,
that inimitable underground fungus, does not appear on this
continent, and the fat geese of Strasbourg have no counterparts here. But excellent *pâtés* can be made using, instead
of goose, chicken or turkey livers with or without mushrooms.
One pâté that we like very much is made by using the
electric blender to reduce the sautéed chicken livers to a
paste. With it I put softened sweet butter, fresh lime juice,
brandy, salt and pepper. Sealed with a layer of fat this
keeps as long as moral fiber allows.

In my personal hierarchy of dishes the one that stands at
the very peak, the flag on the culinary Everest, is a hash.
It is at once one of the simplest dishes known, in that it uses
in addition to seasonings only four ingredients, and one of
the most elaborate, for it presents five different textures. It
can be made in one day, but I prefer to divide the operations
over two days. Now don't be dismayed, for it's both absorbing
and rewarding to create a version of

CIRCASSIAN CHICKEN
1) On the first day simmer until tender a stewing chicken,
   adding to the water in the kettle: one whole large onion

stuck with a clove or two or a piece of cinnamon, salt and pepper, and tarragon or chervil, if you fancy more flavor.

2) Let the chicken cool completely in the broth; remove to a plate and chill thoroughly so that the meat can be easily sliced.

3) The next day, slice off and set aside as much meat as will make good-looking slices around the edge of the platter which will be used for the finished dish. Remove all the rest of meat from the bones.

4) Put all the bits of meat through the grinder using medium, fine, then very fine blades. Measure then divide this minced meat into two equal portions.

5) Take the same bulk of fresh walnut meats as you have of minced chicken. Reduce them to a paste by grinding and mashing. The electric blender makes this a simple operation. Squeeze the paste in a cloth to get as much oil as possible. The fresher the nuts, the more oil they release.

6) Soak the crumb of fresh white bread, the same amount as there is of chicken, in chicken broth. Squeeze gently when moist to drain out excess liquid. Mix half of this panada with one half-portion of minced chicken. Mix the other half with half the walnut paste.

7) Now mix the remaining half portions of walnut paste and chicken together.

8) Thin the crumb and walnut paste with broth to make a thick creamy "sauce."

9) Arrange the slices of meat around the edge of the platter. With dampened fingers mold in the center the mixture of chicken and crumb. Flatten the top and on this mold the chicken-and-walnut mixture. Make a depression in the top of this layer. Now cover the whole mound with the crumb, walnut and broth sauce. In a shallow depression in the top pour the bit of walnut oil. Add a sprinkle of paprika if the oil isn't red of itself. Serve cold but not chilled, or the oil would be too thick.

For a hot summer night this is the perfection of fine eating, particularly if it follows a few oysters or clams, and is accompanied by a chilled, almost dry white wine, and followed by a morsel of sharp cheese. And if it can be served in a garden with scented stock in a nearby border and fireflies pricking the dark beyond the table, neither you nor your guests will ask more of paradise.

The original and classic Turkish dish is simpler and marvelously good to eat. To make real

CIRCASSIAN CHICKEN

Proceed through steps 1 and 2 of the preceding recipe then,

3) Lay the slices on a platter.

4) Remove the rest of the meat from the bones and grind very fine. You will need three grindings to take the place of the chopping then grinding in a mortar which is the Turkish technique. Measure.

5) Take the same amount of walnut meats reduced to the texture of coarse flour. This is done easily by a blender. Squeeze the ground nuts in an oiled cheese cloth to get a few drops of oil. The fresher the nuts the more oil they release.

6) Soak the crumb of fresh white bread, the same amount as there is of chicken or walnuts, in chicken broth so that when squeezed gently it is a soft paste.

7) Mix all three ingredients thoroughly and season with salt and pepper to taste.

8) Mound the resulting "sauce" on the chicken slices and sprinkle with the walnut oil—or mix sweet paprika with olive oil and sprinkle.

Sea food of all sorts has been hashed in numberless dishes, but one of the most interesting I've known is still

MIDYE DOLMASI (Stuffed mussels)

1) Scrub 1½ doz. fresh mussels. Force open the shells

enough to remove the "beard" and the "black" with a slim sharp knife. Chop flesh roughly.

2) Make a Wedding Pilav, using a fish bouillon if possible, but water alone will do if the seasonings are stepped up; ½ cup of rice is sufficient.

3) Poke into each bivalve as much of pilav as possible, then tie the shells securely with thread.

4) Pack the mussels upright in a pan which will just hold them, being careful to stand them with the hinged end on the bottom. Pour in enough water to cover—but just barely. Put a plate on top to prevent dolmas floating. Cover the pan and let simmer for about 20 minutes.

5. Let the dolmas cool in the pan before draining off the liquid. Remove the thread.

6) Chill. Serve with a few drops of lemon juice squeezed over the slightly opened dolmas.

So far we've examined hashes in which the ingredients are coarsely chopped and loosely bound in a thin sauce, or more finely chopped and held together with a binder such as egg, flour or crumb of bread. Another binder for hashed ingredients is gelatine, and when this is used the mixed bits may be either small or large. Gelatine is used for cold dishes either in the main part of the meal or for dessert. Not many entrées can match in glamour a well-turned mold of chicken, fish, or ham, chic with a garnish of greens. For an entrée aspic, there are two absolute essentials: the stiffened liquid must be perfectly clear, and the texture of the bits suspended in it must be firm. To achieve the first, the visual characteristic, the broth used may be cleared with egg white and shell, then strained and strained again through cheesecloth. The second essential, the textural, can be left to the cook's judgment, but in general it can be said that fresh-water fish have too flimsy a texture for a perfect aspic dish; shellfish and meats are ideal.

When beef or veal is used with gelatine the resulting aspic

is often called a *daube,* and the use of a *daube* is identical
with that of an aspic. Whether the mixed bits are fish,
chicken, ham, beef or veal plus their flavor and texture accompaniments, the transparent medium in which they are
suspended is every whit as important as the solid bits themselves. A visually handsome aspic or *daube* can be faked
with bouillon cubes, water and gelatine. The only trouble
with such a dish is that it will taste exactly like bouillon
cubes, water and gelatine. The exacting cook will prefer to
make her dish really her own, so despite the time required
she'll probably start with fish or meat and bones, seasoned
with her own choice in vegetables and herbs, spiked with
lemon, vinegar, or wine, coddled slowly through several hours,
skimmed lovingly, cleared briskly, and at last mixed, if
necessary to stiffen completely, with more gelatine than that
provided by the meat and bones.

Related to the aspics are the mousses, where bits of solid
are suspended in infinitely delicate custard. Mousses require
much finer chopping or grinding than do aspics, and except
for the dessert mousses are always served hot. The texture
of a mousse is uniform throughout; it's impossible to say
where the bits leave off and the custard begins; so the special
skill required here is the reduction of the hashed bits to a
paste which will unite imperceptibly with the custard. In
some cultures the mortar and pestle are used to get a smooth
paste; here we rely on the grinder or the blender.

The word mousse means froth or foam, so the best recipes
for such a dish are those that give the finest texture, are
richest in eggs beaten to cloud nine lightness, and baked gently
to stability. A mousse is the combination, then, of two basic
techniques: the hashing technique of reducing a number of
ingredients to a blend of perfect balance, and the baking
technique of the soufflé. Whereas a ham soufflé, for example,
has small bits of the meat added to the basic soufflé, a ham
mousse adds a paste of ham and other seasonings.

Taking hash to mean, as I do, a dish of mixed bits, chopped, ground or mashed, we may subsume under this heading vegetable or fruit dishes as well as those made primarily of flesh. Vegetable flavors being fairly delicate for the most part do not benefit particularly from close association with each other. There are certain standard simple combinations which are well known, like peas and carrots, or lima beans with corn, or string beans with green pepper or almonds, but the wise cook generally presents the vegetables of the meal more or less intact; the European cook often serves the vegetable as a course by itself.

However, vegetables can be hashed most successfully for relishes and pickles. Pickles are likely to use the vegetable primarily as a textural base, but the relishes, uncooked vegetable pickles, feature the vegetable flavors. There are two such in the Pennsylvania Dutch cuisine that I use frequently as small chow to accompany curry. The first is called, appropriately,

PEPPER HASH or PEPPER SAUCE

1) Chop cabbage very fine until you have 1 cup. This will take about ½ a small cabbage less the hard core.
2) Chop 1 green pepper into tiny dice. Combine with the cabbage.
3) Add 1 heaping tsp. of sugar
   1 tsp. of salt
   1 tsp. of yellow mustard seed
   ¼ tsp. of ground cloves
4) Cover with cider vinegar.

The second is

COLD CATSUP

1) Peel and squeeze through your fist into a bowl 5 lusciously ripe tomatoes.

2) Chop into tiny dice:
   2 green peppers
   1 medium stalk of celery
   1 medium-sized onion
3) Add 1 tsp. of salt
   3 tbsp. of sugar
   ¼ tsp. of black pepper
   1 tsp. of mustard seed
   ¼ tsp. each of cloves, cinnamon and mace or nutmeg
4) Cover with cider vinegar.

If there is no celery, substitute 1 tsp. of celery seed.

Fruits, as well as vegetables, seem to me to be more honestly dealt with when they are served simply, but that does not rule out combining two or even three fruits. More than three, however, I find makes for a confusion of flavors. There are certain simple combinations of fruits that I put together with the hash technique that have proved successful. One that I use quite often in the spring and summer is

PINEAPPLE-STRAWBERRY HASH

1) Scrub a pineapple and split it vertically, foliage and all, and remove the flesh from the shell.
2) Cut the meat into small wedges.
3) Hull 1 pt. of strawberries; leave whole if small; cut in halves lengthwise if large.
4) Combine pineapple and strawberries with ½ cup of confectioner's sugar and pour over all ¼ cup of Maraschino liqueur.
5) Serve in the pineapple shell halves.

A similar dish, but utterly different in flavor and appearance, can be made by substituting blueberries in place of the strawberries.

The blender hashes up fruits superbly, but the resulting purée is generally more useful as a sauce rather than as a dish in its own right, but for a fruit ice you can't do better than to blend apricots, bananas, lime juice and sugar.

Perhaps the best known fruit hash is one that few cooks now attempt, yet there is nothing better and more useful to have on hand than homemade

MINCE MEAT

1) Cut into chunks, cover with water and simmer until tender 5 lb. of lean beef—top round is best.

2) Cool the meat; strain off the broth and set aside.

3) Grind the meat with the medium blade of the grinder.

4) Grind 2½ lb. of beef suet, trimmed of membrane.

5) Peel the rind from 2 oranges and 2 lemons; trim off the white pulp, and chop into short narrow strips about ½″ x ⅛″.

6) Squeeze and strain the juice of the oranges and lemons.

7) Peel, core and chop 6 or more apples into pieces less than ½″ cubes.

8) Chop, don't grind,

1 lb. of raisins

1 lb. of currants

½ lb. each of candied citron, lemon, orange, cherries

9) Put into a large kettle the meat and broth, all the fruits and juices, 1 cup of the suet, a jar of tart jelly, 1 pt. of grape juice or cider, 3 lb. of brown sugar, 1 cup of white sugar, and 1 tbsp. of salt. Bring all this to a boil, stirring until everything is smoothly amalgamated.

10) Put the mincemeat into a crock of 4 gallon capacity to leave room for stirring.

11) Now add while the mincemeat is still hot:
      2 tbsp. of freshly grated nutmeg
      2 tsp. of cloves
      2 tbsp. of cinnamon
      2 tsp. of ginger
      Stir well.
12) Last of all when almost cool add the rest of the suet
    and a fifth of brandy, ½ cup of Maraschino liqueur
    or 2 tbsp. of almond extract.
13) Cover the crock with a loose-fitting lid and leave it
    in a cool place.

The melted suet will form its own seal over the mince meat,
and the brandy will preserve it anyway. If all the suet is
put into the kettle and melted there will be a thick cake of
suet on top of the mince meat when it cools, which will have
to be chopped each time a pie is made. Heating the brandy
would evaporate the alcohol on which we're relying for pres-
ervation.

This mince meat keeps indefinitely—well, at least from
November until March—and will provide the fillings for a
dozen or more pies, depending on size. Though expensive,
compared to the emasculated and often dehydrated kinds on
the grocery-store shelves, it's well worth the cost and the
effort. And how simple it is to whip up an elegant dessert or
a batch of cookies when there's a crock of mince meat on
hand.

Fruit conserves can by an extension of meaning be included
among the hashes. They are mixed bits held together in a
syrup—a sugar sauce. But generally the only ingredients that
are truly hashed are the nuts and rinds; the fruits are stoned
or seeded but not really chopped. In my mother's jelly cupboard the jars that outranked all the others were filled with

PLUM CONSERVE

1) Stone 3 lb. of large blue plums or the small tart red ones.
2) Peel the rind from 2 oranges and chop both rind and fruit.
3) Chop ½ lb. of English walnuts.
4) Put all but the nuts into a large saucepan, adding 3 lb. of sugar, and spices:

   1 tbsp. of cinnamon
   1 tbsp. of mace
   1 tbsp. of allspice

5) Bring slowly to the boil, then cook, stirring occasionally, until thick.
6) Add the chopped nuts, pour into jars, and seal.

Hash from scratch is a legitimate—indeed, a noble—technique. When the term is used opprobriously it usually refers to dishes born the wrong side of the blanket, illegitimate by reason of the mismating of ingredients or extreme age. Good healthy honest leftovers, though, can be made into quite excellent dishes by employing the hash technique. One of the favorites of my childhood was the Monday-night dinner that followed the Sunday's pinbone roast of beef. This cut, now alas all but obsolete, provided lovely solid chunks of meat with no gristly streaks, so it could be chopped into ½" cubes very easily. Mother always roasted extra potatoes on Sunday which on Monday were chopped like the meat into small cubes, the brown crust providing a nice textural element to the

BEEF HASH

1) Chop onion into fine bits and sauté until golden in a very little butter.
2) Add flour to take up the remaining butter, then the

brown gravy from the roast of the day before. Thin
with a bit of hot broth or water.

3) Add the chopped beef and chopped roasted potatoes.

4) Season with salt and pepper and let bubble before
serving.

Croquettes are a form of hash from leftovers that is generally acceptable, and of all croquettes chicken are the ones
most frequently encountered. The major bit of labor in preparing them is that of getting the meat off the frame. Once
that chore is out of the 'way it's really rather fun to make

CHICKEN CROQUETTES

1) Put through the fine blade of the meat grinder all the
bits of flesh that could be salvaged from the frame.

2) Cover the frame with water, add an onion, a stalk of
celery and seasonings, and simmer as long as needed to
get a good broth.

3) Make a medium thick velouté sauce using the broth for
the liquid. Enrich this with an egg yolk beaten in when
the sauce is cooked.

4) Combine each 2 cups of chicken meat with ½ cup of
sauce.

5) Add a pinch of tarragon or ½ tsp. of powdered dry
dill—or 1 tsp. of cut fresh dill leaves—plus a good
sprinkle of white pepper freshly ground, and a pinch
of nutmeg or mace.

6) Form the croquettes in cones or balls and roll in flour,
then dip in egg beaten smooth with a tsp. of water. Roll
in finely ground breadcrumbs. This operation may be
repeated for more crust. Let stand for at least an hour
so that the egg dries and sets the crust.

7) Fry in deep fat; or use buttered crumbs and bake in a
hot oven (450°) until browned.

Mousses, which use ingredients worked to a homogeneous paste, may be more readily prepared from leftovers than from scratch. Aspics, too, require meat that has been already cooked, and therefore are more easily approached the day following a roasted chicken or a baked ham, or a rather over-sized fish.

The hashing technique's being one of preparation does not preclude any of the cooking techniques. And if hashing is a labor of love, then it deserves the further labor of imagination to be added to it, that the result may be delight.

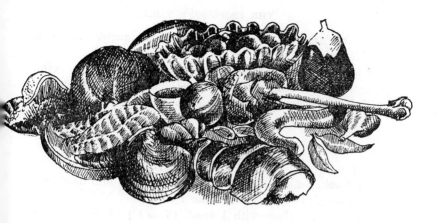

6. Stuffing and Boning, either separately or

in combination, are glamorizing and face-lifting techniques.
Stuffing I take to mean either filling a cavity or wrapping a
container around some other food. Boning is self-explanatory.
You may wish to consider these two techniques for the sake
of elegance or you may be driven to do so for other reasons.
Consider Cook A, wife to the enthusiastic gardener, faced with
the eternal glut of summer vegetables, fruit and flowers; or
Cook B, wife to the happy fisherman; or Cook C, victim of
her own economical impulses to concentrate on chicken, say,
while it's cheap; or Cook D, of limited purse and a conviction
that the cheaper cuts of meat are really the most flavorsome.
At wits' end, the cook of any of these categories turns at one
time or other to stuffing.

Gardeners in English novels have always been portrayed
as absolute tyrants. My semi-domesticated gardener, then,
runs true to type and with his harvests decrees my durance
in the kitchen at just that season when the lucky apartment-
house dwellers are lying on some sunny strand or breathing
bracing mountain air. But when the meal is ready much if
not all is forgiven, for even a vegetarian menu can be lifted

to nearly ambrosial heights by use of the ancient and honorable technique of stuffing.

Clean and cool at last, you relax on the terrace before dinner with a long drink of something sharp and icy, and with it you provide a simple selection of hors d'oeuvres which might include

STUFFED CUCUMBERS

1) Cook, drain, and force through the food mill or grinder enough baby beets to make 1 cup.
2) Combine these with 1 small (3 oz.) package of cream cheese and 1 tbsp. of finely chopped onion. (The blender does this chopping nicely but wastes a certain amount.)
3) Add about 1 tsp. of fresh dill leaves and flowers, cut with scissors or put into the blender with the onion, ½ tsp. of salt and a little freshly ground pepper.
4) Chill this mixture thoroughly.
5) Cut fresh and chilled cucumbers (about 1½″ in diameter and 8″ long) in half across. Hollow out the seedy inside.
6) Fill the cucumbers with the cheese mixture, packing it in solidly.
7) Slice across into pieces about ⅓″ in thickness.
8) Serve fairly soon, or the cucumber flesh will "melt" from the effect of the salt.

With the cucumber harvest come the nasturtiums as well, so the next evening you may wish to serve

STUFFED NASTURTIUMS

1) Crush ½ small clove of garlic with ½ tsp. of salt.
2) Add a small package (3 oz.) of cream cheese and work smooth with 1 tbsp. of cream.
3) Add 1 tsp. of finely minced parsley.

4) Fill clean, chilled nasturtium blossoms with this mixture. Chill again to stiffen the cheese filling.

The pepperiness of the nasturtium plant is present in the flowers, so this makes a very tasty as well as pretty hors d'oeuvre.

Earlier in the season you may have made Yalanci dolmas, those stuffed grape-leaf delicacies native to the Near East, but by now unless you had the foresight to preserve some of the leaves these are beyond your means. Cabbage leaves, however, may be treated much the same way and served hot as a main dish. Or perhaps that morning you have been presented with two pretty zucchini, several firm tomatoes, the first bell pepper, and the first rather small eggplant. All these may use the same filling, and all but the tomatoes take about the same time to cook, so you decide on a dish of assorted

DOLMAS

1) Cut the tops off of the vegetables and reserve to use later as lids.
2) Scoop out seeds of the peppers and discard. Chop or mash the flesh of the other vegetables.
3) Stew onion wedges, pine nuts and currants in butter, olive oil, sesame oil or corn oil.
4) When the onion begins to color add washed and drained rice. Stir it about so that each grain is coated.
5) Add the chopped vegetable flesh and seasonings:
   salt and pepper
   parsley
   dill and mint
6) Let cook for a few minutes until some of the vegetable juices have evaporated.
7) Stuff the vegetables and pin on their lids with toothpicks.

8) Pack them closely upright in a pan that will just hold them, putting a plate on top to keep them from bobbing about. Fill the pan with water and add a tablespoonful of olive oil to the water. Cover all with a lid and simmer for about 40 minutes—except in the case of the tomatoes.

When using tomatoes, let the filling cook nearly completely by adding water to the rice in the skillet. Stuff the tomatoes with the all-but-cooked filling, and finish by cooking the tomatoes about 10 minutes.

If the dolmas are to be served hot use a little lamb, finely ground, and browned in the pan when you start the onion.

The Mediterranean countries have dozens if not hundreds of ways to serve eggplant. The Turks give us one of the most epicurean of all stuffed dishes and call it delightfully

IMAM BAYILDI (The Priest Swooned)

1) Using 4 slender medium-sized eggplants, wash them and wipe dry. Make a slash on each side almost from top to bottom and piercing to the middle of the vegetable.

2) Sauté in oil 3 medium-sized onions cut in thin wedges, 1 large clove of garlic, sliced in thin chips, 2 tomatoes skinned and roughly cut in wedges, salt, and some chopped parsley.

3) After the vegetables are somewhat cooked and blended, stuff the mixture into the eggplant through the slashes in the skin.

4) Lay the stuffed eggplants in a shallow casserole, cover with water to which is added ¼ cup of olive oil. Cover the casserole and let simmer until the vegetables are tender.

5) Allow the dish to get cold before serving.

Served as a course by itself on a hot night this dish is as satisfying as a roast at midwinter, and the hungry gardener asks for very little more in the meal.

Not all the riches of the garden come in the summer, luckily. The real cabbage harvest comes with the first cool nights, and, if there's a root cellar in the house, lasts well into the winter. In addition to using cabbages for Pepper Hash and Cole Slaw you may have made sauerkraut by putting it "down" in a large stone crock or barrel, or putting it "up" in glass jars. In either case you have a cabbage pickle: cabbage preserved in brine. For the crock or barrel method of preparing

SAUERKRAUT

1) Use mature heads of cabbage, and after removing the curled-back, coarse outer leaves cut the cabbages in halves and shred the leaves very fine; the ideal shreds are hardly more than 1/16" wide.

2) Using 2 tsp. of salt per lb. of shredded cabbage (about ½ lb. of salt to about 20 lb. of whole cabbages), pack the mixed cabbage and salt fairly firmly into a crock or barrel so that it comes within about 2"-3" of the top. The crock may be lined with the large outer leaves of cabbage.

3) Cover the crock with a large cloth which will hang down over the sides of the crock, then with a plate or hardwood board. Put a stone or other weight on top, so that as the liquid accumulates and rises and fermentation takes place the cloth will absorb it. A scum will collect against the cloth which must be washed and replaced. This scum is the accumulation of undesirable bacteria which grow where the air touches the liquid, therefore it must be removed and not allowed to come into contact with the vegetable. The cabbage must be

kept submerged in the brine and not permitted to float and be touched by the air. The weight atop the plate serves to achieve this end. The plate, or board, and weight as well as the sides of the crock must be cleaned each time the cloth is washed. Fermentation is complete when no more bubbling is detectable and the liquid around the vegetable is clear and still.

Apples, Malaga grapes, and caraway or cumin seeds are sometimes added to sauerkraut, but I prefer to add such flavors in the cooking rather than in the pickling stage.

As long as the brine has really pickled the cabbage there is no need for further processing. A crock of sauerkraut should keep all winter if the temperature of the storage room is not too high. We keep ours in the root cellar where the temperature stays between 40° and 50°.

Nowadays in the Pennsylvania Dutch country housewives quite often make sauerkraut in glass canning jars. The cabbage is shredded, mixed with salt, packed firmly in the jars, and the lids left only half screwed down so that the excess liquid will overflow during the fermentation period. The jars are kept in a large pan until fermentation stops, then sealed tightly and stored.

Having got the sauerkraut, you may now use it in a number of ways, and one of the most interesting is to make a festive winter dish of

SAUERKRAUT-STUFFED GOOSE

1) Clean the goose, setting aside the giblets for gravy.
2) Cut out of the cavity, which is large in this bird, the large lumps of fat, and stuff the goose with sauerkraut. If the sauerkraut is very salty, rinse and drain in a colander. A goose weighing 8–10 lbs. will take a quart or more of sauerkraut to which add a peeled, cut-up apple, and perhaps 1 tsp. of caraway seed.

3) Tie up the bird after closing the vents with pins or sewing with thread.

4) Roast slowly and long on a rack over the roasting pan. Six hours is not too long for a large bird, for a goose should be very dark in color when served. Basting with water will crisp the skin, but I have never seen the need for this; the skin just naturally crisps with the exudation of the fat.

The objection that liverish people have to goose is its fatty richness. If the heat during the roasting is low, the fat oozes out beautifully. It may be helped out in various ways, the easiest being to press the blunt back of a knife over the surface of the bird from time to time. In any case, even the fussiest diner need not eschew goose, for the fat lies in layers under the skin and this can always be cut away on the plate. The flesh itself is juicy but not greasy.

Other birds, chiefly chicken and turkey, are stuffed with plain or fancy, traditional or individual flavors and combinations of flavors. Boning them before stuffing raises them to the level of *grand luxe*. The first time one bones a bird it's wise to work on a fairly large one so that an unskillful slip of the knife won't tear a hole through thin delicate layers of flesh. A sharp-pointed knife is an essential to successful boning, and it should be one with a blade about 4″–6″ long; too large a knife is unwieldy, especially for a novice. So let's choose a young turkey of about 8 lb. and proceed

TO BONE A BIRD

1) Lay the bird breast down and make a cut the full length of the backbone.

2) Working on one side of the bird only, and with the knife always slanted against the bone, separate the flesh first from the side of the backbone then from the ribs.

3) Having reached the joint where the thigh bone is attached to the frame, with the point of the knife cut away the flesh from around the joint, then cut through the cartilage that holds the joint in the socket. Slide the narrow blade of the knife down the length of the thigh bone and around it, and in the manner of peeling off a stocking turn back the flesh to expose the next lower joint. Cut through the ligaments binding the upper and lower leg bones, leaving the drumstick intact in the flesh.

4) Now repeat this process at the wing, removing the upper bone but leaving the lower one in the flesh.

5) Working again toward the front, continue to separate flesh from bone until the breast meat is loosened to the middle of the breastbone. You are now halfway.

6) Repeat the whole process on the other side of the bird.

Set the frame to cooking gently with the neck and wing tips. The resulting broth you may use for soup or bouillon, aspic or gravy, or you may store it for seasoning later dishes.

You are left facing a large shapeless piece of meat with four projections: two lower wing parts and two legs.

Having providently prepared a stuffing earlier, you may now proceed to fill the bird. I start by sewing the neck opening with coarse white button thread, used in a large darning needle. When the bird is sewn about a third the way down the back I begin to put in the stuffing. This helps to hold the flesh up so that the rest of the sewing and stuffing is easier. Finally, with the stuffing and sewing complete, the legs and wings may be folded against the breast and the whole trussed with thread or string—but gently, gently—and there's nothing left but to roast or poach the fowl. All the natural shape of the bird has been restored as the process is completed, and the first time you do it, it will seem a miracle that it should be so.

Since there are no bones to interfere with the penetration of heat the cooking will take less time. Three hours is plenty of time to allow for cooking a boned 10-lb. turkey.

Carving a boned bird is a breeze. Most carvers will be spoiled after once serving it. They won't wish to return to the more laborious operations of finding for themselves the joints and separating the legs and wings, getting neat slices of breast and fair servings of stuffing. There will be no fragments of meat and crumbs of stuffing scattered around the platter and on the festive cloth, and no need for special spot removal by the reluctant laundress.

The only objection to a boned bird is the enormous amount of stuffing required. This makes, too, for a disproportionate amount of stuffing with each serving of meat. So what you may do the next time is to bone two birds, the smaller one stuffed first, and the larger one sewn around it with a layer of stuffing between the small one and the larger. If you fancy that still less stuffing is desirable, you may even use three birds, starting, say, with a Cornish game hen and stuffing it into a chicken which is then stuffed inside a turkey. The inner birds of this monumental dish must be completely boned; that is, the lower wing bones and drumsticks must be removed as well before the stuffing is put in. If this is not done the carver runs into obstructions.

Besides plain roasting of the stuffed bird there are two other major treatments. One is to serve it *en croute*, covering the trussed bird with a rich pastry bound together with egg, and baking it in a moderate oven. The other is to make it into a galantine by wrapping it in cheesecloth and poaching it in stock. Allowed to cool in the stock, chilled, set in a mold, and covered with a clear aspic, it can be turned out later and served cold.

Given the sharp slim knife, boning is considerably less trouble than the finished dish suggests, and it does make for immeasurably easier serving. The same boning technique can be used for fish if you prefer to serve fillets rather than a whole fish. Cut the fish from head to tail along the backbone and, keeping the blade of the knife always slanted against bone, work your way toward the ventral cavity. In surprisingly little time, you will have two beautiful boned fillets. You may even fillet a shad thus, surely the boniest of fish and frustratingly difficult to eat neatly or hot.

When it comes to stuffing fish, though, I prefer to leave the skeleton in and stuff simply the ventral cavity. Fennel or dill added to the stuffing lifts the finished dish well above the average.

Meats are less often stuffed than birds and fish, partly because they do not present obvious cavities to the eye. But meat may always be flattened out and rolled around a filling of some sort, in much the same way that grape and cabbage leaves are folded around a stuffing of savory rice. Everyone is familiar with a rolled stuffed shoulder of lamb, for instance. Boning of meat proceeds by the same technique as boning of poultry or fish. Starting with a major bone and working always with the blade of the knife slanting against the bone, free the meat gradually. Roll or fold it around the stuffing, tie it securely and proceed to cook it by whatever method is suitable.

A hearty and delicious meal-in-a-dish is made by the Pennsylvania Dutch, but in this day of packaged foods and supermarkets it isn't easy to come by the essential ingredient: a pig's stomach. And if a butcher can be found to supply the stomach, there's still quite a bit of preparation to be done before the dish can be assembled. Given the availability of a pork butcher, persistence on the part of the shopper, and patience on the part of the cook, it is wonderful to dine on

STUFFED PIG'S STOMACH (Dutch Goose)

1) Having acquired with extravagant expenditure of time a pig's stomach, wash it under cold running water to remove the viscous surface, then remove the inner

lining of the stomach, using a sharp and pointed knife at the stomach openings to start the peeling process. (I don't know of a use for the stomach lining, unfortunately, so I discard it.) Wash the stomach again and soak it overnight in salt water. You now have a beautiful translucent bag with one large opening and one small. The small one I sew up right away with button thread. The bag will hold about two quarts of material, which you may balance as your taste directs.

2) Set a few pieces of spare ribs chopped in small pieces to brown with some sausage meat—or use only sausage meat.

3) Mix the browned but not thoroughly cooked meat with a roughly equal bulk each of shredded cabbage and raw diced potatoes. About 1½ lb. of meat, half a cabbage, 4 potatoes, and a good-sized onion chopped fine will account for the filling. Season well with salt and pepper and a leaf or two of sage cut up.

4) Stuff the filling into the stomach and sew up the large opening.

5) Cook the pudding by either of two methods:

   a) Place on a rack in a large kettle and simmer until tender—about 3 hours. Drain, and brown in a bit of butter or lard.

   b) Roast on a rack in the oven in a moderate oven (325°) for about 3½ hours. Baste if necessary with the drippings in the pan.

6) You may make a gravy to serve with the dish from the drippings in the pan.

The pork flavor and the exquisite texture of the delicate skin holding the pudding together is inimitable.

This dish is very similar to the haggis made in Scotland, where the sheep's stomach with its honeycomb tripe lining is turned inside out then filled with chopped lambs' kidneys and suet, heart, liver, lung, or any selection of these, onion, oat-meal, some sharp fruit seasoning like currants or damson plums, salt, pepper, and probably a spice, nutmeg for choice. The whole is moistened with broth and mixed thoroughly before being stuffed in the stomach. The uncooked oatmeal will swell, so the stuffing should fill not more than half of the cavity. In addition, the stomach should be pricked all over with a fork to allow the steam to escape or the bag might burst. As with the pig's stomach, it must be placed on a rack, for contact with the hotter metal of the kettle might tear the delicate skin.

Whatever is it that constitutes elegance in a dish? It certainly isn't the amount of work that goes into the preparation; if it were, then haggis or stuffed pig's stomach would be elegant. It isn't chiefly rarity or delicacy of flavor, for that would admit tripe and onions or the delicious mashed cod's liver of the Eskimos. It isn't appearance alone, though eye appeal based on good cooking technique has a great deal to do with it. It isn't the preparation of food in individual servings, for what could be more truly elegant than a great baron of beef exposing its rosy flesh, or a whole salmon quivering in straw-colored aspic? True elegance partakes perhaps of all these elements, but is incomplete for any single dish. What ensures distinction to a dish is what surrounds it —the rest of the menu. But given one fine dish and a modicum of care to the rest of the meal one is off to a good start.

For a combination of boning and stuffing that is very hard to beat for both elegance and flavor the Russian cuisine offers

KIEVSKI CUTLETS (Chicken à la Kiev)

1) Flay the meat from the breast and wings of a frying chicken, leaving the lower wing bone intact in the flesh. Cut off the wing tip. Split the meat down the

center of the breast, thereby getting two cutlets. Remove the skin from the meat.

2) Pound the cutlets on a block very carefully. This flattens the cutlets and somewhat enlarges them.

3) Somewhat cream sweet butter and form small cylinders of it about ½″ in diameter and 2″ long.

4) Place the butter on the cutlets and roll each one up so as to enclose the butter completely. Skewer only if absolutely necessary. The final shape now resembles a leg of chicken, the lower end of the upper wing bone looking like the end of the drumstick.

5) Wet the hands and toss the cutlet between them to dampen the flesh slightly.

6) Dip the cutlets in seasoned flour, then in egg beaten smooth with a little water, then in fine breadcrumbs Repeat the egg-and-crumbing.

7) Let stand until the egg has dried and set the surface.

8) Fry in deep fat.

Since most frying baskets will not hold more than two cutlets at a time, keep the earlier-cooked ones hot in a warm oven until all are ready.

Approach the cooked cutlet cautiously. When the fork pierces the crust there may be a miniature fountain of melted butter.

There is a whole area of stuffing that is moderately well known even to substandard cooks. This is the stuffed-pastry department. Two-crust dessert pies are probably the most familiar, but meat pies of all sorts—from pastries to enchiladas and empanadas—can be included. The meat turnovers made with Syrian bread dough, the tiny dumplings of China, Cuban mojete, the sausage roll of England are all stuffed dishes, and so is the superb Italian dish of

RAVIOLI

1) Put about 1½ cups of flour and ¼ tsp. of salt into a bowl.
2) Work into the flour about 1 tbsp. of butter.
3) Make a well in the middle of the flour and break into it 1 whole egg. Add 1 tbsp. of water and start working the flour from the sides into the egg and water in the middle. Use the tips of the fingers of the right hand only, keeping the left hand free for pouring in any more liquid that may possibly be needed.
4) When the dough is smooth and quite stiff, knead it for 2–3 minutes, then cover it and let it rest for 10–15 minutes.
5) Divide the dough into two equal portions and roll out into very thin sheets. This is more easily done with a baton roller.
6) For the filling, mix thoroughly
   ½ cup cooked minced chicken
   ½ cup cooked chopped spinach
   ¼ cup breadcrumbs
   ¼ cup grated Parmesan cheese
   1 small clove of garlic mashed with ½ tsp. salt and some freshly ground pepper
   herbs such as parsley or chervil, or any others you prefer
   1 whole egg, beaten
7) Place the filling by teaspoonfuls on one sheet of the pastry leaving about ½″ between the mounds. Cover with the second sheet of pastry, and press with the fingertips around each mound to seal the dough. Cut the packages apart, preferably with a pastry cutter.
8) Drop gently into lots of rapidly boiling salted water, and let them cook for about 10 minutes.
9) Remove with a slotted spoon or a leaking ladle.

Serve these with a simple

TOMATO SAUCE

1) Sauté 1 tbsp. of chopped onion in olive oil.
2) Add ½ can of Pomodoro tomato paste and double that amount of chicken broth.
3) Add seasonings: salt, pepper, basil and oregano.
4) Let simmer until ready to use, adding more broth if the sauce gets too thick.

Here again the container is folded around the stuffing. This does not vitiate the principle of stuffing: that both container and contained are edible.

Fruits are naturals for stuffing for they contain inedible pits or cores that on removal leave very inviting cavities. Most fruits can be stuffed for pleasant desserts or sweetmeats, but there's one fruit that in the Near East is stuffed with meat to make a delicious main dish. I don't know its proper name so I call it just

STUFFED QUINCES

1) Wash the quinces, cut off the tops to use later as lids, and core the fruit, taking out enough of the flesh to leave a cavity that will hold about 2 tbsp. of filling.
2) Brown finely ground lamb and chopped onion together in a skillet.
3) Add to the somewhat cooled filling breadcrumbs, in the proportion of ¼ cup of crumbs to 1 cup of meat and onion, a whole egg, and a little broth. For seasonings use salt and pepper, a pinch of dill and one of oregano.
4) Put into each quince a pinch of sugar or 1 coffeespoonful of honey, then the meat filling. Cover with the quince lid, keeping it in place with a toothpick.

5) Bake in a moderate oven (350°), basting from time to time with a bit of hot water in which sugar has been dissolved (¼ cup of sugar to 1 cup of water is about right) or with honey thinned with water.

The quince skin holds together all through the baking and the fruit provides a built-in sauce for the meat. The cores and flesh of the quinces covered with water and cooked tender yield enough juice for a small amount of jelly.

An eager cook quite dotes on stuffing and if there is no natural cavity to fill, she's bound to create one.

Part II

The Cook's Repertoire, made up of an extensive list of dishes, is built gradually over the years upon a foundation of cooking and preparation techniques modified by three major factors. The first one is the routine cooking required for three meals a day for a family. The young housewife who has never even boiled water soon learns not only how to master that skill but also how to bake potatoes, broil a steak, fry eggs and bacon, and make simple stews and sauces. When she has covered these elementary aspects of cooking she becomes aware of a twin problem, that of surplus —generally at first in the form of leftovers—and lack, quite often presented by the appearance of an unexpected guest. This double problem of surplus and lack leads her to a consideration sometimes of more elaborate techniques, and sometimes of quick ones. Finally, secure in a wide area of cooking techniques, the cook begins to work on the well-planned menu for a carefully devised party.

Every cook's repertoire is distinctively personal. Her routine family dishes are chosen according to the exigencies of time, income, numbers to be fed, and the tastes of her cooking audience. Matters of surplus and lack differ by reason of geography and climate, urban or rural location, and the interests and occupations of the household. In a highly

145

sophisticated city market goods from all over the world are available; near the ocean there are quantities of fish to be had; a household that grows its own vegetables or fruit is quite often threatened with a deluge in one area or another; amateur botanists or passionate picnickers bring home edible treasure trove at frequent intervals.

When it comes to the planned party meal the cook's constraints are likely to be seasonal to some degree. Otherwise, the kind of life she lives and the kinds of guests she entertains decree the dishes she will choose to offer.

Section A

Windfalls and Emergencies account for a great part of the cook's activities *qua* cook. Whether it's a case of feast or famine, an embarrassment of riches or sheer embarrassment, the do-it-yourself-gourmet employs every resource of technique and invention, then seasons to taste.

7. Something for Nothing has a strong

appeal for most people. When the something is food free for
the gathering, I'm right there at the head of the queue. The
first of our free meals for the year comes in late April or early
May with the appearance of the small mushroom called inky
cap. Many otherwise cheerful and kindly people are inclined
to complain about the damp cold of spring in these parts, but
in our household we put off spading, weeding or laundering
the curtains to go mooching about the campus and lawns
for a harvest of *Coprinus micaceus*. These exasperatingly small
fragile mushrooms come up overnight in dense tawny clusters,
their fresh pointed caps glistening as with frost. They are
so crowded that the base of each cluster holds nearly the
mushrooms' own weight in sand and gravel, so the cleaning
of them is laborious. But when they come to table all the
work of preparation is forgotten in the aroma and flavor of
the dish. About a half bushel of these will make a dish for
six people.

You will need the largest heavy skillet you can find, and
even so you may have to cook these delicate bits in several
batches. They must not be crowded, or the result will be a

black soup—very good, too, but not the dish we're aiming at, which is simply

COPRINUS MICACEUS IN BUTTER

1) Clean the mushrooms first by separating them at the base and cutting away the united stems which hold the soil.

2) Rinse them in lots of water to which you've added some cider vinegar. This seems to inhibit the further development of the mushroom, which left to itself grows rapidly dark and inky underneath. All the specimens to be used for cooking should be either white or silvery gray as to gills.

3) Drain them in a colander and even spread on paper toweling to dry further. The less extra moisture in your skillet beyond that in the mushroom flesh, the better the dish.

4) Heat butter in the skillet until it bubbles, toss in the mushrooms and cook rapidly until they begin to color. Using a pancake turner or spatula, turn them gently.

5) Remove to the serving dish and sprinkle with whatever seasonings you like. We use salt only, or a fine sprinkle of sweet basil. They seem not to need pepper, but the basil reinforces the exquisite natural flavor of the mushrooms.

Sometimes the find is just a stray clump of these small caps, in which case you might better toss them raw into a green salad with a simple Italian dressing.

Cooked in butter and puréed, they make a rich black mass which added to a sauce made with browned flour makes a wonderful dark mushroom soup. If you don't bother with browning the flour the soup comes out mauve—a rather unpleasant color for the table.

With the violets in clearings in the woods, or around old shaley stone walls under trees, or in abandoned orchards where the undergrowth is not too rank, you may come on morels and jack-in-the-pulpits. I wouldn't dream of picking a jack-in-the-pulpit, but morels don't seem to have been forbidden as yet by conservation departments. They are sometimes called the sponge mushroom, but we aficionados call them by their proper name, *Morchella esculenta*—transliterated, morel. You may look in vain for hours in a patch of land that you *know* grows morels and not see them, until suddenly your eyes are opened and there they are, perhaps not many, but a few are a feast. We handle them gently, for they are quite brittle. A soft brush is the most efficient tool for cleaning them, with plenty of water to wash away the grit. After that we proceed to cook the

MORELS

1) Slice the morels into cookable pieces. I halve or quarter them lengthwise.
2) Using a shallow pan, skillet or earthen casserole over asbestos, heat butter until it foams. Put in the morels, leaving enough room to turn them over comfortably.
3) Turn down the heat to medium after a moment or so and cook them until they color prettily, turning them as they cook. But don't fidget them about too much or they will go limp.
4) Sprinkle with salt when nearly cooked, and take to table in a warm dish.

These golden bits glistening with butter, crisp, yet succulent inside, taste faintly nutty and sweet, and unlike any other mushroom.

"Weed and Feed" carries a connotation for us quite different from that in the garden columns of newspapers and magazines. About the first of June, when the race to get in the garden and grades is at its peak, when visitors to the University who have gone neglected all year are about to depart and must now be entertained, when winter blankets and clothes have to be packed away, and one hasn't a single presentable summer costume, then comes Nature's great push. Weeds in bewildering variety and fearful profusion spring overnight in lawns and flower beds, and the good gardener gets up betimes and works until dark, pulling them up and laying them neatly in compost pits, piles or heaps. We, being gardeners with a difference, carefully consult books and botanists and find that a surprisingly large number of weeds are edible. Occasionally we collect enough dandelions from the lawn for a mess of

DANDELION GREENS

1) Stew a chipped clove of garlic in olive oil until soft but not brown.
2) Toss into the oil the washed and drained young dandelion leaves and a few tight buds.
3) Sprinkle with salt and pepper and toss and turn the greens for a few minutes until cooked and a bit limp but not melted.
4) Put into a warmed dish and sprinkle on them a few drops of lemon juice.

This is an Italian technique, and it suits dandelions perfectly. It may also be used for garden sorrel—in which case omit the lemon juice—and for spinach or "Chinese greens," a variety of mustard.

The big bought dandelion greens I generally do by a method of my grandmother's. She made a boiled dressing, Pennsylvania Dutch style, and put into it the cleaned raw greens. Here is the way she made

BOILED DRESSING

1) Break an egg (or two) into a pan and stir in with a spoon:

   1 scant tsp. of salt

   2–4 tbsp. of sugar, depending on taste and the dish. (Dandelions want 2 tbsp.; cabbage wants 4.)

   1 rounded tsp. of flour, and some pepper

2) Add 1–2 cups of milk, depending on the number of eggs used and the amount of sauce desired.

3) Add about 4 tbsp. of cider vinegar—or less if you prefer the sauce less sharp, and stir all together.

4) Put over a low fire, increasing the heat gradually until it is at its highest, stirring rapidly *all the time*.

5) The sauce is done when it boils and is thick and smooth. It won't curdle if you keep it moving rapidly as the heat is increased.

This is the sauce that Grandmother made for Hot Cole Slaw too. But frequently she would toss in a small piece of butter for the Cole Slaw sauce. For that dish she chopped the cabbage on a board with a very large sharp knife and got the loveliest finest shreds of cabbage you'd ever wish to see—and quickly and neatly, too. The modern shredders don't do anything like so pretty a job as Grandmother's big old sharp knife.

After the dandelions come the lamb's-quarters (*Chenopodium album*) ugly little weeds, glamoured up by a frost of silky hairs that give them a blue cast against the yellow green of late spring. These grow chiefly in poor soil, and in the last few years we've been noticing a decline in our crop. Whether that means that we're improving the soil or increasing our appetites I'm not quite certain. Like most wild things of delicate flavor, they demand simple treatment. This is how I prepare

LAMB'S-QUARTERS (Greens)

1) Wash the greens and put them directly into an empty pan. As with spinach, the water on and in the leaves is sufficient for the cooking. If the plants are young the stems may be used, but the older ones have tough, fibrous stems, and these should be discarded.

2) After a very few minutes of rapid cooking the water will have almost disappeared and the greens be cooked and limp. They should be turned once or twice during the cooking, preferably with a wooden fork.

3) Chop them in a wooden bowl until they are as fine as your patience will allow.

4) Now melt some butter in the pan in which the greens were cooked and return the chopped greens to it, adding salt—and pepper if you like, though they don't really need pepper. Stir the greens in the butter until they are thoroughly hot, then serve.

The flavor of these humble greens is haunting and exquisite, and served with chicken or fish they make a memorable menu.

Purslane, (*Portulaca oleracea*), that pretty little succulent weed that accounted for a lame back during many a weeding season, now pays its way by coming to table in the same fashion. Meatier than lamb's-quarters, it is also less elegant, but even so it's a dish fit for at least a little king.

About this time, too, come the pods of the Judas tree or redbud (*Cercis canadensis*). The flowers are said to be edible, but I can't bring myself to rape that gaudy blossom for the table. As for the pods, pick the clusters, not single pods; for when you come to prepare them, each tiny pod must be stripped of its dried blossom and stem, and it's much easier to cut all four or five in a group with a pair of scissors than to pick off each blossom-end separately by hand, for it takes a weary many pods to make a dish. Having rinsed the pods in a colander and drained them, proceed to the cooking of

REDBUD PODS

1) Heat butter or a bland oil such as sesame in a shallow pan or skillet.
2) Throw in the pods and toss them with a fork or pancake turner several times in the very few minutes it takes to crisp them. Don't let them brown too much.
3) Sprinkle with pepper and no salt.

When they're a week older, the pods will need to be cooked in a small amount of water before they're crisped in the butter. Use a covered skillet, and when the water is absorbed, proceed as above.

Redbud pods make a wonderful accompaniment to chicken or fish dishes, for there is a slight sharpness of flavor about them that sets off the blandness of the meat.

In a lucky year, when I've managed to keep the rhubarb going by cutting the blossom stalks, I generally take off a day to collect wild angelica (*Angelica atropurpurea*), and return home with armfuls of the fragrant stalks, which are then added to the rhubarb to make

RHUBARB AND ANGELICA JAM

1) Clean and cut into short lengths equal amounts of rhubarb and angelica stems—not the flower-bearing stems in either case, just leaf stems, and these well before the flower stalk is threatening to bloom.
2) Put these into a large kettle and warm slowly until the juice is released. Then turn up the heat to cook the flesh.
3) Add the same amount of sugar as you have fruit. Stir this in and bring to a boil. Boil rapidly until thick and clear.
4) Let cool for about 5 minutes and pour into clean hot jars.

Candied angelica gives a pretty fillip to a festive Trifle, and the candying of fruits and flowers is much simpler than it looks or sounds. Again, gather the angelica before the flowers bloom, and do not use the woody blossom stalk at all for

CANDIED ANGELICA

1) Cut the stems into convenient lengths—about 6″— weigh, and blanch in boiling water for about 3 minutes. Drain, saving the liquid.
2) Measure by weight the same amount of sugar as you have of stems.
3) Put the pieces into a large kettle, cover with the sugar and add the water in which the stems have been blanched to make a heavy syrup (1 lb. of sugar to 1 pt. of water).
4) Simmer until the stems are tender.
5) Drain on a rack over a pan to catch the drips—I use a roasting pan and rack—and when almost dry slit the stems to flatten them.
6) Strew sugar over the stems and place again in a pan and cover with the syrup that has been drained off of them previously.
7) Now cook gently again until the stems are translucent and a clear, bright green.
8) Repeat the draining, sugaring and simmering process until the angelica dries into stiffened strips, but do not repeat so often that the sugar dries in crystals on the stems. Three or four times should be enough.
9) Drain finally, cool, and store in a dry place between layers of waxed paper.

When Thanksgiving or Christmas meals come along we sometimes serve a trifle for dessert as a change from the more conventional pumpkin or mince-meat pies. The candied angelica makes a spring-green accent on the topping of whipped cream and bright candied fruits in red and orange.

What typical British understatement to call such a dish a "trifle"! Or was it so named, perhaps, as a tribute to the texture? "Trifles light as air . . ."

If you can command the time it's rewarding to make the ladyfingers and almond macaroons from scratch and then proceed as follows to assemble a

TRIFLE

1) Make a rich boiled custard and set aside to cool.
2) Line a serving dish with ladyfingers or small sponge cakes and drip a rich Madeira wine on them; Boal is excellent.
3) Spread the macaroons with raspberry jam and arrange in layers in the dish.
4) More Madeira or Maraschino liqueur is dripped over the macaroons.
5) When the custard is cool, pour it over the dish so that all the crevices are filled.
6) Top with lightly sweetened whipped cream and arrange candied fruits, slivered almonds and angelica to make a pleasing pattern.

By mid-June most of our meals are eaten outdoors, and since there's a patch of wild strawberries just a few feet from the back door it inevitably suggests a lunch of

HOT STRAWBERRY SHORTCAKE

1) Make baking powder biscuit in a cake tin.
2) With a fork carefully split the cake of biscuit horizontally and butter generously the exposed crumb of the lower half.

3) Cover this half with the wild strawberries which have been crushed, using a potato masher, with confectioner's sugar.

4) Cover with the lid of biscuit; butter this and top with the remaining half of the sugared berries.

Served with mugs of cool milk this is a perfect lunch, even for guests.

When we pick strawberries away from home, we keep our eyes open for fox-grape vines (*Vitis labrusca*), for this is just the time to find the leaves in perfect condition for preserving. In the winter months they'll be used for making Yalanci Dolmas, that delectable hors d'oeuvre of the Near East. Nothing in the whole realm of cookery is easier than

TO PRESERVE GRAPE LEAVES

1) Choose leaves that are not insect-bitten. If they are dusty, wipe them gently with a dry cloth.

2) Pile about a dozen clean, dry leaves one atop another, then roll them up, and if necessary to keep them rolled, tie the roll with soft string.

3) Stand the packages on end in screw-top canning jars. About 4 packages of a dozen leaves each fit snugly into a pint jar.

4) Screw top on very tight.

The natural acid in the leaves preserves them.

When these are to be used, rinse the leaves in warm water and go ahead with the manufacture of

YALANCI DOLMAS

1) Lay the leaves out on a counter or platters to drain

somewhat. Trim the stems if necessary to about $\frac{1}{2}''$ lengths. Make sure that the leaves are smooth and lying with the back, or "wrong" side of the leaf uppermost, the stems toward you.

2) Sauté in olive oil some chopped onion.

3) When the onion begins to color, add washed and drained rice, salt, pepper, chopped or dried dill and chopped or dried mint.

4) Stir the rice about until all the grains are coated with oil but not brown, and remove from the fire to cool.

5) Put about 1 tsp. of the rice mixture on the medium-sized leaves, less on small ones, and more on outsize ones.

6) With the stem nearest you, fold the leaf as follows: the lobes to left and right of the stem are turned up and over the rice; the sides of the leaf are folded over the rice, in toward the middle; then roll, not too tightly toward the tip of the leaf, allowing the butt of the stem to keep the package loose. You end with something that looks like a stubby cigar.

7) When all the little rolls are finished, put a couple of grape leaves flat in the bottom of a fairly deep pan and pack the dolmas standing on end. The pan should be deep enough so that the dolmas can be completely covered with water. They must not be packed in too tightly or the rice, swelling as it cooks, will burst the leaves; nor must they be so loosely packed that they fall on their sides and come open. A small cup or glass set in the middle of the pan often solves the latter problem.

8) Put two or three more leaves on top of the packages, cover the dolmas with water, put in a little salt and a tsp. of olive oil, then put on top of the dolmas a plate nearly the diameter of the pan; this is to prevent the dolmas' floating and opening. Cover the pan, bring to the boil, turn down to simmer, remove the lid, and allow them to cook covered just by the plate until all

the liquid is absorbed. This takes about an hour or a little longer.

9) When cool enough to handle remove from the pan and lay them on their sides in the dish in which you'll serve them. Sprinkle a little confectioner's sugar on them and a few drops of lemon juice, and if you like a few more drops of olive oil.

10) Chill and store until ready for use. They're better after some hours than they are immediately.

The dolmas are even better made from fresh vine leaves, in which case the leaves should be blanched in boiling water to soften them enough to roll. Leaves preserved in brine should be rinsed.

There are many variations to this basic Turkish recipe. Some peoples in the Near East add pine nuts and currants to the rice mixture; some season with cinnamon; some add tomato to the rice, but they're all really the same dish, and all are good.

Vine leaves make another dish that the Greeks do superbly. The technique is quite similar, but minced lamb is added to the rice and onions, the mint and dill are replaced by other herbs—parsley, oregano, or thyme, and the dolmas are served hot with an egg and lemon sauce called in Greek

AVGOLIMONO SAUCE

1) Mix with a fork 3 whole eggs and about 2 tbsp. of the cold stock in which the dolmas have been cooked, and the strained juice of a lemon. A little sugar helps to make our more acid lemons resemble the mellow Mediterranean variety.

2) Add hot stock gradually, beating with a whisk, and put over a low heat or over a pan of hot water, beating constantly until the sauce is thick and smooth. As long as the sauce doesn't actually boil it won't curdle.

3) Season with salt and pepper and pour over the hot dolmas, now drained and lying in a hot dish.

Such dolmas take naturally to one of the resinated Greek table wines, and eaten out of doors in shade on a brilliant day allow one almost to believe himself in a *taverna* on the shores of Greece.

When we go into the woods anticipating the first summer mushrooms, we're often disappointed, but we never come home completely empty-handed. One of the items that we collect at this season is sassafras. The young leaves we dry, preferably in sun, and pack in jars to crumble later into creole dishes for the authentic gumbo flavor. Sassafras also is a slight thickening agent in a stew or sauce. The filé of New Orleans is powdered sassafras leaf, to be put into a dish just minutes before serving, whereas okra, another New Orleans staple, exerts its thickening power during the whole cooking period.

Living inland has one real disadvantage; sea food comes too far or too frozen to be the delectable item it is on the coast. Only by marrying, breeding, or cultivating a fisherman can an inland cook assure a satisfactory supply of fish, and of course only freshwater fish. One of these is much neglected and in plentiful supply. The fishermen we've cultivated are trying to rid the nearby ponds and lakes of carp, so we are offered this creature quite often and we rarely refuse it. Indeed, a gift of a carp generally sparks a dinner party, for this large fish, though bland of flavor and of a soft texture, takes well to sharp or highly seasoned sauces. It is said to have a muddy flavor in certain seasons, but having taken the precaution of rinsing the gutted fish in a bath of vinegar and water we've never noticed any objectionable taste—far from it. This is how I prepare

CARP IN ASPIC

1) Having washed the scaled and gutted fish in vinegar and water, put it in a roomy kettle along with the head, tail and fins. Cover it with water to which add: salt, pepper, bay leaf or tarragon, onion, carrot, and a generous amount of white wine. If there is no—or not enough —wine on hand, use lemon juice or a small amount of vinegar—something acid, anyway.

2) Bring slowly to a boil, skimming off any scum that rises as it heats. This will insure keeping the broth clear.

3) Turn the heat to low, so that the liquid just simmers, and cook until the meat is about to fall off the bones.

4) Lift out the fish and allow it to cool before you separate the flesh from the skin and bones.

5) Strain the broth through a piece of cheesecloth or old linen. If it is not perfectly clear and bright, clear it with egg white and crushed egg shell, as follows: To the cooled broth add egg white and shell in the proportion of one egg white and shell to each quart of liquid. Bring slowly to the boil, whisking constantly. Allow to boil, now unwhisked, until the egg curd is completely cooked, then strain through a cloth into a clean container.

6) Make an aspic with plain gelatine and the clear broth in the proportion of 1 tbsp. of gelatine to 3 cups of broth. (The bones of the fish will have provided for some natural jelling.)

7) Rinse a mold in cold water, and pour some aspic into it. Tilt the mold so that aspic coats all the inside of the form. This tilting and coating should be repeated during the period of the stiffening of the aspic.

8) Chill the mold until the aspic is viscid, then lay in it the flesh of the carp and cover with the remainder of the aspic.

Chilled and turned out onto a platter, garnished, and served with a herb-flavored mayonnaise, nothing could be more attractive and satisfying on a hot night.

Carp, being large fish, have gargantuan amounts of roe. Uncooked, the roe is a muddy color and sandy texture, but sautéed in butter it turns a brilliant orange. It is delicious, like all roes, but it does need salt. We also like a sprinkle of lemon or lime juice with it.

Carp is widely used and highly valued by the Chinese, and they have a technique for cooking it that we like. My version I call

CARP CHINOIS

1) Scale and clean the fish, trimming off the fins but leaving on the head and tail. Make several slashes through the backbone, so that the heat will penetrate quickly into the flesh while cooking. I generally make as many slashes as I want pieces to serve. This makes for easy work at table.

2) Heat a bland oil (peanut or sesame) in a large skillet to the depth of about ¾".

3) Dry the fish well with paper toweling and dip it in highly seasoned flour so that it is completely coated.

4) Lay the fish in the pan and fry at a fairly high temperature for about 3–5 minutes on each side. The time depends on the size of the fish. The oil should bubble at least halfway up the side of the fish. Remove the whole fish carefully and drain on a rack covered with paper towels.

5) Pour off all but a tbsp. or so of oil and sauté in this some sliced scallions or shallots, or onion.

6) Mix about 1 tsp. of cornstarch and 1 tbsp. of sugar in a coffee cup with 4 tbsp. of good soy sauce; fill up the cup with dry sherry.

7) When the scallions are tender, pour in the cornstarch and liquid mixture and stir rapidly until the sauce is

clear and a little thickened. If the pan is large, you may need to add a little water to make up for liquid lost by rapid evaporation.

8) Put the fish on a large platter, pour over it the sauce and bring to table.

You may play many variations on this theme, by combining sugar and acid like vinegar or lemon juice for a sweet-sour effect, or by serving the fish on a bed of chopped greens, or garnishing with any tidbit that you fancy. Or you may wish to slice the fish before it's cooked (in which case discard the head and tail), marinate it in a seasoned sauce, then fry or bake or broil it.

A snapping turtle is a gruesome creature to prepare for table, but once cooked and served it makes not one but several dishes that linger in the highest heaven of memory. These are large animals, and the only times we're offered them are in early summer when the females come out of the water to lay their eggs on land. The friend who brought us our first turtle had shot it in the head and kindly removed at least that part, for in his youth he'd been bitten by a "dead" snapper, and he carries the scar to this day.

Complete novices that we were in the art of butchering turtle, we were appalled at the way the headless thing pushed away the knife with its flippers. It took two of us to remove the shell and skin the beast, and by that time I feared that the man of the house would never be able to eat turtle meat. However, after twenty-four hours of soaking in salt water, the meat and the scrubbed shell had lost their horrid connotations for him, and we and our guests thoroughly enjoyed

"GREEN TURTLE SOUP"
(So called by reason of the color, not the species of turtle.)

1) Bring slowly to the boil then simmer the scrubbed shell and the flesh of turtle with onion and celery, skimming off the scum as it rises. Cook until the meat is loose from the bones.
2) Separate the bones and discard, and return the meat to the kettle with salt and a bag of crushed spices and herbs such as basil, coriander, peppercorns, and whole mace. (Note the "sweet" herbs.)
3) Shortly before serving remove the bag of herbs and spices, add Madeira and the turtle eggs.

This is the clearest, most delicate green soup, and well worth the preliminary horrors both aesthetically and gastronomically.

This one turtle yielded 1¼ lb. of meat, 22 eggs, 2 oz. of liver and heart, and ¾ lb. of shell with meat shreds attached. It served ten people heartily.

In late June, when the elderberry bushes flower, there is a rare dessert treat in store. Gather about a dozen of the wide, heavily fragrant umbels for a batch of

ELDER FLOWER PANCAKES

1) Strip the flowers from the stems and stemlets, and you'll find that you have about one cupful from a dozen umbels.
2) Make a rich pancake batter without baking powder and adding about 1 tbsp. of sugar for each two eggs. Add the cupful of elder blossom to it.
3) Bake on a lightly greased griddle as for any delicate pancake.
4) Roll up and sprinkle with sifted confectioner's sugar.

These taste somewhat like almond or pistachio and will mystify and gratify the most sophisticated palate.

In July begins the great spate of wild mushrooms which over a period of twenty years we've learned to recognize. The harvest keeps coming all through the summer and early fall and finally peters out at about Thanksgiving except for the delicious winter mushroom, *Collybia velutipes,* recently re-classified as *Flammulina velutipes.* If the weather at Thanks-giving is too cold for mushrooms to grow, we stuff the turkey with some of other species that we've dried in the generous days of July or August, but the ones we like best for that purpose are the large inky caps, *Coprinus atramentarius.* They impart to the basic rice stuffing a basil-like flavor that goes beautifully with turkey. This filling I call

MUSHROOM PILAV STUFFING

1) Wash and drain rice and sauté for a few minutes with chopped onion in olive oil.
2) Add half as much water as rice; cover and cook slowly until the water is absorbed and the rice has begun to swell.
3) Add the clean whole raw mushrooms, a pinch or so of basil, salt and pepper to taste, some pine nuts, and washed and drained currants.
4) Stuff the turkey with this mixture and proceed to roast as usual.

The juices of the bird and the liquid in the mushrooms should provide enough more liquid to finish cooking the rice.

If dried mushrooms are used they must be re-hydrated before being added to the rice. Use the water in which the mushrooms have soaked—if there's any left—to cook the rice.

We dry chanterelles (*Cantharellus cibarius*) or fairy-ring mushrooms (*Marasmius oreades*) by spreading them, either whole for small ones or cut for large ones, on a piece of screening set on sawhorses in the sun. They may also be dried in the oven on trays or racks. Or if the weather is damp, they may be threaded on string and hung in a dry airy place like an attic. Be sure, in this case, that the mushrooms do not touch each other, or soon the whole string will be spoiled.

The chanterelles, those large solid fragrant fungi, last well into the wild-fruit season. We often find nearly ripe May apples (*Podophyllum peltatum*) when we're hunting for them. Now May apples are relished by the woods creatures, and if you wait to gather them when they are dead ripe you'll get a very small harvest, for squirrels, or deer, woodchucks, or whatever it is that delights in them are up earlier in the day than human beings. So we gather them when they're still pale yellow and fairly hard, pack them loosely in plastic bags and bury them shallowly in the herb border on the south side of the house. After about ten days, we dig them up and use them. Now they are a deep yellow in color and soft and dent-able, almost squashy. Alone or combined with other fruit, peaches particularly, they make a superb jam or jelly. They have lots of pectin in them, so that any other fruit with little pectin may be used with them to make a jelly. This is how I go about making

PEACH AND MAY APPLE JAM

1) Stem and cut open the May apples and separate the seed mass in the center from the flesh and skin. Put the seeds and tissue in a pan with enough water to keep them from sticking. Cover, bring to the boil, turn down the heat and simmer for about 10 minutes.

2) Strain out the seeds and add the liquid to the May apple flesh which should be cut into strips about $\frac{1}{4}''$ wide. I use kitchen shears for this. Do not peel the fruits.

3) Peel, stone, and cut up the peaches and add them to the May apple and the liquid from the seed and tissue.

4) Add enough water barely to cover the fruit, and bring to the boil.
5) Add sugar, the same amount as the total amount of fruit.
6) Bring again to the boil and let boil quickly until the fruit is clear and bright and the juice jells as it drips from the spoon.
7) Let the jam cool for a few minutes in the pan so that the fruit won't float, then pour into clean warm jars and seal.

There is a flavor to May apples that is reminiscent of pineapple, so the affinity with peach is understandable.

August is the picnic time *par excellence,* and we make the most of the assured good weather to go early and stay late away from home. It's pleasant, though, to come home at about dusk with baskets of mushrooms and berries and sit about the floor with books, knives and mushrooms, trying to identify new ones and checking old acquaintances. It's even pleasanter if you have a glass of pink sumac "lemonade" to sip from while you work.

What we collect seems to be *Rhus typhina,* the staghorn sumac, with velvety stems and clusters of berries like crimson plush. It's something of a chore to clean the cone-shaped berry clusters as they're quite often infested with minute insects, but once that is done it's not too tedious to make

PINK LEMONADE

1) Put sumac berries into a deep bowl or wide-mouthed pitcher, cover with water, and crush with a solid wooden potato masher.
2) Strain the faintly pink liquid through cheesecloth into another pitcher and sweeten to taste.
3) Serve cold.

The very last picking of wild blueberries coincides with the ripening of the large black wild cherries, the rum cherries, *Prunus seratina*. These make a good jam but require an extravagant use of sugar; but they make a most superior cherry liqueur, rather like that made in the Near East from the morella cherry. In good rum-cherry years I try to get around to making

CHERRY LIQUEUR

1) After stemming the cherries put them into a jar or crock and cover with sugar.
2) Crush the cherries and sugar a bit and leave for a day or so, covered with a cloth, to ferment slightly.
3) Pour on brandy, cover closely with a lid, and leave as long as your patience allows.

By Thanksgiving, if you can wait that long, you will be rewarded by having very dry cherry brandy to serve at the close of the feast.

Anyone who grows squash in a kitchen garden is appalled at the rate of production of these plants. Luckily we learned long ago that the blossoms are edible as well as the fruits, so now when we are threatened with a surplus of squash we pick the flowers and make

BATTER-FRIED SQUASH BLOSSOMS

1) Make a good rich pancake batter of
   2 or 3 eggs
   1 cup of flour
   1 cup of milk
   salt

2) Dip the clean, dry blossoms in the batter and fry in deep fat.
3) Drain on paper and serve hot.

These taste very delicately of squash and are the prettiest things imaginable to serve.

With the longer cool nights of early autumn come the giant puffballs. These huge fungi are perfectly safe to eat as long as they are solid and white inside, for they cannot be confused with any poisonous mushroom. Most of the people who dislike them have been misinformed about the method of cooking them. The soft flesh will absorb any amount of butter, so it must be insulated if you want to get its distinctive but mild flavor and not too much fat; therefore, to prepare

PUFFBALLS

1) With a very sharp knife, cut about 1″ thick slices and peel off the tough outer skin.
2) Dip each slice in egg and water, then in seasoned flour, then again in egg and water, and finally in fine crumbs.
3) Fry quickly in butter until golden.

Classes start again in late September, formal social life resumes, the multitude of tasks to be picked up for the winter lands on us all at once, but Nature still provides a wealth of fruits that can be used if we can find the time to process them. One such delightful plant is the Japanese quince (*Chaenomeles lagenaria*), which makes an excellent tart jelly. The fairly large fruits are remarkably free of insects and worms, and they are so rich in pectin that the pale amber jelly is ready in just a few minutes after the sweetened juice comes to a boil. Another of our favorites is the fruit of the lovely dogwood (*Cornus mas*), which makes a brilliant crimson jelly, indescribable as to flavor and as tart as currant. We find it simpler to wait until the dark red oval fruits drop to the ground than to pick them from the trees. Even the dead-ripe fruit is full of pectin, and once the juice is expressed it's a matter of only a few minutes before the jelly is poured into the glasses.

Then there are the fox grapes and the hips of the *Rosa rugosa*, both of which are best after they've been touched by the first light frost. The fox grapes make a dark purple jelly, and the rose hips make a deep amber jam or jelly. I make a

PURÉED ROSE HIP JAM

1) Using a little more than half as much water as hips, cook until the fruit is soft.
2) Rub through a sieve or put through a food mill to remove the hundreds of little seeds.
3) Add to the purée half its bulk in sugar.
4) Heat to simmering, stirring well to dissolve the sugar, and continue cooking until thick and somewhat clear— about 10 minutes.
5) Pour into clean warm jars and seal.

There is said to be a large amount of vitamin C in rose hips. This seems to have a relatively short life, so if you're vitamin-conscious use the jelly within a few months. Even six months after making, however, the flavor is still superb.

There comes a day with a bite in the air, and we know it's going to freeze hard overnight, so the last job of harvesting the garden is done just before dinner. The great dry overgrown zucchinis are picked to be made into

MARROW JAM

1) To remove the hard rind, first cleave the marrow in half, then, cut side down on a board, chop off the rind.
2) Cut the flesh into ½″ cubes, and put in a large bowl in layers separated by layers of sugar, allowing 1 lb. of sugar to each lb. of flesh. Leave for 24 hours. In this time the fruit will have expressed its juice and will look a bit shrunken or withered.
3) Add lime or lemon juice and rind and either fresh or preserved ginger in the proportions you choose.
4) Put all this into a preserving kettle and boil to a clear amber.

By this time the jam cupboard is bursting and the pantry shelves are packed jar atop jar with all the luxuries we've processed in the growing season, and we're set for high days and holidays all through the months until the first little inky caps show again.

8. By-products

of activities and interests quite outside the kitchen frequently enhance our diet. Prime among these are the mushrooms that we gather from April on—sometimes into January. In a good year we have dried more than a bushel of the little *Marasmius oreades*, and anyone who hasn't done so has no idea of the suffocating pride with which we view the strings of tiny caps looping through our attic. And the fruity fragrance when a jar of dried chanterelles is opened brings back all the magic of a hot July day tempered by the deep shade of the woods where we gathered these honied morsels, quite often in thick patches of poison ivy. There is no greed like that of the true mushroomer. He'll climb rotting trees, descend crumbling cliffs, dare insect venom—anything—to get his paws on a particularly good specimen.

The professional mycologist is quite often wary of eating the mushrooms he collects, while the amateur in his protective armor of little learning enjoys his harvests in innocent abandon. We have been poisoned only once in twenty-five years, and then not badly. This was, too, the result of taking a deliberate chance on one species that we knew might be unwholesome but not fatal. But any reference to the gathering and eating of wild mushrooms should not be taken as a recommendation to the uninitiate to go and do likewise. Each separate species must be known—not guessed at—to be safely eaten.

Besides drying certain species of mushrooms, we process others by canning. The larger varieties of inky caps, *Coprinus atramentarius* and *Coprinus comatus,* have too much moisture to dry successfully, but young solid specimens if processed immediately can wonderfully and keep their flavor well for four months and moderately well after six months. Like the chanterelles, these are rather sweet mushrooms and lend themselves to dishes made with tomatoes. Like tomatoes they are improved, if that is possible, by a modicum of basil.

The polypores, unlike the gilled species of mushrooms, are generally edible—or at least not poisonous. They are likely to be large, so if a tasty one is discovered it does for a large number of diners. One grisly autumn evening the breadwinner arrived home, wet and loaded with a bulging brief case, assorted groceries and an enormous muddy *Sparassis crispa* looking like a much overgrown tawny-gray cauliflower. It must have weighed about ten pounds, and indeed, though we gave three parties on it during the week that we housed it in the root cellar, we actually tired of it before it was used up.

A beefsteak mushroom (*Fistulina hepatica*) however is none too large for two greedy people. But then it really is the main dish of a meal. This is how I prepared a memorable

BEEFSTEAK MUSHROOM

1) Wipe off the slimy upper surface with a damp cloth.
2) Put whole into a large skillet in which plenty of butter is bubbling but not smoking.
3) Turn once only—as for pancakes.

Nothing could be simpler or better. There is a slight acidity in this thick juicy mushroom which makes it taste like steak with a sprinkle of lemon juice, and the red succulence of it heightens the illusion. Season this dish after cooking. I like quite a bit of pepper with it but very little salt. It is almost as satisfying for the meat craving as steak itself, and regarded as a mushroom it is unique and superb.

The so-called field mushroom, *Agaricus campestris,* is so similar to the commercially produced variety that it can be treated in the same ways. During one year when we had a glut of these in the neighborhood, after canning two bushels of them, I hit upon a Polish and Russian technique that made a pleasant change from the sautéed, broiled, scalloped and creamed mushrooms which we'd been having *pro forma* at every dinner. This method employs sour cream of course, and I have modified it to include wine as well. I call it

MUSHROOM STROGANOV

1) Clean but do not peel the mushrooms; then slice them vertically or not at all.
2) Slice onion or shallots into a skillet or shallow casserole in which butter is bubbling, then cook until soft over lowered heat.
3) Throw in the mushrooms and turn the heat high again. When the mushrooms begin to color push them aside, tilt the pan and add enough flour to absorb the little butter remaining.
4) Add sour cream and white wine and stir smooth. To 1 cup of sour cream use about ⅓ cup of wine.
5) Season with salt, pepper, and a pinch of dried dill leaves and flowers, or a little more of fresh.
6) Turn heat low and let the sauce thicken.

Beloved or even merely long-lived pets in a household become entities in the family as much as their servants, the humans. One caters to their tastes and whims as well as to their needs. The kitten that ate all the pretty crimped crust from two Thanksgiving pumpkin pies is thereafter rewarded by having crust specially baked for him well into his middle age. Conversely, when he disdains his favorite dish of raw lamb's kidney with that inimitable gesture of pawing the floor by the dish, head turned well away, as if he were burying some loathsome relic—why then his family provides canned salmon and eats the kidneys themselves. Unfortunately, what remains in his dish is cut too small for our purposes, but cooked it goes on the dog's plate. No, it's the remaining four and a half kidneys that we use for

KIDNEYS IN WHITE WINE SAUCE

1) Chopped shallots, for preference, or sliced onion for second choice, are stewed gently in butter until they begin to soften.
2) Turn up the heat and toss into the pan veal or lamb's kidney sliced about ¼″ thick. These must brown before they cook through. We prefer them a touch rare.
3) Push aside the meat and rub into the remaining butter enough flour to absorb the fat.
4) Add broth or milk, and white wine in equal proportions. Stir and let thicken.
5) Season with a very small pinch of dry sage and salt and pepper. Or if you have fresh sage in the garden, two leaves cut in thin strips crosswise can be put into the pan when the kidney slices go in.

A variation of this made with sour cream is also very good.

A pet by-product which I fear may never again be duplicated was quail. A year or so ago, one of the government departments interested in correcting some imbalance in the ecology of our natural surroundings, released great numbers of quail here. These charming plump birds paraded through the garden in devoted couples and we enjoyed watching them. But one windy cold fall day, one of them, probably neurotic, committed suicide against one of the large windows, and before a neighbor's boxer slavering in the background could reach it, our high-minded cat retrieved it—we like to think— for us. At least he gave it up to us with a minimum of persuasion.

I had read of quail baked in vine leaves, and luckily I had some on hand at this time; certainly they must have been preserved ones. There was also some lean ham in the house. After the bird had been plucked and cleaned I set about preparing

BAKED QUAIL

1) Fill the cavity with a few sweet mushrooms which have been added to chips of onion and currants cooked in butter and seasoned with a little salt and pepper.
2) Butter or oil the bird well and wrap it in vine leaves, then tie it up with soft string.
3) Put it in a well-buttered dish in a hot oven (450°).
4) Baste after 10 minutes with 1 or 2 tbsp. of white wine and leave for another 10 minutes.
5) Meanwhile sauté the tiny whole giblets in butter for not more than 3 minutes.
6) Having removed the vine leaves, carve the quail in half and serve each half on a thin slice of lean ham, pour over it the drippings and wine, and garnish it with the giblets.

Veal tongues are another staple of the cat's diet, but good as they are, they pall for him after a day or two. We look forward hopefully to the time when our spoiled black beast says, "I'll have tuna tonight; I'm tired of tongue."

These morsels, peeled, cut in bite-sized pieces and served in a white wine and cream sauce with mushrooms and perhaps a touch of tarragon are a real treat.

But our greatest dividends from the pet-investment are the soups. These are never named soups. They are the result of simmering first veal tongues, say, then perhaps chicken gizzards or veal hearts in the same stock. To this I add vegetable trimmings, the outside leaves of lettuce, an odd carrot for the dog once in a while, the tops of fennel, or the hard stalks of asparagus, a few elderly sprouting peas, dribbles of wine, a half cup of coffee left from breakfast, and so on. After boiling these for a few minutes once or twice a day for several days the stock is rich and brown and gives off an irresistible aroma. The fat is skimmed off every evening and added to the dog's dinner plate, so that when the soup is ready for us all I need do is strain out the debris. If we want a really clear soup, I add an egg white and the crushed shell to each quart of the strained cold broth. This I heat to the boiling point, stirring with a *wisp* or metal whisk, then let it boil for a few minutes before straining it through cheesecloth. There are very few days in the year that we have no soup available, even though I use it constantly in making other dishes. When I have started a new lot with just chicken gizzards I take advantage of the chicken flavor to make a Wedding Pilav. But the generalized broth, called by one of our friends "the percolating soup," comes in very handy for sauces, for basting, or for adding to bland vegetables. When we have a dish of endive the heads are always cooked in broth rather than water, and of course any bits left from that cooking are returned to the soup pot. It's a two-way operation.

Ham is such a versatile meat and keeps so well that I like to have it on hand fairly often. And surely the ham bone makes a fine split-pea soup. But we find that it is actually improved if chicken-gizzard broth is used to cook both bone and peas. If there should be, as there has been in our house, a half cupful of tired beer on the counter when I'm finishing the soup, I add it, and then questions follow as to the "mystery" ingredient.

Though I sometimes think that I couldn't cook without a soup pot on the stove, not everything goes into it by any means. I avoid using any of the cabbage family, for long-cooked cabbage flavor is both overpowering and unappetizing. Beets, unless used specifically for borscht, are both too sweet and too mauve.

During the last war most of us in this country made the acquaintance of margarine. In those days, when it came out of its wrapping livid and waxy, it was supremely unattractive. Of course we learned to color it, but nothing ever persuaded me that it was as good as butter. It didn't melt the same way, it didn't brown like butter, and it neither smelt, felt, nor tasted like butter. Also at that time our diet was higher in carbohydrate foods than in protein, and the first signs of added weight appeared, so we began to think that perhaps we didn't need the unhomogenized Guernsey milk that we were used to drinking each noontime, but skim milk did not taste like proper milk to us. Eventually we compromised. We continued to buy the rich Guernsey milk, but now we poured off the full cup of cream in every quart, shook it in the wedding-present-cocktail-shaker never used otherwise, and got both really skimmed fresh milk, or buttermilk, and butter. This was *real* butter which melted, browned, smelt, felt and tasted right. Since that time we've continued to make butter. It takes about ten minutes of shaking—a man's job, I say—then it is drained of the remaining milk, rinsed in ice water, and is ready to use. Jack Spratt drinks what's left in the bottle after the cream is poured off; his wife drinks what's left in the shaker after the butter is made; the butter, unsalted is used for cooking the dishes that benefit from the use of sweet butter—puff pastry or croissants, and certain sauces.

Gardening is the chief activity that provides edible by-products. I've mentioned in the previous chapter the uses of certain weeds and vegetable flowers when the crop threatens to overwhelm us, but there are a few plants that we keep strictly for ornament that don't know their places and insist on providing us with an embarrassment of produce. The most spectacular one is the flowering quince bush, which gives us huge crops of fruit each fall. When I've made all the jelly we can use and give away, there is still enough fruit left to do something with. Then I make a quince paste called by the Portuguese

MARMALADA

1) Cook the quinces, cut but neither peeled nor cored, in water to cover until the fruit is soft.
2) Put through a food mill or strong strainer to get a purée.
3) In a large, fairly shallow pan over medium heat cook the purée with sugar in the proportion of 1 cup of sugar to 1 cup of purée. This must be stirred often to prevent scorching.
4) When the bubbles insist on plopping bits over the stove and the aproned cook, remove the pan from the fire and pour the very thick jam onto an oiled cookie sheet or into a large shallow pan.
5) Ideally this should be set in the sun to dry thoroughly, but failing sun, a low heat in the oven will dry it in time.
6) When it is no longer juicy or "weepy" it may be stored between layers of waxed paper or aluminum foil until needed.

This paste can be used for a quick winter dessert. Cut into strips and served with sour or whipped cream it makes a pleasant change from the usual winter fruits.

The same process of drying can be carried further and the paste dried to the point where it is like leather. It is then even called "Quince Leather." The slab is cut into small strips which are then rolled in powdered sugar. The result is now a confection very useful for Tricks or Treats.

Arranging flowers and keeping the bowls and vases attractive and fresh-looking has never appealed to me as what I believe is now known as a "creative outlet." But I must confess to a low craving for applause when I proffer a dish which represents a major effort. One of the more spectacular ones is a platter of stuffed nasturtiums, so in order to keep the flowers coming I try to pick them at regular intervals. Eventually there comes a period when they're let go because of the press of other demands, and before I know it there's a crop of swelling fruit pods. These I gather and pickle to make a variant to capers, different but just as good. To make

PICKLED NASTURTIUM PODS

1) Put 1 cup of green pods into a brine of ½ cup of water and 2 tbsp. of salt and leave them for 2 days.
2) Drain the pods, put them into clean jars, and pour over them ½ cup of vinegar and ½ cup of sugar heated to boiling point.
3) Seal as for any pickle.

The leaves of nasturtiums are also flavored like the flowers and seeds and may be added to a salad of greens for a peppery effect. There can hardly be too much of this useful plant in the cook's flower border.

In the little "wild" garden under the trees we have introduced a number of pleasant native plants. One, the wild ginger (*Asarum canadense*), has become a thick ground cover and needs thinning once in a while. I try to do this job in the early fall when the apple crop is beginning. There is a lovely spot we know where the apple trees of an abandoned farm still produce delicious but anonymous fruit, though there's no longer any other sign of cultivation or habitation. Coming home in the late afternoon we sample the apples and decide which ones to use for applesauce, which for jelly, which for pie or apple butter. The tartest ones are reserved for jelly. So the next morning we thin out the wild ginger patch and I proceed to make

WILD GINGER JELLY

1) Cook the cut-up but not peeled or cored apples in water to cover easily.
2) Drip or press out the juice.
3) Meanwhile scrape the ginger roots to remove rootlets and hard bumps, then cut them across into tiny chips. Scraped, the roots are hardly over $\frac{1}{8}''$ in diameter.
4) Add the ginger-root chips to the juice in the proportion of 1 tsp. of root to 1 cup of juice, and bring to the boil over medium-high heat for 2 or 3 minutes.
5) Add sugar in the proportion of 1 cup of sugar to 1 cup of juice. Turn the heat to the highest possible and boil until the jelly comes. This will take less time on a dry, bright day than on a dark, damp one, as evaporation is faster.
6) Let cool for a minute or so, and skim off any fluff before pouring into clean warm jars. Distribute the ginger chips more or less equitably.

Served with bean dishes like pork and beans or cassoulet, this jelly is ideal. I use it too as a topping for a sponge cake as a dessert.

In various herbals borage (*Borago officinalis*) is mentioned as a useful salad herb. The leaves are supposed to have a fresh flavor similar to cucumber. But either ours is not the same species or my overcivilized tongue is not tough enough, for I can't enjoy the bristly prickles on the leaves. I keep the plant in the herb border for its dark green silver-brushed leaves, and the brilliant blue of the flowers. Occasionally I use the flowers in iced tea or a fruit punch. The single drop of sweet nectar in each one reminds me of sucking honeysuckle blossoms on a hot summer day in childhood. The deep blue stars of the blossoms are pretty in any case, though they contribute very little in flavor.

I am frequently surprised at the particular sorts of surpluses that mount up in different households. One person has an unending supply of stale bread, another is regularly troubled by a selection of fruit just on the verge, another has bits of meat left over and not enough of any one kind to do anything with. But the one who has my heart and undying gratitude is that friend who seems to use nothing but the yolks of eggs. Periodically she asks me if I'd like some egg whites. I always say yes, please, for egg whites seem to me wonderfully useful. Once I can command four egg whites and half a pound of arrowroot (God bless S. S. Pierce!) I set about putting together a

SCOTCH SNOW CAKE

1) Cream ½ lb. of butter thoroughly. I do it with my bare hand.
2) Add ¼ lb. of sugar and the ½ lb. of arrowroot; continue beating until the mixture is pale and light in texture.
3) Whip 4 egg whites very stiff with ½ tsp. of salt and add to the mixture. Use an electric beater now and beat for 5–7 minutes, or by hand for 20 minutes.
4) Add vanilla or lemon extract.

5) Turn into two buttered layer tins and bake in a moderate oven (325°-350°) until set and crisp.

This, though a butter cake, is completely unlike a cake made with flour. It's somewhat reminiscent of shortbread, though not so dense. I generally put the layers together with a rather tart jam between them and frost the top and sides with sweetened whipped cream lightened with a fifth beaten egg white.

As for stale bread, in addition to drying it and grinding the crumbs, or toasting buttered dice of it for croutons, or soaking the crumb for bread sauce or açorda, there is always pudding, nice, wholesome, unimaginative bread pudding. Not that it need be "mere"—here is one that does for six people which I call

LEMON BREAD PUDDING

1) Crumble the crumb of bread—no crusts—into a bowl until you have 2 cups.
2) Pour over it ¼ cup of lemon or lime juice in which is dissolved 2 tbsp. of sugar.
3) Beat up 3 whole eggs with ½ cup of sugar and ½ tsp. of salt, then add 2 cups of milk and mix it in.
4) Add the custard mixture to the bread and juice and pour the pudding into a buttered baking dish.
5) Bake in a moderate oven (350°) until set and the top is golden.

Pineapple slivers and juice added to the bread are another variation, in which case cut down on the sugar. A sprinkle of brown sugar over the top when the pudding has half cooked makes for an interesting crust.

Even a suspicious guest would never dream that this started out as a desperation measure.

9. The Sudden Guest can cause havoc in

the kitchen even when it is well-hidden behind baize-covered
doors, as mine is not. It seems to be the housewife's fate
to have nothing but oddments on saucers in the refrigerator
when the Dearly Beloved brings home unexpectedly the
former roommate who has become all but unbearably illustrious. Like as not he has an ulcer to boot, but the cook of
sense will rise above concern for it. Having applied a bit of
lipstick when she heard voices raised outside the door, she
presents a cordial and serene exterior to the guest and her
spouse no matter what emotions seethe beneath the surface.

There are three crucial aspects of this problem of the Sudden Guest. First of all comes quantity; what will just stretch
for two moderate feeders will not be enough, much less look
enough, for three. Something must be done to extend the
planned dish or dishes, or they must be scrapped and the
frantic cook must start afresh. And starting afresh means
working against time; this is the second aspect. Now many

dishes may be prepared at short notice, but the bulk of them do not present the cook's best aspect. In his own home your Sudden Guest might relish creamed dried beef on toast, but that's not going to make a memorable impression on him— or his wife, when he reports to her. (Like as not, you think bitterly, she has a daily maid, too, and a Cordon Bleu course under her belt.)

The pantry and refrigerator well stocked by the woman of foresight can buy time for the cook, but no matter what wealth of resources there are the dinner hour must not be too long postponed, for liquid hospitality offered by the happy host can destroy all the ingeniously contrived impact of the cook's success. So how to juggle this threefold problem and survive to cook another day is the matter of this discourse.

Extension of quantity may be achieved in three ways: by adding extra courses to the menu; by adding "fillers" in the dish; and by adding "bases" or accompaniments to the dish. The easiest of these is the first, and herein lies the reward of the well-stocked pantry. When drinks are proffered, you bring on your first extension. Everybody knows that olives and nuts are natural accompaniments of preprandial drinks, so I keep on hand some ripe olives that are bought in bulk. Just as they come, packed in brine, they are good, but prepared as the Mediterranean peoples do them they are delightful.

OLIVES IN OIL

1) Rinse the brine off the olives by putting them in a strainer and flooding with water. Drain and put them in a jar large enough to hold them loosely.
2) Put a peeled, cut clove of garlic in the jar.
3) Put a coffee-spoonful of crushed red pepper and 1 tsp. of oregano on top.
4) Pour in olive oil until all the olives are covered.

These keep indefinitely. When you are ready to serve them,

lift the olives out with a slotted spoon onto paper toweling and mop off the loose oil before turning them into a serving dish, but be sure to serve a napkin with them for they will still be oily.

If there are some shelled nuts on hand, preferably almonds or pecans, it takes only minutes to prepare

GARLIC NUTS

1) Heat oil (salad or olive) in a large skillet.
2) Toss in the nuts and toast until light brown, stirring so that they brown evenly.
3) Turn out onto paper and shake over them lots of garlic salt.
4) Let cool a moment to crisp before serving.

Crackers or Melba toast with spreads, or potato chips with dips are other useful extenders. Leftover bits of fish, too little to be used for a main dish, can be reincarnated as spreads or dips the following day, and I always welcome an extra mouth to feed on these occasions, for shad, swordfish, halibut, mackerel, or whatever, make an "ooh-aah" change from the ever-ready tuna fish or sardines.

FISH SPREAD

1) Mash the thoroughly boneless and skinless fish with a fork.
2) Blend in mayonnaise in the proportion of about 1 tbsp. of mayonnaise to 4 tbsp. of shredded fish.
3) Add about 1 tsp. of chopped fresh dill or 2 pinches of dried flowers and leaves to shad or halibut, for example; or add ½ tsp. of fresh chopped tarragon or 1 pinch of dried to swordfish.
4) Pepper, freshly ground over the top and not blended into the dish, adds a pleasant piquancy.

Much the same thing can be done to make a dip, using instead of mayonnaise, sour cream or yoghurt, or cream cheese smoothed and thinned with cream or milk. With a dip, a bit of onion or garlic flavor is good.

Leftover bits of finely minced meat require a different technique. When the roast will no longer provide presentable slices, I take the remaining meat off the bones, throw the bones into the soup kettle, and grind the meat. The ground meat is more compact and easier to store than the loose chunks and has the virtue of being ready for a quick transformation into something else. If you grind up onion with the meat you are still further along the way to a new dish, but don't plan to keep this mixture long after grinding unless you freeze it.

So your Sudden Guest coming when you'd planned to have a nice simple mish-mash, you look at your paltry bit of ground meat and decide that it just won't do. Before whipping up the soufflé or whatever for the main dish then, you use the white of an egg, a few crumbs and seasonings, and quickly form small balls of what was to have been your small-hash-for-two. Dip the balls in the egg yolk mixed with 1 tsp. of water, roll them in crumbs, and put them on a greased pie tin about six inches below the broiler. While you're beating eggs or slicing tomatoes, or otherwise advancing your main course, these little croquettes are browning. When you make your next foray into the living room you can take them with you piping hot and stuck with toothpicks. And you'll probably discover that although your absence was noted you'll not have been really missed in the time these operations have taken.

These hors d'oeuvre extensions have added another course to your dinner. If you need still more time, or quantity of food, the next thing you can do is to add a soup course. Nor do I mean that you should open a can. This is not to disparage the canned soups, which are doubtless very good and nourishing, but really, who ever heard of a memorable canned soup?

You are out to impress and delight your guest; you can do neither by offering a standard dish.

The soup kettle is a must for the ever-ready hostess, and along with the kettle a large piece of cheesecloth. Even the most provident cook cannot keep exquisitely clear bouillon always at hand, and the good stock in the kettle will have particles of meat and vegetables in it. But several layers of cheesecloth will strain out all but the very finest solids, and these will hardly be detectable in a dark bowl and by candle-light—both excellent aids to attractive but *ad hoc* dining.

A good rich meat stock needs little dressing up. You may achieve glamour by adding to "clear" (as distinguished from "cleared") soup a touch of dry vermouth. To a dark soup thickened with flour—known prosaically in England as "gravy soup"—add sweet vermouth or Madeira. With all meat-stock soups go lightly with the salt, for the meats themselves deposit salts in the broth. Sherry will do to add to soup, but these other wines will make it sparkle.

Garnishes should always be added for the sake of flavor rather than merely for looks or bulk, but they often serve all three purposes. I like paper-thin carrot slices—raw and unpeeled carrots—added to clear soups with a strong beef base. Or if the base is chicken, float a thin slice of lemon or lime in each bowl. Minced herbs are not useful for clear soup. They tend to detract from the visual appeal, but a cream soup with a chicken base is lifted to glory by a sprinkle of finely chopped fresh tarragon or chervil. The dull appearance of dried herbs will make the surface look merely littered, however, and won't contribute all that much in flavor, so don't bother with the dried forms.

If you have chicken stock on hand you're quite likely to have a bit of chicken meat. Tiny balls of minced chicken, bound with egg and fine crumbs and seasoned with a sugges-tion of herbs and onion, can be poached for a few minutes and served two or three to a bowl.

It isn't often that you'll have a good fish stock on hand

when a guest appears unexpectedly, but should such conditions meet, try slicing cucumber thin into each bowl of soup—or if it's just enhancement of flavor that you're concerned with, add a dollop of good gin to the broth.

Egg dripped through a very small funnel or from a fork into boiling chicken broth makes a pretty garnish, and a good textural offset, but does little to enhance flavor.

One soup that almost anyone would take for Borscht can be made in practically no time at all if you have on hand some stock, uncooked beets, and cream, fresh or sour. Here's how I make

INSTANT BORSCHT

1) Peel uncooked beets, and cut up roughly into cubes, using 1 medium-sized beet to 1 cup of stock.
2) Drop these cubes into a good meat stock and boil for about 5-10 minutes, depending on the size of the beet chunks.
3) Put into an electric blender and run until the mixture is homogenized.
4) Pour back into the saucepan and add 1 cup of cream, fresh or sour, for each 2 cups of beet and stock.
5) Season and serve.

If you have only fresh cream but should prefer sour, add a few drops of lemon juice.

The addition of a salad course is Standard Operating Procedure for the cook who wishes to extend the quantity aspect of a meal, and I might as well confess straight off that in this department my interest flags. There is for me but one salad: the salad of greens with French dressing. This is noble food, but all other salads with bits of other food either mounded on greens or mixed in among the leaves reduce me to unwilling admiration without any urge to go home and do likewise. Fruit salad is very good, but to me it is a dessert. Potato salad can be superb, but it takes the place of bread, potatoes, or rice in the meal. Tomato salad is a vegetable dish, shrimp salad a fish course, and so on. All these are good dishes, but a salad course is green edible leaves dressed with oil and acid and seasoned with the reliable old S and P. And certainly it is an admirable way to extend quantity in an otherwise meager meal.

A cheese course at the end of the meal is another valuable extender, and in addition it adds a touch of elegance served at a cleared board, with perhaps unusual plates and small pretty knives. A cheese course may substitute for dessert, eminently so if fruit in some form accompanies the cheese. In the fall when the Japanese quinces ripen I make at least one sheet of quince paste (Marmalada) and this is reserved almost exclusively for emergency desserts. It is particularly good with a sharp cheddar, but a mild "texture" cheese like the soft Monterey Jack is very appealing too.

Besides adding a course or courses, quantity may be extended by using fillers in a main dish. In its most primitive form this may mean simply adding cut-up vegetables like mushrooms, onion, celery, green pepper or tomatoes, to whatever you are planning to have. But there is often some limiting reason why this simplest of all principles won't do: too many flavors in the dish, overbalance of vegetable flavor for the meat to which you're committed, the time needed to blend flavors or reduce liquid; or some other. The most effective way of adding fillers to a dish is really to scrap the technique you'd planned and substitute another. In our small household we are bound to the use of leftover meats, for we insist on having good roasts, which means large ones, and the inevitable consequence is cold meat. Luckily we enjoy cold sliced meat accompanied by pickles or relishes, and this seems quite good enough to offer a guest if the slices are generous and attractive as on the night following the hot roast. A rather unusual pickle that goes particularly well with cold beef is

TOMATO SOY

1) Chop into quite small dice, ¼", 8 medium-sized onions and 2 cups of sour cucumber pickles.
2) Put these and all the following ingredients into a large kettle:
    2 quarts of skinned tomatoes
    3 cups of sugar
    2 cups of cider vinegar
    2 tbsp. of black pepper
    2 tbsp. of Worcestershire sauce
    1½ tbsp. of salt
    1 tbsp. of cinnamon
    1 tbsp. of ground mustard
    1 tbsp. of turmeric
    ½ tbsp. of allspice
    ½ tbsp. of cloves
    ½ tbsp. of sage
    ¼ tbsp. of crushed red pepper
3) Boil together for 2 hours and bottle.

After the second day of a roast though the meat may still be succulent, the slices may look a touch shopworn. What to do?

If your oddments of meat are beef, rather rare, and you can provide mushrooms, onion, sour cream, white wine and dill, you're already in business with

BEEF STROGANOV

1) Sauté onion and sliced mushrooms in butter until the

onions are soft and both vegetables have taken a trace of color. Use ½ an onion to about 1 cup of meat.

2) Make sure there is about 1 tbsp. of butter in the pan then add an equal amount of flour, stirring it smooth.

3) Add the 1 cup of liquid necessary to make the sauce, using sour cream and white wine in the proportions of 3 to 1.

4) Add ½ tsp. of dried dill leaves and flowers or 1 tsp. of fresh, salt and pepper.

5) Add the rather rare meat cut in strips about ½″ x 1½″. Heat thoroughly and serve.

Perhaps, though, you'd had that the previous night and used up all the sour cream. You do have green peppers on hand, however, so what about a Chinese-like dish of

PEPPER STEAK

1) Using thin slices of beef, the rarer the better, sear them quickly in a little lard or bacon fat, along with very thinly sliced onions and squarish chunks of green pepper.

2) Add to these after the vegetable juices begin to sputter in the pan, vertically sliced mushrooms. Keep the heat high so that the vegetables will not go limp, and cook for just a minute or so.

3) Mix in a cup ½ tsp. of cornstarch and 1 tbsp. of soy sauce for each cup of liquid you need. A 12″ skillet containing 3 cups of solid will take about 1 cup of liquid and thicken and cook the sauce sufficiently in about 3 minutes. Stir the sauce and the mixed meat and vegetable bits to the desired consistency and serve immediately.

The liquid for this dish may be water or stock. The addition of a wee bit of sherry does no harm at all.

If there's broccoli in the house, make the whole main part of the dinner oriental in effect by omitting the mushrooms from the pepper-steak dish and cooking them with the small chunks of broccoli—also in a skillet, and using a bit of peanut or sesame oil as the lubricant. The cooking of both these dishes will take under 10 minutes, so be sure to start the rice that you'll serve with them about 20 minutes earlier, so that it will have time to steam dry after cooking.

If your meat is pork, the "stir-fry" technique works equally well. With pork, green pepper, onion and mushrooms are good; so are celery and onion. You may approximate the sweet and sour sauce used in Chinese dishes by adding a bit of brown sugar and vinegar to the soy sauce, cornstarch and liquid.

Another Chinese dish that stretches gratifyingly is

SHRIMP AND PEAS

1) Using 1 lb. of shelled uncooked shrimp, mix them in a bowl with 2 tbsp. of vegetable oil and 2 tbsp. of sherry, and salt.
2) Fry for no more than 5 minutes.
3) Add cooked peas, fresh or frozen; allow the shrimp and peas a moment to blend, and serve hot. The bulk of peas should be just about the bulk of shrimp.

Whereas 1 lb. of shelled shrimp served as a separate dish will be barely enough for two, served with the peas and accompanied by rice they will feed three people easily, if not four. I don't quite know why, but combinations of foods seem to be more filling than the same things served separately.

Using fillers in the dish is probably the most satisfying method of extending quantity, but there are two other extension principles to consider. These may be used separately or in conjunction, and they are 1) adding a serving base to the major ingredients, and 2) adding a sauce.

When you add a "base" to a dish it is more than likely
to be a carbohydrate in some form, for a *mirepoix* made of
vegetables takes too long both in preparation and in cooking
time. The first base that leaps to mind is toast. This simplest
of all bases is an admirable texture foundation for a dish
of minced meat. For maximum effect the meat must be
minced to a paste or as close to that as possible. For this
operation a blender is a godsend. We particularly like leftover
liver reincarnated as

HOT PÂTÉ

1) Blend small pieces of cooked liver with stock until the
   two make a smooth paste.
2) Add 1 whole egg to each cup of minced meat and stock.
3) Add ½ tsp. of grated onion, salt and pepper and a
   discreet pinch of crumbled sage.
4) Put the mixture into the top of a double boiler and
   stir occasionally until all is smooth and thick, adding
   more stock if necessary. A tsp. of brandy stirred into
   the thickened paste will add the party touch. This may
   now be left to wait your convenience.

The same technique can be used for minced chicken, tongue
or ham, omitting the sage and using instead one of the milder
herbs.

If you have thickened gravy on hand, you may use it for
the binder instead of egg, in which case no double boiler is
necessary and the pâté can be heated over the direct flame.

Biscuit and pastry are invaluable as lids for second-day
stew, in which case stew becomes pie, the very name adding
glamour to the dish. Biscuit made by the technique described
in Chapter 2 takes only a couple of minutes, uses only the
mixing bowl and a spoon or spatula, goes into the oven 20

minutes before you plan to serve it and leaves you free to join the gentlemen in the living room while they have their second drink.

But perhaps you don't mind a bit of really extra work, as this particular Sudden Guest seems to be a man of taste. For glamour-in-a-pinch you decide on having crêpes as the base for your main dish. These are particularly good with something like crab, lobster or shrimp in a rich sauce. Let us assume that crab is on the menu. Here then are

KING CRAB CRÊPES

1) With heavy kitchen shears separate the claw at its joints. Slit the shell and lift out the meat. If you're careful when separating the joints, the "feathers" pull out cleanly. Cut the meat, still with scissors, into appropriate bite-size pieces. (All this should have been done before the return of the lord and master.)

2) Make a sauce using 2 tbsp. of butter and 2 tbsp. of flour, ½ cup of cream, ½ cup of milk, and ½ cup of white wine, salt and white pepper.

3) Put this over hot water and beat into it 2 egg yolks. This may now be left to itself.

4) Add the chunks of crab meat long enough before serving to get hot through.

If I know that I shall want mushrooms in the dish, I sauté them in butter before the sauce is made, but in an emergency, when the mushrooms are wanted at the next-to-last minute this can't be done. For one thing, I'm generally forced to rely on dried ones, and this means covering them with water and leaving them to re-hydrate for about 10 minutes. They may then be put over the fire and boiled quickly for about 3 minutes, drained, and added to the sauce. Now for the

CRÊPES

1) Put ¼ cup of flour and 1 tsp. of salt and ½ tsp. of sugar into a bowl.

2) Break into this 3 whole eggs and mix.

3) Add 1 cup of milk and beat smooth. A Dover beater does the job in just a moment or so—no need to get out the cumbersome electric mixer.

4) Heat a lightly greased griddle—the larger, the quicker the job—and when it is hot but not smoking bake the crêpes on it, pouring the batter from a large cooking spoon, one that holds about 1½ tbsp. of batter. To ensure a circular cake, pour the batter from the point of the spoon, not from the side.

5) Turn the crêpes just once, when the batter has somewhat dried over the top. Leave for just a moment to brown on the second side.

6) Remove the crêpes to a warm platter and leave in a warm oven.

7) When ready to serve, put the crab mixture over one crêpe, cover with a second, and top with more of the crab.

It's so much easier to serve this on the individual plates in the kitchen that I recommend it rather than serving a platter of the "filled" crêpes, which will only get cold on the table and will present an untidy appearance after the first ones have been parceled out.

Crêpes make one think too of other batters. Suppose you were planning "sausage and mashed" for your simple dinner. You don't now wish to fuss with mashing potatoes at the last minute, even though you have learned how simple it is to put boiled potatoes through a food mill or ricer, or whip them with an electric mixer. Instead, you vote to have Toad-in-the-Hole, using either the batter given in Chapter 1 or the Yorkshire pudding recipe in Chapter 3. Each is good, but they give different effects. In either case, whatever the meat used, it should be browned before it goes into the baking dish.

All too often the Sudden Guest emergency finds the cook reduced to hamburger or cans. By all means, then, choose to work with the hamburger. In supplying the kitchen with this meat I take it that you have reasoned your way through the false economy of mere ground beef with its wasteful bulk of fat, to the more expensive, leaner meats that go so much farther.

Our household really likes good hamburger, but we much prefer it cooked in one big cake, difficult to turn over, but so much more succulent than when it is cooked in small individual patties. But here is the first hurdle: how to serve three from what was to have been cleaned up by two? Spreading the cake thinner will deceive only the eye. First of all, start re-hydrating a generous quantity of dried mushrooms, the equivalent, say, of ¼ lb. of fresh ones. Sauté these with thin wedges of onion and remove. Then cook the meat and when it is ready put it on a hot platter and quickly transfer the already cooked onion and mushrooms to the pan in which the meat cooked. Now mix up 1 tsp. of cornstarch with 2 tbsp. of cold water, stir it into the fat remaining in the pan and add meat stock or water and 1 tbsp. of red wine. (The bottle has already been opened to "breathe" before drinking it with dinner, and 1 tbsp. won't be missed.) Pour the sauce over the meat on the platter and take to table.

Even so, you've not extended your main dish by very much. So if you could broil a few smallish tomatoes while the meat is cooking these will add more bulk and look very attractive surrounding your rather small steak. Just a pinch of sugar dropped into the hollow where the stem of the tomato has been cut out will improve the flavor and aid in browning the tops before the vegetables collapse into a purée.

Not all the problems of the *ad hoc* company meal are concerned with the main dish. The vegetable dish can be a problem, too. Parched corn, an old pioneer standby, is a most useful supply to keep on hand. If there's no glut of corn from your own garden in that nervous week or two before the first frost, go to a truck gardener for a supply and return immediately to your kitchen to start the processing.

TO PARCH SWEET CORN

1) Husk the ears and remove the silk.
2) Cut all the grains off the cobs. You'll want about 12 cups.
3) Scrape the cobs and add the "milk" to the corn.
4) Pour over the corn ½ cup of cream, the richer the better, and stir until all the grains are coated.
5) Spread on baking sheets and dry the corn slowly, stirring once in a while to make sure that the drying proceeds evenly. This is best done out of doors on bright days, using a screen or loosely woven cloth to keep off the wasps and flies. But it can be done with almost as good results in a very slow oven, below 200° if possible, or over a hot air register. If you use the oven make up your mind to wasting heat and leave the door of the oven somewhat ajar to ensure a circulation of air. The corn is dry when it rattles on the sheet. It may then be stored in a muslin sack or in a jar or can.

Some cooks advise sprinkling sugar over the corn when the cream is added, ½ cup to 12 cups of corn, but if you have freshly picked and really ripe corn this isn't necessary.

When it comes time to prepare the dish of corn measure out whatever amount you want into a wide shallow container and re-hydrate it by covering it with warm water. This takes about 15–20 minutes, unless the corn has been long stored, in which case it's no use for an *ad hoc* dish for it will take an hour or longer to re-hydrate it. Set the corn over the heat, add a generous lump of butter and cook until tender. This will take 5–10 minutes in a skillet. If you've used just the right amount of water to re-hydrate the corn, use a cover over the skillet. If you've used too much water, don't cover it. The appearance of the finished dish should be like that of canned creamed corn.

But let's face it, sooner or later there is an emergency when there is no vegetable in the refrigerator or pantry presentable enough for a guest, and we must resort to frozen or canned ones. There are always home-canned string beans in our storage cupboard and these can be presented *à la Turca* to add interest to their humble nature. I call them simply Fasulya, the Turkish word for green beans, but they taste just as good in English.

TURKISH STRING BEANS

1) For 1 pt. of beans, sauté a finely sliced medium-sized onion in olive oil barely covering the bottom of an 8″ skillet.

2) When the onion is soft and beginning to color add the beans and the liquid from the can, no salt, but some freshly ground black pepper. Also crumble over the beans 3–4 pinches of dried dill leaves and flowers and a little less of dried mint leaves. Or if you have the fresh herbs on hand, cut with the scissors herbs to the amount of 2 tsp. of dill to 1 tsp. of mint.

3) Cover, and after bringing to the boil, simmer for 10 minutes. If there's too much juice in the pan, uncover it and turn up the heat until it reduces to about 1 tbsp.

This is the same technique as that for fresh beans, except that the fresh ones take longer to cook. The dish is served either hot or cold.

Creamed turnips make another dish that can be got up in

a hurry if the turnips are cut in small chunks and put to cook with little water in a shallow pan. After draining them, put them through a ricer or food mill instead of mashing. They can then be mixed with cream and butter, seasoned with salt, pepper and a drift of cinnamon, put into a shallow greased baking dish and heated in the oven. For the last minute or two turn on the broiler so as to toast the top slightly.

From a good bit of the foregoing discussion it will be clear that the Sudden Guest holds few culinary terrors for the cook with a well-stocked pantry. This is particularly so when one comes to the dessert department. Whereas alone we might omit dessert, when a guest appears one likes to tie up the company meal with a sweet.

If the main part of the meal has been Spartan this course can explode with richness, and will if you make Zabaglione. Once the eggs, sugar and wine are mixed, this can be set over hot water and beaten to the required consistency in very short order. One recipe for this dish is given in Chapter 1, but there are a number of versions of the custard. The amount of sugar to egg varies. Some recipes call for only yolks of eggs; others use whole eggs. Marsala wine is typically used in the true Italian dish, but in America sherry is often substituted. Some recipes even call for vanilla, but I cannot see the point of cluttering this exquisite custard with any flavoring other than the wine. Served in small glass bowls or large wine glasses this makes a very pretty dessert as well as a rich one.

The cook who keeps on hand her own plain cake mix never lacks for a dessert. I make one by blending sugar and vegetable fat, flour, baking powder, and dried milk in standard plain-cake proportions. When I need a cake in a hurry, I beat up eggs with a bit of salt and add them and the required amount of water, and a flavor like vanilla or almond to the cake mix. For a plain cake to be used as cottage pudding, I use 2 eggs. When the cake is ready to serve I spread a jar of ginger marmalade, plum conserve or lemon butter over the hot cake. For a richer cake, I melt 2 tbsp. of butter and add it to the batter before baking, and of course I've already increased the number of eggs. If I wish a lighter cake I separate the eggs and fold the stiffly beaten egg whites in at the end.

In our household very little goes to waste. If cake is left and goes dry and stale, I dry it completely and grind it into crumbs. To these I add the crumbs that accumulate in the bottom of the cookie crock. Thoroughly dried, these sweet crumbs keep indefinitely and are available for further use. So when the Sudden Guest appears, if dessert is the hole in the menu, I can make a "pie" very quickly by melting ½ cup of butter in a pie tin, adding a cup of cake crumbs, and frying them a moment or so before patting them smooth to make a crust. Into the crust I put a jar of home-canned fruit seasoned very likely with 1 tbsp. of rum. Over this I drift some cinnamon and put the pie into the freezer chest for about ¾ of an hour. Spread with sour cream or whipped cream just before serving this makes a quite elegant dessert.

The Sudden Guest will nearly always present the cook with some problem, but it is one that is extremely rewarding to solve successfully, and it clearly admits of fairly ready solution. With a well-stocked pantry and a command of techniques, seasoned with imagination any such meal should be delightful and quite possibly even memorable.

Section B

Guest List implies meticulous planning, and these carefully constructed menus to be enjoyed by choice spirits make the greatest meals of all the year. In cold weather they are eaten indoors perforce, but in summer they may be served outdoors at home or abroad in the country—in a meadow, on a hilltop, by a stream, in a clearing in woods or on a beach.

Feasts in winter are generally the solo performances of the virtuoso cook, with varying degrees of assistance from members of the family, the modern counterparts of the Victorian kitchen slavey. Picnics in summer are legitimately cooperative affairs; indeed, that is implicit in the meaning of the word. One does not "give" a picnic as one "gives" a dinner; rather a group of people "take" a picnic, each one providing some part of the rather extraordinary meal.

Both feasts and picnics deal in larger quantities than everyday household meals, and thereby automatically exclude certain dishes or suggest others. In each case the food is probably unusual: the festive food stemming from the *haute cuisine*, picnic food from less exalted tradition. The picnic, depending as it does on good weather, has about it also an aura of the *ad hoc*; the feast is planned to the least crouton or smallest branch of parsley.

10. Of Feasts,

the first is Thanksgiving, which comes on the heels of the changeover from outdoor to indoor living. Children are settled into heavier clothes and new school programs; the house is more or less in order for the winter with windows cleaned and curtains freshly laundered and copper and brass newly polished. Hems have been let down or taken up; the garden is put to bed; the dog and cat have stopped shedding and the last flea has been tracked down. Now it's time to set about entertaining new members of the department, or eminent visitors to the university, or some of the people you never got around to all last year. The first guest list might well be made out for Thanksgiving.

On this holiday, turkey is a must for the majority of us Americans, and the daring cook who would bypass turkey must outdo Escoffier to satisfy her guests—not that it can't be done. . . . But granted turkey, how does one proceed to create a magnificent feast, keeping well within the great tradition but lifting the menu from what has on occasions become a conventional rut?

First of all, the turkey itself must be superb, and it's unlikely to be so if the poor bird has been consigned to a deep-freeze for several months. So have a fresh turkey if possible, or at worst a recently frozen one. A short freezing period has the effect of "hanging," in that the meat is thereby made more tender than that of freshly killed poultry. Frozen for too long a time the meat dries out and loses flavor, so that it is merely the conveyance for stuffing and giblet gravy. An excellent bird to start with needs little dressing up and no extraordinary care in roasting to make an equally excellent dish to eat.

Now any cookbook will tell any novice cook how to roast—really bake—a turkey. For a bird up to 15 lb. bake 15 minutes for each pound. Heavier birds should be baked 18–20 minutes per lb., and big old tough birds may take up to 25 minutes a lb. Presumably cooks follow these directions and still notice variations of excellence. The process of baking is merely the penetration of the flesh by dry heat. Where the flesh is thin and bone close to the surface as in the wings, legs, and back, it may be necessary, in order to prevent the drying out of the meat, to slow down the rate of penetration of heat below that required for the fleshy breast. Some cooks bind the legs and wings with protective wrappings and some wrap the whole bird in greased cloth, parchment, or foil: then if the perfectly cooked bird is not brown enough at the end of the cooking period it can be browned in a very few minutes just before serving by putting it under the broiler. To wrap a bird too tightly with foil, however, defeats the purpose of baking; the effect is to steam the meat as when cooking *en papillote*. Some cooks prefer an exaggeratedly low heat for 10–12 hours so that the natural juices are not evaporated too quickly. Some prefer basting often with additional liquid and fat. This method does crisp the skin rather quickly and seals the pores, so that juices remain in the flesh, but you may end with an unbecomingly brunette bird. Having tried various methods, choose the one that seems to you to give the best results and cut the cloth of the rest of the menu to fit the demands made on you. Provident cooks like to have everything under control at all times, and I prefer the method of

OVERNIGHT TURKEY

1) Stuff and truss the turkey and place it on a rack in an uncovered roaster.

2) Cover the whole thing, roaster and all, loosely with foil so that heated air can circulate about the roast within the foil seal, and at 10:00 p.m. place it in the middle of an oven heated to 400°. After ½ hour turn down the heat to under 200° (I use 150° in an electric oven) and leave until ready to serve at midday or shortly thereafter.

If when you peek at, say, 11:00 a.m., the bird seems at its apogee, re-cover it and turn out the heat entirely. It will keep quite hot for another hour in a well insulated oven.

Some turkeys when you're working on them can be seen to need additional fat. This is more likely to be the case with smaller and younger birds than with large older ones. I take precautions with a small bird by pouring into the cavity about ¼ cup of good olive oil and sloshing it about before I stuff it. What oil drizzles out when I hold up the carcass to drain, I smear over the skin of the bird. A filling made with sausage will contain enough additional fat to lubricate the inside of even a young bird.

The stuffing in the turkey serves one purpose only: to add another taste and texture experience to the dinner; so the stuffing must be considered as one of the several side dishes that are served with the meat. A consultation with the cellarer is in order before the cook decides on these accompanying dishes. Whereas turkey alone will take a fairly dry wine, when it is served with a number of sweet accompaniments a dry wine, no matter how excellent, will be too tart for maximum pleasure. The way to get the most palatal excitement from the feast is to serve the bird, stuffed with the proper filling and accompanied by its sauce, as a course along with the wine, but since that is a form of service little used in this country the best compromise is to use a softer, sweeter wine—whether red or white is up to the committee of cellarer and cook. Then having agreed on the wine, the cook decides on just which stuffing to use in conjunction with just which other dishes. The standard bread stuffings flavored with onion, herbs and butter can be excellent. We prefer our bread stuffings made of a good strong bread, ideally homemade, and the crumb cut in $\frac{1}{2}$" dice. Instead of salt, I frequently mince a few anchovy fillets, and rather than melt the butter I cream it and mix it lightly into the crumb with my fingers. This results in a stuffing of rather light texture, not the solid pack of standard restaurant fare.

Quite often we choose to have a pilav stuffing (Chapter 7), especially when the mushroom crop has been abundant and we can either gather fresh large *Coprinus* mushrooms or tap a jar of those canned earlier.

A chestnut stuffing is rather more trouble, for peeling chestnuts is time-consuming, but if you make up your mind happily to using time in that way, remember to keep the chestnuts hot and work on only a few at a time. I like a touch of onion flavor even with chestnuts, so when the nut meats are put to cook I add a shallot for each pound of nuts. I also prefer Madeira to stock as a moistening agent when the purée is mixed with the seasonings.

A simple rice stuffing will benefit from a pinch or two of Spanish saffron and a bread stuffing from $\frac{1}{2}$ teaspoonful of curry. A cornbread stuffing is delightful with mashed liver and ground nuts, especially filberts.

The stuffing chosen, the cook now turns to the remaining side dishes: sauces and vegetables. We probably couldn't get away from serving cranberries in some form even if we wanted, and certainly the clear rich red of cranberries turned from an attractive mold makes a sparkling color accent on the table. Since they have so much pectin, cranberries are no trouble at all to make into jelly, and I wonder that the cranberry-canning industry survives. I make up four molds of jelly before Thanksgiving, and cover each with paraffin to have on hand for several winter menus. We prefer the form in which the cooked berries are not puréed; the slight bitterness of the skins is very pleasant. A stick of cinnamon cooked with the berries adds another piquancy. But sometimes as a change—though it's really better with goose—we like to serve an old English

CUMBERLAND SAUCE

1) For about 1½ cups of sauce, cut into fine shreds the peel of an orange and that of a lemon both freed completely of the felty white part of the rind, and put to cook in a saucepan with the juice of both fruits to which is added ¼ cup of stock or water. After bringing this to the boil simmer for about 5 minutes.

2) Strain through a fine-meshed sieve and return the liquid to the pan adding ¼ cup of port wine, ¼ cup of red currant jelly, ¼ tsp. of salt. Heat again to blend and serve hot or cold.

If you like, you may add one or two tbsp. of vinegar and ½ tsp. of prepared mustard; cayenne pepper or ¼ tsp. of ground ginger; and even, according to some recipes, ½ tsp. of Worcestershire sauce. Any or all of these additions are optional. Some recipes call for adding when the sauce is cold 2 tbsp. of chopped candied cherries. I prefer the simpler and less sweet versions.

An interesting modern development of this sauce has come about through the use of the blender to homogenize all the ingredients.

The other sauce traditionally served with roast turkey is gravy made from the drippings in the roasting pan plus the giblets, flour and water. Many recipes call for boiling the giblets, but to me it seems sacrilege to boil tender heart and liver. Instead, I sauté these in butter for just a few minutes, so that they remain a bit rare. Chopped, they may then be added to the pan drippings and the sauce made as usual. The flavor is infinitely superior to a gravy with boiled giblets added.

Of the other side dishes customarily served at Thanksgiving, winter squash is the first that comes to mind. We raise the dumbbell-shaped butternut squash in the garden, store them in the root cellar, and rarely touch them until Thanksgiving when they head the winter's vegetable parade of cabbage, turnips, beets, brussels sprouts, carrots, broccoli and last, but far from least, parsnips. For a festive dish here is how I prepare

CREAMED BUTTERNUT SQUASH

1) Hack up three good-sized squash, remove the seeds and skin and put on a rack over water in a kettle to steam soft.
2) Drain and put through a food mill or mash.
3) Mix about 4 cups of puréed squash with ¼ lb. of butter, ½ cup of cream, and ¼ cup of Madeira. Add salt and pepper and reheat before serving, giving a good beating with a slotted spoon to fluff the purée.

Since squash is rather sweet, it's unlikely that you will also serve sweet potato, but you may wish to serve white potato. Here is one place where I find that the small canned Irish potatoes answer a felt want. They come graded evenly in size, a particular boon for a festive table. These I put in a large skillet in which butter is bubbling but not smoking. There should be enough butter to bubble halfway up around the small potatoes when they're dropped in. Lightly salted and generously covered with freshly ground black pepper they do not take long to brown. They must be turned once or twice during the browning period. Of course, the same treatment goes for fresh potatoes but the pieces should be parboiled for about 10 minutes then drained on paper toweling before being dropped into the bubbling butter.

If your taste runs to mashed white potatoes, be a bit extravagant and add for 8 medium-sized potatoes, mashed, mixed with butter, cream and salt and pepper, 4 egg yolks, or more, well beaten. Turn this into a greased dish and put under the broiler for a few minutes to toast the top before serving.

The other festive mashed potato dish is French and calls for great quantities of garlic stewed gently in butter to melting point, puréed, and added with salt, pepper, more butter and cream to the mashed, riced or puréed potatoes. Each medium-sized potato used asks for 4-6 cloves of garlic. A conservative feeder will reject this dish out of hand, finding it impossible to imagine that the robust garlic could submerge its personality sufficiently in the mild potato. Just try it once, if you are such a one. The cooked garlic is very delicate, all its fiery raw power transformed into a sweet and subtle warmth.

With any other but a chestnut filling for the turkey you may wish to serve a chestnut puff in place of potatoes or squash. The basic preparation is the same as for any chestnut dish. First the nuts are shelled, skinned, and cooked. For chestnut puff they must also be puréed, seasoned, mixed with well-beaten egg yolks, then have folded into them the stiffly beaten egg whites. For 1 lb. of chestnuts in the shell you'll need 4 whole eggs, more, if you want the puff to come closer to a soufflé. Just before folding in the egg whites I add cream and Madeira, about 2 tbsp. of each for the pound of chestnuts. If a dry white table wine is substituted for Madeira use 4 tbsp. This takes about 20-25 minutes to bake in an ordinary 3"-deep casserole set in a moderate oven (350°).

This technique works equally well for spinach which might well be the green vegetable of a Thanksgiving menu, but not

of course at the same meal as the chestnut puff. It is simply
a development of

CREAMED SPINACH

1) For 2 lb. of spinach, washed and drained, put into a
   saucepan about 1 tsp. of onion chopped or the equivalent
   in thin wedges. Add the spinach leaves, cover, and
   start sweating the vegetable over fairly low heat.

2) When enough juice has leached out of the leaves to
   begin steaming, after about 5 minutes, turn the spinach
   over in the pot and turn the heat high. Continue cooking until the mass of leaves is tender, about 3 minutes
   longer.

3) Drain in a colander and press out the loose juice with
   the back of a large spoon. This should be done into
   the soup kettle; a little spinach flavor in soup is very
   good.

4) Now chop (don't purée in a food mill) until the spinach
   is an even paste. This is moderately tedious, but the
   operation may be performed early in the day, before
   crises are likely to descend on you.

5) Melt in the spinach saucepan, which you have not yet
   washed, about 2 tbsp. of butter; add 2 tbsp. of flour,
   and blend and cook over moderate heat for a moment
   or so.

6) Mix in about 1 cup of milk or cream, and stir and cook
   until the sauce is perfect. Blend in the finely chopped
   spinach, season with salt, pepper and a sprinkle of
   mace or nutmeg, and serve.

Proceed with this as a base to make spinach puff by using
4 eggs or more to the 2 pounds of spinach—now much reduced in bulk. Bake like the chestnut puff, or put into small
greased custard cups set in a pan of water.

If you have timbale irons and someone to help in the kitchen you may wish to bake individual custards—for that's roughly what the spinach puff is—and serve them in timbale cases made of a good batter and cooked on the timbale irons in deep fat. The custards when turned out must be the same size as the cases, but this you will have worked out well ahead of time.

Spinach makes a strong visual contrast with the creamy, blond and golden tones of the potatoes, squash and turkey. So does another dish, very simple, and when properly prepared very beautiful to the palate as well as to the eye. In a good tomato season there are always lots of green fruit to be gathered before the first freeze. The large green tomatoes we wrap loosely in clean tissue paper or newspaper, first making sure that each one is dry and clean and free of blemish. Then every available flat surface except the floor in the basement is put to use, and the wrapped fruits are ranged with a clear space around each package. If they can be put on racks so that the air may circulate under as well as around them, the chances of their ripening evenly are thereby increased. By the time Thanksgiving comes you will still be having fresh tomatoes, probably not quite so sweet as those ripened on the plants, but firm and fine otherwise. So you may serve at your feast simple

STEWED TOMATOES

1) Quarter but on no account skin tomatoes, allowing two or three per serving, and put these with a goodly allowance of butter (1 tbsp. for 6 tomatoes) in a large shallow pan over moderate heat. They should not be more than 1″ deep in the pan.
2) When a bit of juice has gathered, turn up the heat as high as it will go, and cook until the tomatoes are of an almost creamy consistency. They will need occasional stirring, for they must cook quickly to evaporate the undesired moisture.

3) These tomatoes ripened off the plant will benefit from the addition of a bit of sugar, about 1 tsp. for 12 good-sized tomatoes. Do not oversalt, but they can tolerate an extra grind or so of pepper.

Tomatoes done this way will be not soupy but saucy, so they may be served on the dinner plate.

If you feel that the meal requires a salad for flavor contrast or refreshment of the palate, remember that by this time people are going to be physically satisfied, so it should be a light one. In fact this is the place in the meal for those dishes of vegetable tidbits: radishes, spring onions, celery, olives or gherkins. This period of celery-munching gives the hostess a chance to clear the table and make order in the bursting kitchen. And it gives each guest a chance to catch his breath before facing what he knows will be a fairly substantial dessert, for what would Thanksgiving be without pies? (Much less bad for the waistline, perhaps. . . .)

Now let's see, what pies shall we choose? Theoretically it need not be pie for dessert, but traditionally and conventionally it is. At the least daring level it will be apple or pumpkin pie, the apple, tart and spicy; the pumpkin, creamy rich and spicy. (Don't let's broach the mincemeat crock until Christmas!) But how about trying a dessert just a little different. I occasionally make something that seems a bit lighter as the ending to a feast. I call it

APPLESAUCE PIE (8″ tin)

1) Make a crust by melting ½ cup of butter and blending into it about 1 cup of stale dried cake crumbs rolled or ground to a fine even consistency. The mixing can be done right in the pie tin on top of the stove using a low heat and the crumbs stirred about for a minute or two to cook in the butter. They are then patted

evenly around the sides and over the bottom of the
tin. A little freshly grated coconut added ties the crumb
crust together and adds another subtle texture and
flavor.

2) Fill the shell with applesauce (I season mine with cinnamon), and put the pie into the refrigerator until
ready to serve, or into the freezer chest of the refrigerator for not more than an hour.

3 When ready to serve, spread sour cream over the pie
and sprinkle the top with a dust of cinnamon or grated
orange or tangerine rind.

Another pie that seems a lighter touch for a festive meal
is a meringue crust filled with fruit. If you're lucky enough
to find persimmons, you may care to make a custard of the
puréed flesh and eggs, well spiked with lemon juice and rum.
Paint this lily with sweetened whipped cream at your peril.

Now you may serve the coffee, probably one demitasse
apiece being all that by this time any frail human frame
can hold. If the guests are stretched on the floor—as I have
known at least one to be—by all means provide pillows and
a thimbleful of brandy as well.

Between Thanksgiving and Christmas the housewife-cook,
if not her guests, will lose all the extra calories she took on
at the first great feast of the year. There are all the usual
chores attendant on Christmas: the shopping for, tying up
and mailing of packages; the endless writing of Christmas
letters or greeting cards; the problems of decorating the house;
and in addition there is the looming feast. Christmas too has
its food conventions, but they are more flexible than those
surrounding Thanksgiving, for Christmas is celebrated not
just by Americans, as is the earlier holiday, but by all the
peoples of the Christian world, and we have drawn from many
cultures for the foods we set before our Christmas guests.

The strongest single influence on this feast outside the native Anglo-Saxon is German, so it's fitting at this season to consider a menu featuring goose. Since goose is rich and dusky, the preprandial tidbits should be meager in quantity but of a quality to sharpen one's zest. With the sherry or the single cocktail, then, one might serve

PICKLED MUSHROOMS

1) Wash in water to which a dollop of cider vinegar has been added whole button mushrooms.
2) Steam in very little fresh water for 5 minutes, then drain on paper toweling.
3) Make a dressing of mild oil (a corn oil is, surprisingly, more satisfactory for this than olive oil) and a good white-wine vinegar in the proportion of ½ oil to ½ vinegar. Add a pinch of salt, a grind of white pepper, and ⅛ tsp. of sugar for each ½ cup of dressing.
4) Marinate the mushrooms in the dressing for 2 hours or longer, and leave them in a cool place until ready to serve them.
5) Just before serving lift them onto a paper towel to drain a bit. They should be glistening but not wet.

The herb-addicted cook might add a sprinkle of chervil or basil to the marinade, but more than very little will overwhelm the delicate flavor of the mushrooms.

Another preprandial snack that we find both light and piquant is made from the small canned or frozen artichoke hearts. It is

SIMPLE DRESSED ARTICHOKE HEARTS

1) Having drained and rinsed canned, or thawed the frozen, artichoke hearts, put them in a marinade of

French dressing using first quality olive oil, red wine vinegar, salt, pepper, and oregano.

2) Leave in the marinade in a cool place for 2 hours or longer before draining on paper toweling and serving.

When everyone is seated at the table, bring on the goose prepared as in Chapter 6, but filled on this occasion with a saffron rice stuffing rather than sauerkraut, for you've chosen a side dish of

SPICED RED CABBAGE

1) Cut the cabbage in half and shred finely.

2) Put the shredded cabbage into the largest colander available and scald it with boiling water; drain well.

3) Put the scalded cabbage into a large bowl and add ¼ cup of cider vinegar, mixing well with a wooden fork or spoon.

4) Melt 2 tbsp. of lard or for second choice, butter, in an earthen casserole, add the cabbage with its vinegar, 2 tbsp. of sugar, 1 tsp. of salt, and 1–2 cups of water, depending on the size of the cabbage.

5) Let this simmer, covered, over an asbestos mat for 1 hour.

6) Add ½ tsp. of cinnamon and ¼ tsp. of cloves before serving.

This dish I made for the first time under the direction of a German scholar who translated each step of the recipe into English from an old family cookbook given him by his mother when he left his home for a career in this country. With the enthusiasm of a real foreigner he had adopted one of our horrid mechanical shredders and he insisted that it be used to shred the cabbage. In my own kitchen I have stubbornly shredded the cabbage much finer with a sharp knife.

For a sauce other than the gravy for the goose, if not Cumberland, choose a tart jelly or jam like gooseberry, currant or quince.

The visual impact of a goose dinner is dark and ruddy: the goose "black" and shining, the cabbage red, even the rice stuffing orange with saffron. The other vegetables then should ideally offer visual as well as flavor contrast. One that does so very neatly is

BRAISED ENDIVE AMANDINE

1) Allowing 2 or 3 endives per person, wash them, trim the bases of any brown resulting from exposure, and plunge them into boiling water for about 3 minutes. Drain and rinse in cold water. This blanching allows the endives to retain their delicate fresh green.

2) Put a generous allowance of butter into a large, cold, shallow pan—a large skillet, for example. Lay the endives in and add water to come halfway up their sides. They should lie in the pan with just enough space left so that they may be turned over without being mangled.

3) Cover not too closely and cook over moderate heat until the liquid is almost evaporated. At this point turn them over, re-cover, and let cook until all the liquid is gone and you hear the faint beginning of sizzling.

4) Remove from the pan and lay them in a shallow casserole dish, and sauté halves of blanched almonds in the butter remaining in the skillet. You may need to add butter at this point. The almonds should be golden, not toast-brown. Spread the almonds over the endives.

5) Make a béchamel sauce in the skillet and season it with salt, white pepper, and the merest whiff of cinnamon. Pour the sauce over the endives and almonds.

6) Heat in a moderate oven before serving.

Endives are generally in supply at Christmastime. A rarer but even better vegetable to accompany a goose is

BRAISED FENNEL

1) Wash and trim the fennel and cut across into 1" wide sections. Don't separate the "leaves."
2) Put into a skillet or other wide shallow pan with an extravagant lump of butter and enough water to boil away under a cover, in about 7-10 minutes. This indicates quite high heat.
3) Uncover when the sizzling begins and sprinkle with white pepper. Turn the vegetable so that it takes on a bit of gold color but doesn't stick or burn.

For a more elegant but not more flavorsome dish the fennel may be served in a rich cream sauce and studded like the endives with golden sautéed almonds.

Since the cavity of the goose is large you may not need more than the rice stuffing as the carbohydrate dish of the meal. But should you perhaps have used a fruit stuffing of apples, prunes, apricots, or something similar, you will wish to have another side dish. What could go better with the Teutonic goose and red cabbage than

BUTTERED NOODLES

1) Having made the noodles by the recipe in Chapter 4, proceed to drop them into briskly boiling water, generously salted. Cook them quickly for 5-10 minutes, depending on freshness and thickness.
2) Drain in a colander; melt butter in the pan in which the noodles were cooked; and return the noodles to the pan to heat again in the hot fat. Toss them to coat each strand thoroughly with butter.

3) Turn into a warm dish and now, not earlier, grind all over the top an extravagant amount of black pepper.

With a great meal like this I feel as with the Thanksgiving feast that a salad course is too much. Here again the vegetable tidbits are the most that need be offered, for in a very few minutes you'll doubtless be bringing on a mince pie or a beautiful homemade plum pudding. There are countless recipes for this old English dish, some of the modern ones fairly emasculated. My puddings vary in content from year to year according to the fruity ingredients at hand when I am seized with the compulsion to create. But the proportions are quite constant, and the fat is always beef suet, and I don't like sodden nuts in my puddings. First of all, I chop or cut up (not grind) all the fruits I wish to use and put them in a bowl and stir about with enough flour to keep them from lumping together. This amount of flour is measured and subtracted from the total, which I put in another bowl with salt and ¾ of the brown sugar. Into this I rub the chopped suet—not too thoroughly. The whole eggs are beaten, the last quarter of brown sugar added to them, and beaten again. Then all three units are combined, put into greased pudding molds, cans with lids, or "bags" made of cheesecloth, and steamed forever—about 6-10 hours. When the puddings are cold I pour brandy over them and store them until needed. They're then given another steaming of at least 3-4 hours before they're brought smoking to table or flaming with more brandy or rum, warmed and set alight.

With mince pie we like a piece of sharp cheese, but with plum pudding it must be hard sauce. Calories galore, I know, but I do spread them out a bit by adding stiffly beaten egg white to the creamed butter and sugar before chilling the sauce.

After the coffee and before anyone falls asleep, a brisk walk is in order.

The third great feast of the year used to be at the New Year, but nowadays so many people prefer a different kind of celebration on New Year's Eve that they're scarcely in condition to appreciate a carefully constructed meal the next day. However, should you have reached the age of temperance without ulcers, a New Year's feast can be a delightful one. Let's plan something outlandish around a

SUCKING PIG

1) Make sure the carcass is thoroughly clean, especially the nostrils, ears and feet, and if it has been flushed with water dry it thoroughly.
2) Fill the cavity with the stuffing and sew it up.
3) I prefer to truss the pig in a kneeling position, though the authorities recommend stretching the legs out. Put a stick of clean wood between the jaws if the butcher has not already done so.
4) Roast on a rack in a low to moderate oven (300°-325°) allowing about 25 minutes per lb., even a bit more if the suckling is on the heavy side. The market weights are between 12-15 lb.
5) Baste two or three times during the roasting period by wiping the surface with fat. This may be a piece of pork fat; or the surface may be painted with oil. On no account allow any liquid other than oil to touch the skin, as this toughens it and makes the crackling utterly unchewable.
6) Serve on an enormous platter or on a foil-covered board with a rim contrived of foil. The suckling should have the stick between its jaws replaced by an apple. A wreath of smilax and blossoms, or an herb wreath, should go about its neck.

The traditional English stuffing for sucking pig is sage and onion with bread crumb. The one I most like is just
Inc., 1923), p. 170.

seasoned whole onions. I can't remember where or how I hit upon this filling but even twenty years later it's still our favorite.

ONION STUFFING FOR SUCKING PIG

1) For a piglet weighing about 13 lb. provide about 4 lb. of smallish yellow onions. After trimming off the rootlets, cut a cross in the base of each onion; remove loose torn bits of skin, but do not peel. Wash the onions well, though.

2) Drop the onions into rapidly boiling water and cook for 5 minutes.

3) Take out the onions, slip off the brown skins and return these to the kettle. When the water is colored brown with the skins you will have the basis of a *maigre* broth which you may use in any number of ways.

4) Season the skinned onions with salt and pepper and any herbs you fancy. I like a combination of rosemary and oregano. Stuff into the cavity and sew it up.

No butter is needed, for the piglet provides the lubrication, and of course the onions still contain a great deal of moisture, quite enough with the meat juices to finish the cooking process.

For a sauce with sucking pig we like pears cooked with their skins and cores, then puréed in the food mill. To the purée I add brown sugar rather than white, salt and quantities of ginger.

Nothing goes better with a delicate sucking pig than an equally delicate cornmeal pudding, the soufflé sort, rich with eggs and light as meringue. But if the suckling pre-empts the oven, wild rice is just as good though radically different. This delectable grain takes much, much longer to cook than rice does; in fact it has so little in common with the tame variety that it's a pity to call it by the same name. We like the distinctive flavor of wild rice uncorrected by any seasoning other than salt and the broth in which it is cooked.

The vegetable dish that we find indispensable with sucking pig is Hot Cole Slaw (Chapter 7), but in addition I might serve also the much neglected creamed turnips. People who avoid turnips are generally those unfortunates who have had them straight off a steam table in a cafeteria. The lovingly wrought homemade dish is a quite different article. Turnips must be thoroughly cooked and utterly drained; they must be smooth as a sauce and rich with butter and/or cream. They should resemble, though not imitate, mashed potatoes in texture, be light and fluffy and ivory-colored, not heavy and wet-looking, bluish and grainy. And they should be served soon after the preparation is complete. Allowed to stand too long over heat they will develop the strong flavor and aroma that is objectionable.

After a main course like sucking pig there's little needed for dessert. But you might like to serve a small wedge of

SCOTCH SHORTBREAD

1) Put the dry ingredients into a large bowl:

    2 cups of flour
    ½ cup of sugar
    ½ tsp. of salt

2) Rub into this ½ lb. (1 cup) of butter. When the butter is evenly distributed begin kneading the dough—still in the bowl—and continue to knead until you have a lovely, satin-smooth ball that neither cracks nor crumbles.

3) Divide the dough evenly into 3 pieces and pat these onto cookie sheets. With a rolling pin flatten the pieces into rounds about ⅓″-½″ thick.

4) Prick the rounds all over with the tines of a fork, flute the edges with the fork held upright, and lightly score the cakes across with a knife so that when baked they

will break easily into the desired number of servings. I find that a round of 7"-8" provides 8 pie-shaped pieces.

5) Bake in a low to moderate heat (325°-350°) for about 50 minutes. They should be pale gold and dry, not moist-looking.

6) These must be cooled completely before storing or the steam remaining in them will soften them.

The "secrets" of shortbread are two, and they're perfectly open ones. First, the mixture must be rich, rich, rich; second, the dough must be perfectly homogeneous. Creaming the butter first is completely unnecessary, for it's creamed as you rub it into the flour and sugar, and still further creamed as the dough is kneaded. As for baking powder—away with it! You'll only spoil the exquisite flavor.

If even one little wedge of shortbread seems too many calories to entertain, you might prefer to pass a bowl of cluster raisins and some whole walnuts and your guests may nibble or not while you serve the coffee.

The last traditional feast of the year comes at Eastertime when we might expect, since it follows the Lenten month, an enormous and extravagant meal. On the contrary, at least in this country, the Easter dinner is likely to be the most modest of them all. At this time ham is traditional and often a touch dull. If you don't care to boil, bake, of steam your ham by one of the conventional recipes, there is one method that may appeal to you at least as a novelty. This is known in England as baking in a huff crust, but the same technique is found in other cultures as well. In England (and in Russia) the crust is removed from the ham before serving and is not used as an accompaniment of the meat. In its then state it is utterly inedible, resembling plaster or clay more than anything else. However, the thrifty English farm wife will smash it up and grind it into crumbs which may be used to make a textured surface for that same ham. In France the crust is made rich with fine fat and is not removed but is the distinguishing feature of a dish *en croûte.* The simple huff paste is merely flour and water kneaded to the desired consistency and rolled out to about ½″ thickness then wrapped around the ham and pinch-sealed. It may be elaborated upon, of course, and in Russia it is the device by which the ham is flavored, having rubbed over it the herbs and any liquors desired. For a ham of 11-12 lb. you'll need 4-5 lb. of flour, but you'll have to do without a measure for the water as different flours require differing amounts. Since you'll not be eating the huff crust as crust anyway, all you need worry about is getting the dough to stick together sufficiently to roll out. If you wish to give a texture surface to the ham, remove the crust as soon as the ham is cooked, grind up some of the crust for crumbs and proceed as for any decorated baked ham. But if you're planning to have the ham cold, leave the crust on until just before you're ready to carve and keep all the flavors inside until you serve.

With a country ham a sweet sauce or pickle goes beautifully, but with a Smithfield ham we prefer our own homemade

MUSTARD

1) Boil for 15 minutes a bag of 1 tbsp. of mixed pickling spice and 1 clove of garlic cut in 2 pieces in 2 cups of cider vinegar—adding water at the end of the cooking period to make up the 2 cups of liquid.

2) Meanwhile mix in a bowl 2 cups of dry mustard, ½ tsp. of salt, 2 tbsp. of sugar—more if you prefer a milder mustard.

3) Add oil, either olive or corn, to make a thick smooth paste.

4) Gradually add the seasoned vinegar until the desired consistency is achieved. If more liquid is needed it need

not be heated and it may be water if you prefer the mustard less sharp.

With a hot ham a batter pudding goes beautifully; with a cold one we like a pilav flavored with chicken broth.

Instead of a regular hot vegetable dish I like to serve in a separate bowl a half avocado for each person, the hollow where the seed had been filled with a lemon and olive-oil dressing.

At the end of such a meal, salty and sharp flavors predominating, a bland dessert is in order, and the most satisfying are those in the custard family: plain crème caramel, or crème brûlée, Spanish or Bavarian cream, trifle or, eminently, ice cream. The colder the dessert the more delightful after the stimulation of the flavors in the main course.

Ham somewhat limits your choice of wines, so after a ham dinner something elaborate in the way of liqueurs may be tolerated. If your own wine steward is deft he might be willing to prepare for a small group of diners one *pousse café* each. This jewel-like creation is several layers of liqueurs in the same glass, the densest at the bottom—but it's really prettier to look at than to drink.

With Easter past, the gardening season begins in earnest and we look forward to picnics.

11. Picnics come naturally to us, living as we do in a countryside so rich in geological, botanical and ornithological oddities, not to mention woods, streams, hills and abandoned farms. And what satisfying picnics they are. The ideal number seems to be eight to ten, exclusive of dogs, and of the human participants at least one will have a pair of binoculars for bird-watching; two or three carry knives and plastic bags or baskets for digging up and transporting botanical specimens; one might have a geological hammer or a sketching block; and generally there's at least one geodetic survey map in someone's pocket. But even stamp collectors enjoy picnics, for no matter what the location or the weather there's always excellent food.

After six months of winter a true picnicker can't wait any longer, so the first picnic is projected to see how the spring is coming on. This generally means driving dreamily about back roads in the hills, even fording small temporary streams, and like as not eating in the car, as the rain is very wet in these parts. Such a lunch is a simple affair: no plates, knives or forks, so it's almost impossible to get away from sandwiches. Indeed this kind of picnic is perfected by the sandwich and nobody needs to be told how good it can be who has ever eaten one of homemade bread with a filling whipped up in a few minutes from whatever happens to be on hand. The only axiom about sandwich-making is that the result must be fresh and moist but not drippy or soggy, or conversely, neatly eatable, not crumbly or dry. Neither jelly nor peanut butter does well on a picnic; that's home-snack food. Since you're likely to be far from water faucets it's best not to take along a sweet drink unless you have space to pack a jug of water as well. Milk for the younger set, and unsweetened tea for those of mature years seem to be the best answers, for coffee, too, is thirst-making. Too strong India tea is less satisfying than a China black or oolong. The fragrant Lapsang Souchong is my favorite, but Wu Lung runs it a close second. For dessert either fresh or dried fruit and homemade cookies can't be beat, with maybe a bite of sharp cheddar cheese if there's been no cheese in the sandwiches. And of cookies there is an all but infinite choice. Of course you can't whip up a batch of cookies at short notice, so it's wise, when the thaw begins in earnest, to start providing for those first picnics by baking about 6 dozen

SESAME SEED WAFERS

1) Spread 1 cup of sesame seeds on a baking sheet and toast them in the oven set at 400°. Shake the sheet or stir the seeds once or twice to promote even gilding.

2) Cream ½ cup of butter with your hand rather than a spoon, and add 1½ cups of brown sugar. When the mixture is smooth add 1 cup of flour and 1 tsp. of salt and work these in.

3) Add a whole egg and beat it in—still with your hand.

4) Add the toasted seeds last of all and mix thoroughly.

5) Put bits of the rich dough on the baking sheet by

coffee-spoonfuls, allowing 2″-3″ between the mounds, for these melt and spread out to make lacy-thin wafers.
6) Bake at 325° for about 10 minutes—or until brown.
7) Remove to a rack and cool thoroughly before storing.

Just as crisp but not as waferlike are

HONEY CRISPS
1) Toast 1 cup of rolled oats—any kind—fairly slowly in a moderate oven (350°-375°), until they smell delicious and are pale brown.
2) Cream ½ cup of butter. I always use my hand for this operation; it's speedier and it saves washing extra utensils.
3) Add ¼ cup of brown sugar and work it in, then ½ cup of honey.
4) Add a whole egg and beat it in thoroughly.
5) Add 1½ cups of flour, 1 tsp. of salt, ½ tsp. of baking soda. Beat until smooth.
6) Last of all add the toasted oats and mix thoroughly.
7) Put bits of dough on the baking sheet by teaspoonfuls, allowing 2″ between them.
8) Bake at 375° until toast-brown—about 10 minutes for 2″ cookies.

And just as rich as either and incredibly easy are

CHINESE ALMOND CAKES
1) Sift together
  ½ cup of flour
  ½ cup of rice flour
  ½ cup of powdered sugar

¼ cup of ground almonds. Grinding is easily done in a blender.

2) Work in gradually 2-4 tbsp. of vegetable oil, and knead in the bowl or on a board until perfectly smooth and homogeneous.

3) Roll out about ⅜″ thick and cut into rounds about 1½″ in diameter.

4) Place on a cookie sheet, paint with egg white blended with a little water, and stick a blanched half almond in the middle of each round.

5) Bake at 350° for about 15-20 minutes.

6) Cool completely on a rack before storing in a tin.

The chief requirement of good cookies is that they be rich, repeat rich. If you can't take the calories you have a choice between giving up cookies or taking more exercise, but don't try to compromise by cutting down on the fat in the cookie dough. Not only you but everyone else will be sorry if you do.

In our intemperate northern climate, that first mooching car picnic, while it whets the appetite for more, is likely to be followed by a freeze and maybe even another blizzard of deep wet snow, achingly beautiful but frustrating to would-be picnickers. But suddenly comes that lovely Saturday or Sunday when it's impossible to stay indoors or even outdoors at home. So down tools and books, pack a basket, and walk off as short a distance as you like and eat your lunch on a warm hillside or by a sunny pond. For such a very short-order picnic you can make no preparations to speak of, and since you're walking to your lunch you don't want to carry too much. The only tool you will need is a knife which will do quadruple duty to slice bread, cheese, and perhaps cucumber, and cut any early mushrooms that might be in your way. A pint thermos bottle for milk, tea, or water is all you'll need for two people, which leaves space in the basket for an orange apiece and a small bag of cakes. So very frugal a main course —but note how satisfying and refreshing—can be happily followed by something rich, and since you'll be scattering crumbs for birds and other small deer you needn't mind any slight messiness. So in early May it's a good idea to be fore-armed with

CHOCOLATE CAKES

1) Melt 2 squares of bitter chocolate and ½ cup (¼ lb.) of butter in a large mixing bowl over hot water.
2) Add 1 cup of brown sugar and mix in thoroughly.
3) Add 1 whole egg and beat.
4) Add dry ingredients,
   1½ cups of flour
   1 tsp. of baking powder
   1 tsp. of salt,
   alternately with the 1 cup of milk in which is dissolved ½ tsp. of baking soda.
5) Add ½ tsp. of vanilla and, if you like, nuts, currants or raisins.
6) Drop by tablespoonfuls onto a greased baking sheet and bake at 325° until the cakes have risen and cooked through, about 15 minutes.

These cakes we ice on the flat side, I can't think why.

Unfortunately these go so well with applesauce that they may suddenly disappear at home before the putative picnic can be taken, so if the weather report echoes promisingly in the back of your mind, you'd better have a second string to your bow. I'm likely to think of

ALMOND CAKES

1) Cream ½ cup (¼ lb.) of butter with ½ cup of sugar.

2) Beat in 2 whole eggs and continue beating until very light in color and texture.
3) Add the sifted dry ingredients:
   2 cups of flour
   ½ tsp. of salt
   ½ tsp. of baking powder
4) Butter the smallest-size biscuit tin and spread the batter around the sides and over the bottom.
5) Blend ¾ cup of ground almonds with ¾ cup of confectioner's sugar, and beat into this 3 whole eggs.
6) Put this mixture into the batter lined tins.
7) Bake at 350° for 15 minutes until risen and set and pale gold in color.

These turn out to be completely cake-y when baked, not two textures as when they're put into the pans.

Returning home at four o'clock happily tired you can spread out your trophies of fossil stones or mushrooms and gloat or research while you have a nice nourishing tea which might include

GRIDDLE SCONES
1) Sift the dry ingredients:
   2 cups of flour
   ½ tsp. of salt
   1 tsp. of baking powder
   ¼ tsp. of baking soda
2) Work into this 2 tbsp. of butter.
3) Add sour milk to make a soft dough which can be handled and will not flow.
4) Divide the dough into 4 lumps, and pat these into rounds about ⅓"-½" thick. Cut each round into 6 or 8 pie-shaped pieces.

5) Bake on a medium hot griddle. After the griddle is hot sprinkle some flour on it. If the flour browns in 3 minutes it is just about the right temperature, and the scones should bake on both sides in 15-20 minutes.

Spread with butter and dripping with honey these are better than ambrosia.

The great bonus added to the joys of the active life is that one not only may but must eat more.

By Decoration Day the weather is generally beguiling, and if it weren't for examinations, end-of-term functions, wardrobe demands, the thrusting garden and like imperatives, one might take a picnic nearly every day. In this season though, these forays take on a somewhat different character. They are planned for as to location, time of day, and personnel, and somewhat planned as to menu. They are picnics to which one drives, so there's generally room to transport a few adjuncts to gracious picnicking, like a small grill or a large salad bowl. If it's to be a working picnic following a noon meal—say, to gather angelica for jam and candying—you'll want food that won't require cooking at the site, so you might decide on a menu that features

MOJETE

1) Sauté in butter:
   chopped onions
   chopped green peppers
   sliced garlic
   sliced stuffed olives
2) Add ground meat and cook brown, crumbling the meat with a fork as it cooks.
3) Add tomato paste and let all cook until the meat is thoroughly done and all ingredients are blended.

4) Season with salt, pepper and Worcestershire sauce.
5) Hollow out the crumb of crusty rolls. Fill with the meat filling; press together well and dip in beaten egg-and-water.
6) Fry in deep fat.

After the rolls are fried and drained on paper toweling they may be wrapped in foil then further insulated in a roll of newspaper for transporting to the picnic site.

With this a salad of lettuce greens plus any other greens you might pick up along your route will serve to complete the main course. At this season you will surely find, if you look, dandelion and late mustard greens, maybe even some delicate wild asparagus, probably fiddle heads of bracken, a few small inky caps, and certainly wild sorrel for sharpness. A bottle of ordinary light red wine makes this a meal for an epicure, especially if it's followed by a fancy cookie dessert, perhaps

NUT SMACKS

1) Cream ½ cup of butter with ⅓ cup of brown sugar.
2) Add yolks of 2 eggs well beaten with ½ tsp. of salt.
3) Add ½ cup of flour sifted with 1 tsp. of baking powder.
4) Spread this mixture in a buttered tin.
5) For the top mixture beat the 2 egg whites and add 1 cup of brown sugar and 1 cup of roughly chopped nut meats.
6) Bake in a 350° oven for 20-30 minutes.
7) Score the top of the hot "cake" with a knife, so that it will be easier to cut when it is cold.

A working picnic followed by an early supper can be somewhat more elaborate, for after the work you can relax while a bit of something is cooking. Take along a small grill, if there's any question about the safety of a fire, and the makings for

LA MEDIATRICE

1) Fry oysters in bubbling butter for not more than 3 minutes.
2) Hollow out the crumb of fresh French bread. Butter the inside of the loaf well and heat it in an oven or wrapped in foil in the coals of a fire.
3) Fill the hot loaf with the hot oysters.

This dish may be prepared at home, wrapped in foil then in newspaper, and kept hot for a couple of hours, but it's much better when it's eaten directly from a camp fire.

La Mediatrice likes a bottle of wine—a dryish white. Again a salad is in order, and after it, nothing but fruit, cheese and coffee, then home in the early dark with bundles of angelica headily scenting the warm air.

When the long hot days arrive nothing seems more appealing than dining by a small cascade in a rocky gorge. When the water is low we set up our camp on a platform of stone in the creek bed, and sit on the convenient ledges designed for our comfort by a generous and foreseeing Providence. Here, over proper cocktails accompanied by lazy talk we begin to restore our tissues with Melba toast and

GUACAMOLE

1) Mash a small clove of garlic in a bowl with 1 tsp. of salt.
2) Add the flesh of one large avocado and mash smooth.
3) Add the juice of one lime (or ½ a lemon).
4) Add ¼ tsp. of chili powder or the equivalent in fresh or canned chilis. Or use pepper to taste.
5) Blend well; chill; serve cold.

To this basic mixture may be added onion, chopped or

grated; tomato, skinned and seeded; pimiento, chopped or puréed; olive oil; grapes, or celery. With sour lemon or lime juice I frequently use a pinch of sugar.

The dogs go wading in the stream and even the human picnickers might dabble their feet in the pool below the platform while waiting to be served with the main course, which features this time

COLD HAM PIES FOR PICNICS

1) Mix ground ham and vegetables in the proportions:
   2 cups of ham
   2 tbsp. of chopped onion
   2 raw potatoes unpeeled and put through the grinder
   4 stalks of celery chopped small
   1 whole green pepper chopped fine
2) Add 2 whole eggs, and mix in well with the seasonings:
   coriander, freshly ground pepper, parsley or chervil.
3) Moisten with broth and if you have it a dessert wine like Madeira or a cream sherry.
4) Line a coffee tin with rich pie pastry; fill with the meat mixture; and cover with a pastry top pricked to allow steam to escape.
5) Bake for about ½ hour, by which time the crust should be nicely browned and crisp, in a fairly hot oven (425°-450°).

Cool these pies in their tins and cover with the can lids for safe transportation to the picnic site. They may be turned out onto a plate and sliced across like bread.

With the cold pies we like Fasulya (Chapter 9), kept hot in a jar or crock well wrapped with newspaper, one of the best of all insulators, and one easily disposed of in a small picnic fire.

A rosé wine, kept cool at the edge of the stream in the

running water, goes perfectly with such dishes as these, as does ale. To follow, we'll have some local strawberries, un-hulled, and dipped in a pile of powdered sugar served on each paper plate. Fortified with coffee, we manage to climb the banks of the gorge, the baskets, though now nearly empty, mysteriously more cumbersome than on the way down. As we come out of the woods we find it's only twilight after all, but the rising moon and the huddles of sheep in the pasture invite us home and to sleep.

On breathless, heavy days we like a hilltop for our dining room, where whatever breeze may be can find us and where we can see more distant hills and have an illusion at least of windy space. But even on hot nights a hot dish for dinner is acceptable, especially something like

POLENTA

1) Into 6 cups of rapidly boiling salted water slowly pour 1 lb. of yellow corn meal, stirring constantly to keep the meal from lumping. This must cook for at least ½ hour and be stirred all the time. It will have cooked enough when the mush leaves the sides of the pan. If you're feeling lazy you may transfer the pan to a hot water base and thereafter stir only occasionally, but be warned that it will take still longer to cook.

2) Line a buttered casserole with about ⅔ of the mush reserving some for a top crust.

3) Brown sliced sausage (the fennel-flavored Italian kind is perfect for this dish) and/or ground beef in a skillet along with chopped onion and sliced garlic. One and one-half pounds of meat will want 2 large onions and 2 cloves of garlic.

4) Add 6 or 8 fresh tomatoes and 1 small can of Italian tomato purée when the meat and onions are browned, cover the skillet and let simmer for at least an hour, adding water to keep the texture moist and saucy.

5) Season this mixture with salt, pepper, a pinch of sugar, 4-6 fresh basil leaves (2-3 pinches of dried), a bit of oregano or marjoram, and a whiff of sage.

6) When the filling is cooked, pour it into the casserole on top of the mush lining, moistening it for the last time with a wineglassful of red wine.

7) Cover with the remaining mush; butter the top liberally; sprinkle a generous quantity of freshly grated Parmesan cheese over all; and bake for 20 minutes in a 400° oven.

Arrange to have the dish come out of the oven not more than five minutes before you leave the house. Wrap the hot casserole in foil then in newspaper. It will keep hot for two hours, so even if you get lost on the way to the picnic, as we frequently do, your dinner will still be hot when you come to eat it.

With Polenta, strong with tomato, cheese and sausage, there's nothing so good as a rough red wine, which won't suffer by being swallowed just after a bite of green salad. For a salad of greens there must be; indeed, this is almost a staple picnic dish.

For dessert this time we're having fruit gelatine, made at home of fresh fruit juice and transported carefully to the picnic site in the new portable icebox that one of the picnickers had recently acquired. With the gelatine there are a few plain

BROWN SUGAR COOKIES

1) Cream with the fingers 1 cup of butter.

2) Add 2 packed cups of dark brown sugar and beat.

3) Add 1 whole egg and 1 tsp. of salt and beat—still with your bare hand.

4) Add about 3 cups of flour, and if you like 1 tsp. of cinnamon and 1 tsp. of nutmeg.

5) Form small balls on the cookie sheet, which you needn't bother to grease, as the cookies are so rich. Flatten the balls with your fingers, a fork or a spatula.
6) Bake at 425°-450° for 10 minutes or less, depending on the thickness.

We choose our picnic sites on the basis of weather or temperature, of activity—if any, and sometimes merely for the view. One of the best view sites within twenty-five miles is on a hilltop given over to the cultivation of seed potatoes. For acres down the slopes of these hills there are no trees or shrubs to interfere with the prospect of distant ranges of hills, the woods and the ponds. So we drive along the sandy tracks to reach the top and here surrounded by potato plants we had one of the most memorable of picnics. We still call it the Champagne Picnic, for that is what we rightly drank that evening with a perfect meal. Our sophisticated bachelor who provided the wine also brought proper champagne glasses, each wrapped lovingly in tissue paper. We had iced caviar and chopped onion on Melba toast with the first glass of champagne and followed that with split-pea soup brought in a large thermos jug. Cold fried chicken was the prop of the main course, with tomato salad and thin slices of buttered homemade bread. The coffee ice cream was accompanied by either—or both—jelly roll filled with jelly made from the fruits of *Cornus mas* and Pound Cake (Chapter 2). Hot coffee followed the last of the champagne while we watched a rain squall veil a distant hillside.

A crock of baked beans is moderately easy picnic food and nothing is more satisfying after a stiff walk or climb, especially if there is fresh, buttered homemade saffron bread to use as a pusher, some crisp raw vegetables and a cup of red wine. After a filling main course like baked beans a perfect dessert is

WATERMELON ICE

1) Remove rind and seeds from watermelon and blend the pulp with lemon or lime juice in the proportion of 4 cups of pulp to the juice of 2 lemons or limes.

2) Add a pinch of salt—yes!—and sugar to taste, remembering that the ice will seem less sweet when frozen.

3) Put into trays in the freezing compartment of the refrigerator until frozen, and transport to the picnic in that portable icebox.

With this, thin buttery wafers are good. You might like to try your hand at Brandy Snaps or

LACE COOKIES

1) Put in a commodious saucepan

    ½ cup of golden syrup

    ½ cup of butter

    ½ cup brown sugar, packed

If corn syrup is substituted for the golden syrup increase the sugar to ⅔ cup and add ½ tsp. of salt.

2) Bring this mixture to the boiling point fairly rapidly and remove from the heat immediately.

3) Add 1 cup of flour and blend thoroughly. Chopped nuts or coconut may be added here as well, if you like.

4) Put teaspoonfuls of the dough on well greased baking sheets. Leave about 5″ between the cookies.

5) Bake at no higher than 325° for about 10 minutes or less.

6) Let cool for a second or so before removing to racks, or you may wish to shape them into cones by giving them a horny-fingered twirl while they're still very hot.

For a meal-in-a-dish we like a Near Eastern creation using okra, called

ETLI BAMYA (Meat with Okra)

1) Grind or cut into very small dice 1 lb. of raw lamb.
2) Sauté the meat and stir about, then add 1 medium-sized onion chopped or sliced in thin wedges.
3) When the meat is browned and the onion soft, add about 1 lb. (2 large) tomatoes cut into thin wedges, and water barely to cover the solids.
4) Trim 2 lb. or a bit less of okra of the caps and "tails" and sauté them in a little oil. This *will* spatter.
5) Arrange the partially cooked okra around the margin of a round casserole—head to tail, and another layer on top of the first. If the casserole is deep enough for a third layer so much the better.
6) In the hole in the middle pile the meat mixture and sprinkle it with salt, lots of pepper, and trickle the juice of a lemon over all.
7) Cover closely and simmer about 1 hour or longer, until the whole is tender, savory and saucy—not watery.

The casserole, wrapped in several layers of newspaper and wedged tightly in a basket or carton, can be kept hot for about two hours.

A dry cheese—Greek feta is the type—accompanied by the last of the red wine that you've been having with the okra dish makes a perfect ending for this simple meal. Nothing more is needed but the coffee, and you can lean back on an elbow and watch the first stars come to life behind the bird shadows above the pond.

Another meal-in-a-dish, also Near Eastern, features eggplant. To make

KARNI YARIK

1) Using the small, slender eggplants, with the calyxes removed, fry about six of these 6″ long vegetables whole

in a large skillet with a minimum of butter or olive oil until they are soft but not collapsed. Turn them several times during the process.

2) Cool the vegetables until they can be handled without severe pain, then peel the fat middle portion, leaving a cap of skin 1″ deep at each end. Now make a slash lengthwise with a knife in the peeled part to create a pocket in each eggplant.

3) Fry ½ lb. of minced lamb with 2 medium-sized onions, minced, until the meat is brown and the onion soft. Season with salt and pepper, parsley or chervil, or any fresh herb you may fancy.

4) Stuff the meat into the slashed eggplants, which you have already arranged in a casserole, keeping the slash uppermost.

5) Put a large slice of tomato on top of the gaping pocket-opening.

6) Add liquid (tomato juice, broth, water, or a combination of these) not quite to cover the vegetables, and simmer until cooked through and mellow with sauce. This will take an hour or longer.

This dish is traditionally served hot, so lay in a supply of insulating newspaper again for transporting it to the picnic. But if it should get cold it's really just as good, as long as you haven't used too much oil or butter so that there's a surplus on top of the sauce.

Homemade bread is again a Good Thing to go with Karni Yarik; it sops up that delectable sauce and fills the interstices that seem to be present in every healthy human frame.

Having successfully stretched our stomachs with the foregoing, we like a good solid dessert as well, so we might have an old-fashioned

SOUR CREAM AND RAISIN PIE

1) Beat 2 or more eggs with ¼ tsp. of salt and ½ cup of sugar.

2) Add ⅓ cup of brown sugar and beat it in.
3) Add 1 cup of commercial sour cream and 1 tsp. of cinnamon. Beat smooth.
4) Add 1 cup of raisins which you have lubricated with 1 tbsp. of melted butter before chopping.
5) Put into a pastry-lined tin and bake. Have the oven at 450°, but as soon as you close the door turn it down to 350°. The pie will take about 45 minutes to bake.

Or we might have a cheese cake or, though this is ideally a breakfast dish,

SUGAR PIE

1) Into an unbaked pie shell (9″) put
   1 cup of sugar
   ½ cup (scant) of flour
   ½ tsp. of salt
   Mix this about with your fingers.
2) Dot generously with butter.
3) Pour over all about ¾ cup of milk
4) Bake at about 350°–375° for about 30 minutes or a bit longer. The top should be pale brown.

Or we might prefer something like Date Pie or a pie I've come across only in New York State but which I've seen attributed to Tennessee and called

OSGOOD PIE

1) Divide 3 eggs and beat the whites stiff with a pinch of salt.
2) Mix together:
   1 cup of sugar ⎫
   3 egg yolks ⎬—beaten together
   2 tbsp. of cider vinegar ⎭

½ tsp. of cinnamon
¼ tsp. of cloves

3) Mix 1 tbsp. of melted butter with ¾ cup of raisins and chop.
4) Roughly chop ¾ cup of pecans or walnuts.
5) Mix raisins and nuts with egg yolk mixture.
6) Fold in the beaten egg whites.
7) Bake in a pastry-lined tin at 450° for 10 minutes, then at 325° for 50 minutes.

This may be topped with whipped cream when cold and ready to serve, or one of the egg whites may be reserved and used for a meringue topping. We find that for a picnic no topping at all makes the pie easier to carry safely up hill or down dale.

One Near Eastern dish suggests another, so if it's an outsize in picnics, say 10 people, I like to make in a large oval Mexican casserole the Greek

MOUSSAKA

1) Wash and remove the calyxes from 3 or 4 medium-sized eggplants. Do not peel. Slice them crosswise about ⅓" thick and fry them in olive oil. Drain them and lay them in the casserole.
(In the Near East the slices are sprinkled with salt, piled up, and put under a weight to press out some of the liquid and remove the slight bitterness of the vegetable. I rarely do this with our different species of eggplant.)
2) Using a very little olive oil to lubricate the skillet, sauté 1½ lb. of ground lamb with thin wedges of onion. The onion should amount to about ½ the bulk of the meat.
3) When the meat has browned and the onion is soft add

tomatoes cut in wedges; 1½ lb. of meat will want 5–6 good-sized tomatoes. Also at this time add the seasonings and liquid:

salt and pepper
herbs: oregano, parsley, basil or others
½ cup of white wine

4) Cover and let cook until the sauce is reduced to about half.
5) Make a thick béchamel sauce based on 3 cups of milk, and when it is cooked and then somewhat cooled add 3 whole eggs and beat them in thoroughly.
6) Mix 1½ cups of freshly grated Parmesan cheese with 1½ cups of breadcrumbs.
7) Put the meat mixture on top of the eggplant slices; cover with half the cheese and crumb mixture; pour the sauce over this; cover with the remaining half of the cheese and crumb mixture. Now drizzle all over the top ½ cup of melted butter.
8) Bake at 425° for 20 minutes, or until the dish is hot through and the crust is golden brown.

Moussaka needs no bread, for the custardy topping satisfies that texture requirement.

The water supply of our community comes from a beautiful stream which runs through still another gorge, the seventh in the locality that we have picnicked in. Years ago, before juveniles became delinquent, this area was open to any public hardy enough to clamber the sheer walls or struggle through underbrush that would defy any but an Indian with a machete or an ardent picnicker. We used to go there in late July to find the *Hypomyces lactifluorum*, scarlet lumps of succulence embedded in the gravel, or just to look at a slope brave with *Amanita muscaria* in their thousands. But whatever the purpose of our expedition it always ended with a picnic meal. One day on a high stone platform jutting out over the main gorge, we built a fire and grilled our dinner. Where we got the fresh clams I can't now remember, but that was what we had. Whether it was because of the very hot fire, or because they'd been marinated in oil and their own juice and sprinkled with fresh herbs, or just because we were famished from the hard two-hour climb, they were the most delectable grill of all time. Succulent, but crispy on the edges, they partook of the best of both steamed clams and fried clams, with the smoky flavor raising them to an empyrean of shellfish cookery. I've never done them since then, fearing that it was all perhaps a lucky accident.

But grills in general make splendid picnic food. Humble frankfurters wrapped in bacon taste quite superior cooked over a real fire. The only secret of successful grilling is constant heat and a device for moving the food closer to or farther from the flame, for the food must be thoroughly cooked without being burnt. If you can control the heat you can grill anything better on a picnic than it can be done in a kitchen stove. There's something about a real-life fire that glorifies food. Even food fried in a skillet over the fire takes on a trace of the flavor of the smoke, so if you can transport a few makings and a pan you can have for a fancy dessert after a simple grill a dish that tastes like celestial French toast, sounds like "pamperdy," but looks like

PAIN PERDU

1) Using one slice of stale bread for each serving, soak the bread in 1 cup of milk to which has been added 1 tbsp. of brandy or rum and 1 tbsp. of sugar.
2) Dip each soaked slice of bread in slightly beaten egg.
3) Fry, preferably in lard, until well browned on each side.
4) Serve hot from the skillet with a drift of confectioner's sugar over each slice.

A further touch of elegance is to add a coating of mixed breadcrumbs and freshly grated coconut after dipping the bread slices in egg. The sugared milk can be mixed at home and the bread brought already sliced to the picnic site. While the grill is being eaten, the fat can heat and the bread soak, so that there won't be too long a wait for the end result.

Labor Day is one time when all the children will have to go along on the picnic, and they seem to outnumber the adults. We generally go on this day to an extinct beaver-dam pond which looks like a tarn straight out of *Beowulf*: black water, craggy black stumps of trees and a black snake somnolent on a patch of dark wet moss. But around the pond are sunny pleasaunces: a meadow of cattails, an abandoned orchard at the top of one bank where the apples drop off when a ten-year-old bumps the ancient trunk. On "our" side of the pond the ground is open except for a few blackberry bushes and an occasional young white pine. Here generations of exclusive picnickers have made their fires and we use their ground plan but are not constrained to their choice of menu.

Now children make very reliable collectors of mushrooms if given a sample, and since the *Boleti* are rampant here at this season we set the young ones to hunting for that part of our dinner. The youngest tire early and come back with the first sticky specimens, which we examine for soundness then peel and remove the tubes. It takes at least four adults working as fast as inclination drives to prepare what nine children will gather in a half hour. Either spitted and grilled or sautéed in a pan, or failing fat, simmered in very little water, these are superb, less strong in flavor than the European cêpe, but of exquisite buttery texture. With grilled young turkey that has been marinated in olive oil, white wine and herbs, these boletes make a matchless union. If you aren't sure of your wild mushrooms, come prepared with the bought variety and set the children to collecting apples for jelly or cattails for next year's punk. It's thoroughly foolhardy to take a chance on even one wild mushroom you can't positively identify.

After the first real freeze we do occasionally have a classic Indian summer, the more precious for being doomed to early extinction. A sunny hillside at your back is a must, for otherwise the patches of snow in the hollows when blown on by even a mild breeze could make your picnic too cold for comfort. Even at midday the low sun of early December will not be too strong, so this is another cooking picnic, and since the ground will probably be damp from the recent light snow, we take along a small grill and use charcoal to broil the steaks. This is the easiest as well as the latest picnic of the year but just might be the best of all. While the steaks are broiling we have cocktails and deviled eggs, the latter a variation on the standard theme, using homemade garlic mayonnaise and tuna fish with the mashed yolk. These with celery, raw carrots dug that morning in the garden, Italian or Greek olives (Chapter 9), and some salted nuts make the cocktail course a fairly filling one. By the time the steak is served, the buttered noodles, cooked at home and brought to the picnic in insulating foil and newspaper, have been served as well as the salad. We're likely to have a fairly fine wine with this menu, for after all it's our Sunday dinner. Dessert is fruit with

POPPY SEED CAKE

1) Soak ¾ cup of poppy seeds in ¾ cup of milk. Crush the seeds somewhat with a wooden potato masher or a spoon.
2) Cream ¾ cup of butter with 1½ cups of sugar.
3) Add the poppy seeds and milk, then the sifted dry ingredients:
   2 cups of flour
   2 tsp. of baking powder. Beat well.

4) Add 1 tsp. of vanilla and 4 egg whites beaten stiff with ½ tsp. of salt.
5) Bake in 3 layers at 375° for 20–25 minutes.

For the

FILLING FOR CAKE

1) Beat 4 egg yolks well with 1 cup of sugar.
2) Add 3 tbsp. of cornstarch and 2 cups of milk. Stir in well and put the bowl over simmering water to cook for about 20 minutes or until thick and smooth. Stir often.
3) Cool, then add 1 cup of finely chopped walnuts or pecans.

For the

CAKE FROSTING

1) Mix one egg white with 1 tbsp. of water and ¼ tsp. of salt.
2) Pour this onto 1½ cups of confectioner's sugar and 1 tbsp. of instant coffee. Stir then beat with a spoon to the desired consistency, adding more sugar or water if necessary.

By three o'clock we've burned the paper plates, cups, napkins and newspaper, packed the equipment and are ready for a climb to the top of the hill up the easy track. From there we see the modest towers of our small city gilded in the now slanting rays of sunlight. Completely restored to mobility and feeling the evening chill already, we're ready to get on home again and take up the books and papers we'd put aside for this last expedition of the year.

12. Feeding the Lions

12. Feeding the Lions in an academic community is a rather different business from feeding those in the zoo. For one thing, those in the zoo have nothing else to live for, while an illustrious academic lion can't find hours enough in his days for his commanding interests. He is entertained in our homes and by our best efforts not in order to keep him quiet but to make him talk. We like our lions stimulated rather than somnolent. We also wish to honor them according to the rights and privileges of lions, so the far-from-humble housewife bends every atom of her being to this end. She is not so intent on showing off her virtuosity as in setting off his, which entails careful consideration of elements other than the food at the dinner party: the number and personalities of the other guests, the lighting, the look of the table, the seating arrangements; but what will take most of her time is the actual shopping, cooking, serving and washing up. There's nothing *ad hoc* about feeding a lion.

A somewhat troublesome dinner, but one that gets high marks from all but ulcerous lions, is a curry meal. In winter I base the curry on lamb; in summer it's more likely to be shrimp or chicken. The following dish is my own version; a proper Indian would hardly recognize it as stemming from

his culture. Indeed, I disapprove of it myself on theoretical
grounds, for it contains too many ingredients whose individual
flavors are probably lost to all but the critical cook. Everyone who eats it, however, seems to rise from table the happier
and nobler for it. Right after breakfast, then, I start the

HOT CURRY SAUCE

1) Slice: 2 or more figs, 6 dates, 1 large onion, and 1 clove
   of garlic; and dice 1 apple and 1 green pepper.
2) Sauté these in butter or mild oil (sesame, peanut or
   corn), and when they begin to soften add ½ cup of
   raisins, dark or light.
3) Mix in a teacup or bowl: 2 tbsp. of good fresh curry
   powder or paste, ½ tsp. of ginger, ½ tsp. of powdered
   coriander, ½ tsp. of cinnamon, 1 scant tsp. of salt, and
   1 tbsp. of rice flour. Moisten these to a paste with broth.
4) Stir this into the butter and vegetables and let cook
   a moment or so before adding 4 cups of liquid. I use
   broth plus the milk from a coconut, and, if it's a lamb
   or shrimp curry, tomato juice; or I add 3 or 4 cut-up
   tomatoes to the vegetables in the skillet.
5) Let cook, barely moving, all day. From time to time
   you may need to add water to keep the sauce from
   becoming too thick.
6) I add the meat, already nearly completely cooked, about
   1 hour before I plan to serve the dinner. At this point
   I turn up the heat so that the cold meat doesn't stop
   the simmering, then turn it down again after a minute
   or two.
7) Ten minutes before serving stir in a jar of jelly: quince
   or blackberry seem to me to be best. Also add 1 tsp.
   of almond extract.

A milder curry may be made by shortening the cooking time
and keeping the sauce thinner and more dilute; or by cutting

down on the amount of curry and hot spices like ginger, or conversely, increasing the sweet ingredients of the sauce.

If raw lamb is used, brown small chunks of it in butter, let it cook for 10 minutes, then set it aside until 1 hour before serving when it is added to the sauce. If chicken is the meat, boil the chicken early in the day, cool it, remove the meat from the bones and cut it up into bite-size pieces, or leave the pieces large if you like. Add the meat 20 minutes before serving, or pour the sauce over the neatly arranged slices just before you bring the dish to table. If you are using shrimp, shell them but do not cook them except in the sauce for the last 15–20 minutes before serving. This allows them to retain a crisp but tender texture.

The spectacular aspect of a curry dinner is the array of "small chow" dishes. If you have a dozen or more small bowls roughly the size of Chinese teacups, you may fill them with as many of the following condiments as you have time and patience to prepare. Arranged in approximate order of their popularity with our possibly debased occidental palates are

SMALL CHOW FOR CURRY

1) Bacon, cooked dry and crumbled
2) Sliced bananas, either raw and sprinkled with lemon juice or sautéed in butter
3) Raw cucumber, chopped in tiny dice
4) Chutney based on mango or citrus fruits
5) Chopped nuts: peanuts, walnuts or filberts
6) Riced hardboiled egg yolks
7) Riced hardboiled egg whites
8) Chopped green pepper
9) Fresh grated coconut
10) Raw tomato relish (cf. Cold Catsup)
11) Cooked tomato pickles (cf. Tomato Soy)
12) Powdered dried orange or tangerine rind

13) Chopped fresh ginger root
14) Yoghurt
15) Fresh lime slices
16) Mustard
17) Bombay Duck. If this is unobtainable in your neighborhood it may be approximated by draining anchovies and drying them in a slow oven. When they are completely dried, crumble them to a powder.

It is not necessary to add all these at once to your plate of rice and curry, but you'll find that most guests will! The idea is to contrast the mild and the sharp flavors and the rough and the smooth textures. There are dozens of palatal permutations to be discovered with this selection of small chow.

With the curry there must be a fine dish of dry rice, preferably unseasoned, and preferably the long-grain rice.

We prefer to drink ale or beer rather than wine with a curry dinner. Not only is a fine wine wasted when swallowed with this bewildering array of flavors, but the acid of wine just doesn't go well with such a dish. The beer refreshes the palate far more efficiently.

Something cool and slippery makes a good dessert to follow curry. If you haven't served yoghurt among the bowls of small chow, dessert is the spot for this soothing creation. It is especially good served on or under preserved plums or sweetened strawberries, fresh or frozen.

One adjunct to a curry meal that the well-organized cook can manage if she tries is the unfortunately last-minute job of

CHAPPATTIS

1) Mix white and whole-wheat flour in the proportions of 2 parts of white to 1 part of whole-wheat and add ½ tsp. of salt for 1½ cups of flour.

2) Mix in with the fingers enough water to make a fairly stiff dough.

3) Turn onto a board and knead until the dough is smooth and homogeneous.

4) Cover with a cloth, then with a damp cloth so that the dough won't dry out, and leave for ½ hour to an hour.

5) Roll out small pieces, walnut to egg size, into very thin rounds. A baton roller makes quicker work of it than a regular rolling pin. Additional folding and rolling causes the chappattis to blister attractively while baking.

6) On an ungreased griddle, medium hot, bake the chappattis for just a minute or two on each side. This dries but does not brown them and creates bubbles of air in the cake. Or they may be baked in a very hot oven for less than 5 minutes.

7) Butter the hot cake on each side and toast in a frying pan or on another griddle until golden.

8) Serve as soon as possible, before they cool.

Note how extraordinarily similar this bread is to tortillas.

One charming guest complimented us after a dinner of Pennsylvania Dutch pork and beans (Chapter 4) on "the mealy meal." A curry dinner is not a mealy meal, nor is the Indonesian Rystafel, or a Chinese dinner, or a Smörgåsbord. A wide assortment of flavors and textures satisfies sooner than few. One actually eats more bulk when the menu is steak, baked potatoes and salad, than at a Chinese dinner where there are offered a dozen dishes, say, fish, with a sweet and sour sauce, chicken with mushrooms and peas, pork with bamboo shoots, rice, a broccoli dish, bean curd and perhaps "long rice," followed by egg-drop soup, cakes, lichi nuts and tea. So to keep a lion stimulated and not overfed you may have to expend a certain degree of effort and a sizeable chunk of precious time, which if you're a devoted cook will please rather than petrify you.

Curries, Rystafels, Chinese dinners and Smörgåsbords are all spreads; the dishes are ranged all together before the gratified eyes of the guests. Our more usual approach in the Western world to an important meal is to organize the dishes vertically rather than horizontally, course following course, flavor and texture balancing each other seriatim rather than simultaneously. The impact of a fancy meal, as with a feast, usually relies on building to a telling climax rather than stunning the senses with one glorious blow. But it's perfectly possible to organize a meal vertically and give star billing to one dish which might come at the beginning rather than at or toward the end. Let's suppose that the current lion comes from the Midwest and has infrequent opportunities to sample real sea food. A meal in which The Dish is of fish should stimulate him, but what an embarrassment of riches the cook has to choose from. Shall we start with a fish soup or serve fish for the "meat" course? In spite of the extra dishes to be washed, I like to start off a dinner party with soup. I frequently wash the plates and bowls before the next course, and the guests are so busy talking or digesting that they don't fret at the time lag.

Lately I've been reminded—by being served it by a gentleman cook of my acquaintance—of the creole gumbo. This is the versatile soup of New Orleans, made by a French technique, seasoned by the Spanish, adapted by the Negro cooks of the territory, named by the Choctaw Indians and eaten with relish by anyone. The word "gumbo," said to have been derived from the Indian word *kombo*, originally meant sassafras, and it's the powdered leaf of young sassafras, filé, added to the soup shortly before serving, that thickens the liquid. A gumbo, though, often uses okra rather than filé, for this vegetable also exerts a thickening effect in a liquid. By now, two hundred years after the word's introduction into our language, it has come to mean not only the soup itself but also the vegetable okra, rather than the sassafras of its original denotation, though for generations the creole word "févi" was retained for okra—and for all I know may be still in use today—and one might make a "Gumbo Févi," a soup with okra.

Whatever kind of gumbo (soup) you make it will contain either filé or gumbo (okra), but never both. With a chicken gumbo use okra, but in a chicken and oyster gumbo, use filé. This is not to indicate that any or every shellfish gumbo must use filé, though; there seems to be no discernible principle for using one rather than the other.

Because I generally have stock on hand, I prefer to make even a seafood gumbo with it rather than start from scratch with veal, ham, and pounded shrimp and shrimp shells. Here, then, is how I have adapted the classic recipe to make a

SHRIMP GUMBO FILÉ

1) Peel 3 lb. of green shrimp.

2) Slice an onion of medium-to-large size into thin wedges into a fairly deep earthen casserole in which (over an asbestos mat) is bubbling 4 tbsp. of butter.

3) When the onion is translucent and has barely begun to color add a bit of diced ham. (The Smithfield type is best.)

4) Add about 3 tbsp. of flour and stir it about to a smooth paste, letting it cook gently for a few minutes, until it too looks gold-y.

5) Crush the washed shells of 2 or 3 shrimp which have cooked for 5 minutes in boiling water. The blender is ideal for this operation, for the paste should be very fine. Add to the mashed flesh of the 2 or 3 shrimp and stir into the paste in the casserole.

6) Add about 2 lb. of tomatoes, ideally fresh ones from which you've slipped the skins by scalding them. Canned ones do very well, though.

7) Add 3 qt. of well-seasoned stock, preferably chicken and/or veal, and allow to simmer until the soup is finely blended and somewhat reduced. (A split chili cooked

earlier in the stock will give the authentic Spanish
signature.)

8) Twenty minutes before serving add the uncooked, peeled
shrimp.

9) When the soup has reached the simmer again stir into
it 2 tbsp. of filé. Give the gumbo about 10 minutes to
thicken under the influence of the filé and take to table
in a hot tureen, with finely chopped parsley sprinkled
on top of the rosy soup.

I serve with this a bowl of dry fluffy rice, say a dessert-
spoonful into each bowl of soup.

Following such a hot and hearty first course, something
cool is very pleasant, so if it's a particularly grand lion we're
honoring, I might insert an extra dish between soup and
main meat dish, or serve a cold vegetable course, then the
main dish unsupported but by its own merits. In either case,
what follows such a soup as gumbo is bound to be vegetable
in character. This is historically the position in the menu
for the hors d'oeuvres.

In the states where artichokes grow naturally and come
abundantly and moderately cheap in all sizes, you might like
to prepare this dish from scratch, but the small canned or
frozen vegetables do very well for a dish similar to but more
elaborate than that in Chapter 10 of

FANCY ARTICHOKE HEARTS IN OIL

1) Mix in a pan:

    2 cups of not too dry white wine

    juice of 2 lemons

    ½ tsp. of sugar

    ½ tsp. of salt

    a few peppercorns, 2 cloves, 2 bay leaves roughly
    crushed in a mortar or bowl

2) Put the artichokes (1 can or 1 box of frozen) in this and bring to the boil then simmer for 5 minutes. If you're using the canned artichokes drain the juice out of the can and rinse the vegetables under cold running water. This gets rid of the canned flavor.

3) Drain the artichokes and put in a jar.

4) Crush a few more peppercorns with a few coriander seeds and sprinkle over the artichokes.

5) Fill the jar with olive oil so that the vegetables are completely covered.

Let these stay several days in the oil before using. They will keep more or less indefinitely. When you serve them drain them on a paper towel of the excess oil and remove to a plate. No lettuce is needed for this dish; it merely makes for awkward and messy eating.

The little canned or frozen artichokes need only a fork. If you've prepared your own from scratch you will presumably first have trimmed then cooked the vegetables and finally at great expenditure of time and patience removed the "choke." If I'm obliged to work with the large variety that we generally find in the markets I prefer to trim and cook them, chill them, then serve them with mayonnaise and finger bowls.

By this time any normal lion will be feeling fairly well fed, but he and the other guests will be expecting some kind of "main" dish no matter how astral and filling the gumbo has been. Fowl in some fashion seems to be the answer—not too distending and heavy a meat and one capable of glamour. Here is an ideal spot for

GALANTINE OF CHICKEN

1) Bone the chicken completely. (Cf. Chapter 6).

2) Make a stuffing of the crumbled crumb of white bread and

8 anchovies minced
salt and pepper
oregano or marjoram, ½ tsp.
pinch of saffron worked into 4 tbsp.
   of butter and creamed into the crumb
½ small onion, minced

3) Mound the stuffing on the chicken and fold the two ends and sides over, laying the empty legs and wings close against the back flaps. You will have an oblong package. Now roll this package tightly and neatly in a clean large cloth and tie it well.

4) Cook the package in enough stock or seasoned water to cover. The liquid being at the boil when the chicken goes into it should just simmer for the time it takes to cook—about 1 hour.

5) Remove the package and cut the string away but do not unwrap the cloth. Now press the package under a heavy weight in a dish that barely accommodates it. When it is completely cold next day, remove the cloth.

6) Prepare an aspic by first clearing the stock (Chapter 7). I add more lemon juice before I clear the stock in the proportion of 1 tsp. to each pint of liquid. Use 1 tbsp. of gelatine for each pint of cleared stock. The amount of aspic needed depends on the size of the mold or bowl in which you plan to set the galantine.

7) When the aspic is viscid but not set, put about half of it into the mold, lay the chicken—skinned for extra elegance—breast down in it, and cover the whole with the remaining aspic. You need a deep dish for this so that the chicken when inverted onto a platter will be completely embedded in the pale transparent jelly.

8) Serve on a platter garnished with watercress and thin slices of lemon or lime—both meant to be eaten. The sharpness of the juice and the bite of the cress will heighten delight in the delicate blandness of the meat.

Plenty of people disagree with me, but I like a Barsac with

this dish; if you're not the opinionated type trust your cellarer.

Hot desserts are likely to be tiresome for a hostess. They're last-minute affairs, requiring the 9:00 a.m. kind of attention rather than the 9:00 p.m., and they remove the single-handed *chef de cuisine* from the center of things just when the talk is settling to a high standard of excellence. But following two cold dishes, a hot dessert is ideal; so on with the apron for the next-to-last time this night, and let's have a taste each of

GIANT RUM OMELET

1) Put the platter on which the omelet is to be served in a very low oven while you make the dessert.

2) Pour 1 cup of good dark rum into a small pan and set to warm over very low heat.

3) Beat 6 eggs, ½ tsp. of salt, and 2 tbsp. of confectioner's sugar until thoroughly mixed but not light.

4) Add ¼ cup of water and beat it in.

5) Using a heavy 10"–12" frying pan, heat butter in it to cover the bottom generously, and tilt the pan so that the sides are lubricated as well.

6) When the butter is bubbling but not smoking, pour in the egg mixture, tilting the pan this way and that so as to cover the whole surface.

7) With a spatula lift the edges of the omelet and tilt the pan so that the uncooked egg runs into the emptied space. This is all a much more rapid process than it takes time to tell. In a minute or so all the egg will have cooked on such a large surface.

8) Remove the pan from the fire and quickly sift over the top of the omelet a drift of confectioner's sugar.

9) Now with the pan tilted away from you take the spatula and curl the edge of the omelet nearest you and the handle over on itself, and using the spatula to help it roll, form it into a huge sausage. Continue

rolling it onto the warm platter—now miraculously
materialized from the oven onto the counter beside the
stove. (A third hand is very useful at this juncture.)

10) Sift a drift more of sugar over the omelet-sausage and
    sprinkle a bit of dried powdered tangerine rind on it
    as well.

11) Now light the rum and pour it flaming over the omelet.
    Carry this blazing creation in one hot hand, spooning
    the flaring rum over it with the other as you go blindly
    and slowly to table. If you forgot to whip off the
    apron, be comforted: no one will notice anyway.

I slice this omelet into the required number of servings
and can't say that I've heard any complaints about texture
as a result.

Lions rarely make their formal progresses in summer, but
occasionally an incognito appears, and if a picnic won't
serve for reasons arthritic or obese, you'll have a chance to
show what you can do with a dinner in the garden.

Serving a fancy dinner *al fresco* is fun. It isn't necessary to
use the double-damask dinner cloth and napkins, but paper
ones won't do, for any vagrant breeze is likely to whip an
end of one or the other into the food. Fine crystal and china
are hazards as well, so I use old heavy pressed glass and
heavy pottery dishes. Otherwise the dinner is just what we'd
have indoors, but the more delightful by reason of the cool,
the night sky instead of a ceiling, and the smell of herbs and
flowers relaxing after the heat of the day. For such a dinner
we might start off with something long and cool to drink and
with it serve

PIROZHKI

1) Chilled bread dough, enriched with extra fat and/or

egg is divided into small bits the size of a walnut and rolled out into flat rounds about 2" in diameter.

2) Have ready greased biscuit tins for tiny biscuits, and place a coffee spoonful of filling on each piece of dough, pinch it closed, turn the rounded top in the greased tin, then drop it in the tin with the rounded side uppermost. Let rise at least ½ hour.

3) Bake in a hot oven (400°–450°) for about 15 minutes.

4) Serve hot.

For the filling there are lots of possibilities. You may use seasoned meat very finely ground, cheese of the cottage variety, drained and mixed with egg, raw chopped cabbage with chopped hard-boiled egg, or anything else you fancy. The filling must be finely minced and properly cooked through by serving time. A meat filling may well make use of already cooked or partially cooked meat and onion.

To follow let's have something rich and strange,

WATERCRESS SOUP

1) Cook slowly together, in water to cover, sliced potatoes and onions, the potato three times the amount of onion. When the vegetables are soft put them through a food mill or sieve.

2) Chop a bunch of watercress very fine.

3) Add the watercress to the puréed potato and onion and cook again at simmering point until the watercress-mince is amalgamated with the rest.

4) Put again through the food mill.

5) Add 1 tbsp. of butter for each potato used, put over the heat and just barely simmer again until the butter is incorporated thoroughly.

6) Just before serving add more butter, 1 tsp. of lemon juice for each three potatoes, salt and white pepper.

For outdoor meals a cream soup somehow seems to hold its heat better than a thin one, and this soup must be served piping hot. (Have you an outlet in the garden for an electric hot plate?) What is to follow is icy-cold

LOBSTER

1) Boil the lobsters in lots of salted water until just done. If the rapid boiling never stops this should take not more than 10 minutes.
2) Remove from the water, and when cool enough to handle split them down the underside from head to tail with a very sharp heavy knife. The idea is to cleave the lobster flesh in two without cutting through the shell of the back. If the knife isn't sharp, use kitchen scissors to cut the undershell, then a knife to shear the flesh.
3) Now using a curved grapefruit knife, separate the flesh of the tail from the shell and loosen the coral or liver or both.
4) With scissors cut through the shell the length of the large claws and also the clawlets if you think it worthwhile; I do. The flesh of the large claw can be loosened from the shell just as was the tail meat, with a grapefruit knife.
5) Chill thoroughly.

This extra bit of preparation makes for much less effort on the part of the guests, and much less unattractive manipulation at table, and the chances of unsightly accidents and somersaulting debris are thereby decreased. I put a large bowl by the table so that shell can be deposited in it for easy disposal afterward.

Nothing is needed with the lobster but the proper thing to drink. This I leave to the family wine steward who sometimes serves a still white wine, sometimes champagne, and sometimes no wine at all but a velvety stout.

One sauce that loves lobster, though, is Sauce Verte (Chapter 3), but be warned that the fine mincing of the herbs means a relatively long time with a chopping board and a sharp French knife. The blender merely macerates the herbs and the finished sauce will have unsightly fibres in it. There just isn't any shortcut to mincing herbs.

Following the lobster we'll serve avocado halves with a wine vinegar or lemon juice French dressing in the hollow where the seed had been.

And for dessert let's have a frozen cream which I call

BISCUIT COCONUT

1) For 1 dozen cupcake size units (about 1 qt.), beat 2 egg yolks with ½ cup of confectioner's sugar until pale and light.
2) Stir in 2 tbsp. of dark rum (or sherry).
3) Whip 1 pt. of heavy cream until thick and add ½ tsp. of almond flavoring.
4) Add all but ¼ cup of the following mixture:
    ½ cup of sponge cake crumbs—or cookie crumbs
     1 cup of freshly grated coconut
    ¼ cup of finely chopped but unblanched almonds
    ¼ tsp. of cinnamon
5) Fold in the whites of the 2 eggs beaten stiff with ½ tsp. of salt.
6) Spoon into fluted cupcake papers set in large biscuit tins. Top with the reserved coconut-crumb mixture and freeze in the refrigerator freezing unit.

Yes, this is based on Biscuit Tortoni, but the fresh coconut and the rum make it a completely different taste and texture experience.

If the night is windless nothing will add that touch of elegance so well as a last dish of

PISTACHIO NUTS FLAMBÉ

1) Get from a Near Eastern grocery or confectioner's shop some of those fat, undyed, freshly toasted pistachio nuts.
2) Spread the nuts in a single layer in a very large shallow soup plate or a platter with a deep rim.
3) Heat ouzo or raki in a saucepan.
4) Set it alight and pour it over the nuts, spooning the flaming spirit until all the liquid disappears. About ¼ cup of spirit to a cup of nuts will do.

As soon as the nuts are cool enough to handle they are ready to eat.

Any self-respecting lion will sing for such a supper.

In winter it's probably the main course dish that is featured, and the whole dinner is usually heartier than any of the foregoing, especially if the lion of the day is young and vigorous.

With the preprandial ice-breakers for such a dinner I serve only nuts and olives, reserving the big guns for the table. The first gun isn't all that big, either, but it's sufficient to whet the appetite if it's

TOMATO ASPIC WITH AÏOLI

1) Make an aspic of clear tomato juice and cleared stock (I use veal-chicken stock) in the proportion of 1 tbsp. of gelatine to 1 pt. of liquid—roughly 1½ cups of tomato juice and ½ cup of seasoned stock.
2) Chill this in individual molds and top with sauce in the kitchen before serving; or, mold the aspic in a large ring mold and fill the hole in the middle with sauce, or frost the ring with the aïoli after you've inverted the aspic onto a platter.

For the

AÏOLI

1) Crush in a mortar or bowl with salt 2 cloves of garlic for each cup of finished mayonnaise.
2) Proceed to make the mayonnaise as in Chapter 3, remembering to omit the salt as given in that recipe.

If you use a blender just put the peeled and roughly cut-up garlic buds in the blender and let the machine crush them for you before going ahead with the mayonnaise.

Following aïoli you can afford to have another dish of strong flavor. This dish has traveled around the Mediterranean from the Near East picking up characteristics and ingredients from each culture that accepted it, until finally it is more or less stabilized in Spain as

PAELLA à la VALENCIANA

1) Using a large deep-sided skillet or earthen casserole, sauté until golden a jointed frying chicken along with ½ cup diced pork, salt or fresh, or ham, or bacon. You might even use a lean sausage like the Spanish or Mexican chorizo, or Polish sausage.
2) Add thin wedges or dice of onion (about ½ cup or 1 large onion), and when it begins to be translucent add 2 cloves of garlic cut in thin chips.
3) Add 1 cup of well-washed and drained rice. Stir it about well so that the grains are coated with the fat and oil.
4) Add 2 or 3 ripe tomatoes, about 1 lb., chopped roughly or cut into chunks. Cover and let simmer slowly for 10 minutes, adding a bit of stock halfway through if the juice of the tomatoes is not sufficient to keep the rice from sticking.

5) Add the vegetables, which traditionally include fresh peas and large French beans or scarlet runner beans cut into 1″ pieces. String beans may be substituted. Artichoke hearts are often included, but if you use the small frozen or canned ones don't add them until later. For a one-chicken paella, I should use ½ lb. of fresh peas, ¼ lb. of beans and one artichoke for each piece of chicken. Cover again and allow to cook very gently for 10 minutes more.

6) Now add the shellfish and/or fish. These are likely to be shrimp or prawns, mussels, scallops, eel or a firm white fish, crabs or lobster. When you're unable to get mussels, clams may be used with perfect confidence, but they must be put into the dish at the very end so as to be as nearly raw as hot clams may be. The shells of mussels and clams are tossed in as well. The chopped pimiento goes in now too, in the proportion of 2 canned pimientos to each chicken used.

7) Now presumably there has been about ½ cup of liquid (tomato and/or stock) used in the earlier stage of the cooking. To cook 1 cup of rice completely about 2 cups of liquid is needed, therefore, you will now add about 1½ cups of liquid, either stock or water, into which you have stirred a pinch of real Spanish saffron and any salt and pepper you think is necessary.

8) Cover and let cook quickly now, stirring occasionally and reducing the heat somewhat toward the end of the cooking period.

9) When the rice is thoroughly cooked you may be sure that everything else will be, so remove the pan from the fire, invert a large colander over it and cover it with a cloth to absorb any remaining steam.

10) Take to table in the dish in which it has cooked.

Go ahead and drink a dry white wine with this if you're a

traditionalist, but I prefer to serve a flinty red wine properly *chambré*.

After such a main dish, the felt want is for something smooth and cool and moderately light, and one that answers very well is

JAVA JELLY

1) Make 1 qt. of jelly using 2 tbsp. of gelatine, 3½ cups of perfectly clear strong coffee, ½ cup of lemon juice and 1 generous cup of sugar.
2) Pour this into a 1 qt. ring mold to set.
3) Whip ½ pt. of heavy cream very stiff with a pinch of salt and add 1 tbsp. of brandy and 2 tbsp. of confectioner's sugar.
4) Invert the molded jelly onto a serving dish and cover it with whipped cream topping.

Even a previously famished lion has had enough by this time, so don't serve even a thin wafer with this dessert. But when the coffee has been served you might like to pass around a dish of

FONDANT GRAPES

1) Mix, in a pan larger than needed to accommodate the amounts, 1½ cups of sugar and ½ cup of water. Let stand for an hour.
2) Bring to the boil stirring constantly and brushing down the sugar crystals from the sides of the pan or wiping them away with a damp cloth.
3) Allow the syrup to boil without stirring until it reaches 235° on a candy thermometer. While it boils add a pinch of cream of tartar but don't stir it in.
4) Remove the pan from the heat and let it cool until no

more bubbles rise, then pour it onto a platter or marble slab either wiped with a wet cloth or with an oiled cloth or paper towel.

5) Allow it to cool to lukewarm, about 110°.
6) Stir it about now with a spatula, and you will be surprised to observe how quickly the texture changes from sticky-transparent to creamy-opaque.
7) When cool enough to handle knead the fondant as you would knead bread until it is a satin-smooth mass like pliable clay. Let it rest for an hour covered with a damp cloth.
8) Pinch off a piece about the size of one of the grapes that you are covering, and mould it about the grape. This takes surprisingly little time. You can cover 2 to 3 doz. grapes in a ½ hour.
9) Let these dry on waxed paper over a cake rack for a while before putting them next each other in a dish.

The only good that comes of not having a mechanical dishwasher is that it allows the hostess-cook to unwind before trying to sleep. If the unwinding and the washing up are shared gladly between host and hostess the process is even more successful, for nobody can deny that a good party is work before, during and after. Luckily an ambitious cook welcomes the tension that accompanies her performances just as an actress does. And anyway is she not the mate of a potential Lion?

13. From Ice-breaker to jaw-breaker, the

course of a party for students is an exercise in taut organization. The twin problems are bulk and time. The number of guests is larger than any household cook would choose to cater for; the youthful appetites are invariably voracious; the guests themselves strike a middle-aged person as being somewhat larger than life. The time aspect of such a large party may be suggested by noting that the first arrivals will ring the doorbell ten minutes before the time you had appointed. Nowadays they all come in cars, and a bright lad will figure that to get a parking place he'd better be on hand before the crush. This means that the whole crowd will be in the house—and hungry —before the clock strikes the hour set.

No matter how well students know their professor in the class- or seminar room, when they enter his house they are likely to be overtaken by an unaccustomed rush of shyness to the head. The professor's lady can be of inestimable value here. Let her have studied the list of names never so closely, she will still make ludicrous errors in her introductions, and this comic relief takes the place of alcohol at a middle-aged dinner party. Meanwhile the professor has been pouring out

drinks, soft or vegetable. The sooner these young people have
something in their hands the better. With the drinks salted
nuts and crackers are advisable or you won't have time to
get the buffet set with the hot dishes, for another characteristic of these young people's parties is the jet-speed at which the
food disappears. Therefore, though it's a vicious circle, the
more and better the food the more they eat, and consequently
the more time the cook has to breathe in between courses.

Crackers that go very well with mild vegetable or soft
drinks are

POPPY SEED WAFERS

1) Sift together
   ½ cup of whole wheat flour
   ½ cup of white flour with 2 tbsp. of cornstarch
      substituted for 2 tbsp. of flour
   1½ tsp. of salt
   1 tsp. of sugar
2) Work in with the fingers ¼ cup of butter.
3) Add water to make dough the consistency of pie dough.
4) Roll out thin and spread with about 1 tbsp. of softened
   butter. Fold as for puff pastry, sealing the open edges
   with dampened fingers or by rapping with the rolling
   pin.
5) Roll again and spread with another 1 tbsp. of butter.
   Fold again.
6) Roll out as thin as possible. Cut into small squares with
   a pastry cutter.
7) Place fairly close together on a baking sheet; paint
   with egg white forked smooth with a little water; sprinkle
   thickly with poppy seed.
8) Bake in a hot oven (450°) for about 5 minutes or until
   brown.
9) Cool on a rack and store in an airtight tin.

These wafers can be made several days before the party, luckily, for the multitude of things to do in connection with providing a meal for 25–30 young people could strike an unorganized cook with panic or paralysis.

Remember that though you've invited your young guests to dinner, and though they will certainly eat vast quantities of food in your house, that is not their only reason for coming. Many of them will be curious just to see how the odd academic breed lives. They will want to know about your possessions if they are either rare or makeshift, and they will want to handle your books. They will not care if the rungs of chairs are dusty or if the floors have muddy pawprints on them. So clean the books and rely on candlelight—they love that—and let the rest of the cleaning wait until after the party when the house will be in rather more need of it.

Supple young bodies are even more comfortable sitting on cushions on the floor than in chairs, so your living room and dining room can take on an Oriental aspect for this kind of evening. You may use paper napkins, and paper plates too, if you plan the food for it, though liquids are much safer in glass and china. I introduce a large carton into the kitchen to take the paper debris, and I have a dishpan at the ready in the sink for glasses, silver and china. The glasses used for drinks can be washed, dried and put away by the time the last guest has filled his dinner plate at the buffet table. Before you can fill the professor's and your own, you'll have to replenish the serving dishes, for young guests will always want at least two helpings. A set of serving dishes down both long sides of the table speeds the business of serving and even the last person in line—you—can have moderately hot food.

The kind of food to serve depends somewhat on the amount of time and energy at the disposal of the cook, but there are certain principles useful as guides.

In order that the food may be as hot as possible, any carving should be done well ahead of time and the dish kept hot or be reheated. Even a professor can go to pieces under the tension of carving plus responding to his guests, and the slices may fall from his knife in such coarse slabs that the meat won't go around; or if he resists confusion and achieves symmetrical servings, everything else may be stone cold by the time the meat is ready.

Dinner knives must be eliminated. These large and heavy implements tend to overbalance, and in any case even plastic-coated paper plates will not withstand a too-zealous cut. Butter knives too are hazards, indeed butter itself is dangerous. If bread or rolls are an essential part of the menu, the cook must see to it that any buttering is done before the meal is served.

Beware too of sauces, thick or thin, and sticky relishes. The tidiest and best-coordinated people of any age can be joggled or bumped into an accident, and the consequent embarrassment may spoil their pleasure if not yours.

So much for the negative approach. The positive principle that I have come to rely on is extremely simple: give the student-guests the kind of food that they do not get in institutional catering. This means green salads with real French dressing—not bottled forms, fresh vegetables, not frozen, rice or cracked wheat rather than potatoes or macaroni, and any dessert that you can manage except jello.

When we use ham it is generally a steamed ham done early in the day or on the preceding day. It is served cold and already sliced, and homemade mustard (Chapter 10) is the accompaniment. A carbohydrate dish that goes well with it is

BAKED BULGUR PILAV

1) For each cup of the cracked wheat allow 2 cups of good strong chicken broth well seasoned. Combine these and any further seasonings needed or desired in a casserole.

2) Bake for an hour in a moderate oven (350°).

3) A bit of melted butter should be drizzled over the hot bulgur before serving.

Each cup of uncooked cracked wheat will provide about six servings.

On one occasion I took the trouble to prepare fresh asparagus. This I steamed on the rack in a large covered roaster on top of the stove, and it was a great success with the guests. But nothing I have ever served has had the immediate yet lasting success of a salad of greens tossed with simple French dressing.

If the group isn't too large I branch out a bit from plain sliced ham or turkey and serve a combination dish. One such is a dish of curried eggs, each one sliced in half lengthwise, on slices of ham. This with plain rice is satisfactorily filling yet festive-looking and tasting, and it has the great advantage of being susceptible of early preparation with only the assembling to take care of at dinner time.

Another dish which can be prepared well ahead of zero hour is served in the casseroles in which it is heated in the oven. This is

TURKEY WITH MUSHROOMS

1) Poach a 13–15 lb. turkey, or steam it in a large roaster. Allow it to cool completely before slicing all the meat.

2) Sauté the caps of 3 lb. of mushrooms in butter.

3) Arrange the slices of meat in a casserole and cover with the mushroom caps.

4) In the pan in which the mushrooms have cooked make a sauce using 1 tsp. of cornstarch and 2 tbsp. of water for each cup of sauce desired. (You will need 4 to 8 cups of sauce, depending on the size and shape of the casseroles to be used.) Stir in turkey broth and bring

to the boil, adding 1 tbsp. of sweet vermouth for each
2 cups of liquid. Add other seasonings as desired.

5) Pour the sauce over the meat and mushrooms, and 20
minutes before serving put the casserole in the oven
set at 375° to heat thoroughly.

Desserts for a large party of this sort can be very simple.
Allow a half dozen cookies apiece as a rock-bottom minimum
with ice cream or fruit, which are the two desserts that I find
both popular and easy. The ice cream I buy in the little
paper cups which are so easily disposed of when emptied.
Fresh fruit is well liked, but cores, skins and stems make for
unsightly debris, so I generally take the trouble to prepare
compotes of fruit. Two pineapples mixed with 2 quarts of
strawberries or blueberries are sufficient for a surprisingly
large number of people.

As a change from cookies I sometimes make Pound Cake.
Baked in two small pans rather than one large one, it cuts
to better advantage and the slices are far more manageable.

If you feel that such a mass-produced menu needs topping
off in some way, small hard candies do very well. Chocolate
creams are something of a menace and should be avoided.

By this time you've probably organized the kitchen somewhat, and when you unobtrusively slip among your guests
and find a place to sit you will notice that your party has
taken an alarmingly intellectual turn. Parties of your peers
may descend to a certain amount of easy small talk, but these
young people have little time for chit-chat. They're milking
their professor while they have the chance, and until they
get up to leave, which they do in a body as one man, it is
likely that you'll be allowed to relax and admire from your
ringside seat—unless you too happen to be a professor.

———————THE END ———————

Index

(Recipes are indicated
by capital letters)

AÇORDA, 29.

AÏOLI, 264.

ALMOND CAKES, 229.

Angel food, 37, 64.

ANGELICA: CANDIED, 155; RHUBARB AND JAM, 154.

APPLESAUCE PIE, 212.

ARTICHOKE HEARTS IN OIL, 214, 255.

Ash cake, 43, 44.

ASPIC, 120, 161, 257: CARP IN, 161; TOMATO, WITH AÏOLI, 263.

Avocado, as salad, 224, 262. *See also* GUACAMOLE.

AVGOLIMONO SAUCE, 159.

BASIL SPAGHETTI, 84.

Batter, 59: BREAD, 93; (CORN OYSTERS), 26; DIPPING, 59; FRIED SQUASH BLOSSOMS, 168; (OVEN-BAKED PANCAKES), 60; (TOAD-IN-THE-HOLE), 25; (YORKSHIRE PUDDING), 61. *See also* PANCAKES.

BEANS: ROAST LOIN OF PORK WITH, 91; TURKISH STRING, 199.

BÉARNAISE SAUCE, 77.

BÉCHAMEL SAUCE, 71.

Beef: hamburger, 197; HASH, 126; MEAT LOAF, 114; Steak and kidney pie, 105; STROGANOV, 191; (SUKIYAKI), 110; TONGUE WITH DILL SAUCE, 99; in CANNIBAL MEAT BALLS, 116; in MOJETE, 231; in PEPPER STEAK, 192; in POLENTA, 235.

BEEF-STEAK MUSHROOM, 173.

Beets: BORSCHT, INSTANT, 189.

BISCUIT, 51.

BISCUIT COCONUT, 262.

BLANQUETTE DE VEAU, 102.

BOILED DRESSING, 152: Meats, 100 ff.

Bombay duck, 251.

BONING, STUFFING AND, 129: TO BONE A BIRD, 135; of fish, 137.

Borage, 182.

BORSCHT, INSTANT, 189.

BRAINS SYLVANER, CALVES, 107.

Brandy snaps, 238.

BREAD, 51 ff.: (AÇORDA), 29; BATTER, 93; (CHAPPATTIS), 251; (CORN PONE), 44; CORNISH SAFFRON, 57; (GNOCCHI), 30; (JOHNNY CAKE), 29; (LA MEDIATRICE), 233; (MOJETE), 231; (PAIN PERDU), 244; PIDEH, 55; PIROZHKI, 259; -PUDDING, LEMON, 183; -SAUCE, 80; Spoon, 29; -stuffing, 206; SYRIAN OR TURKISH, 55; (TORTILLAS), 42; YEAST, 52; uses of stale, 183.

BUBBLE AND SQUEAK, 112; BUCKWHEAT CAKES, RAISED, 58.

BULGUR PILAV, BAKED, 271.

Butter, home-made, 178.

CABBAGE: SPICED RED, 215; in BUBBLE AND SQUEAK, 112.

CAKES, 37ff., 62ff.: ALMOND, 229; ANGEL FOOD, 37, 64; ash, 43, 44; BUCKWHEAT, 58; CHINESE ALMOND, 227; CHOCOLATE, 229; CORNISH SAFFRON, 57; hoe, 43, 44; SHORTCAKE, 24, 156; SNOW, 182; SPONGE, 63; oat, 43; plain, mix, 200; POUND, 65; POPPY SEED, 246; VINEGAR, 39. *See also* PANCAKES.

CARP, 160: CHINOIS, 162; IN ASPIC, 161.

275

CAZUELA DE AVE, 101.
CHAPPATTIS, 251.
Cheese: -course, 190; in GOUGÈRE, 36; in pancakes, 62.
CHERRY LIQUEUR, 168: wild, 168.
Chestnut: puff, 209; stuffing, 206.
Chicken: (CAZUELA DE AVE), 101; CIRCASSIAN, 117, 119; CROQUETTES, 127; Curry, 250; GALANTINE, 256; (KIEVSKI CUTLETS), 140; (PAELLA VALENCIANA), 264; (RAVIOLI), 142; TO BONE A BIRD, 135.
CHINESE ALMOND CAKES, 227.
Chinese egg rolls, 13.
CHOCOLATE: CAKES, 229; sauce for fish, 81; SAUCE for PROFITEROLES, 34.
CHOUX PASTE See CREAM PUFFS.
Clams: grilled, 244; in PAELLA, 264.
COCONUT: BISCUIT, 262; grated, for curry, 250.
Coffee in JAVA JELLY, 266.
COLD CATSUP, 122: for use with curry 250.
Cole Slaw, hot, 152.
COOKIES: ALMOND CAKES, 229; BROWN SUGAR, 236; CHINESE ALMOND CAKES, 227; CHOCOLATE CAKES, 229; HONEY CRISPS, 227; LACE, 238; NUT SMACKS, 232; SESAME SEED WAFERS, 226.
CORDERA ASADO À LA MANCHEGA, 88.
CORN: DODGERS, 44; OYSTERS, 26; PONE, 44; PUDDING, 31; to cook parched, 198; TO PARCH, 198; -VEAL PIE, 106.
CRAB CREPES, KING, 195.
CREAM PUFFS, 32: (GOUGÈRE), 36; (PROFITEROLES), 33.
CRÈME BRÛLÉ, 23.
CREPES, 196: KING CRAB, 195.
CROQUETTES, CHICKEN, 127.
CUCUMBERS: for curry, 250; STUFFED, 130.
CURRY, 248: SAUCE, HOT, 249; SMALL CHOW FOR, 250; CHAPPATTIS to serve with, 251.

CUSTARD: BAKED, 22; BOILED, 21; CRÈME BRÛLÉ, 23; Crème Caramel, 22; Floating Island, 22; in TRIFLE, 156; ZABAGLIONE, 21, 200.

DANDELION GREENS, 151.
Daube, 121.
Deep-fat frying: BATTER-FRIED SQUASH BLOSSOMS, 168; KIEVSKI CUTLETS, 140; MOJETE, 231.
DILL SAUCE, 99.
Dogwood (jelly), 170.
DOLMAS, 131: GRAPE LEAF, 157; mussel, 119; QUINCE, 143; tomato, 132.
DUMPLINGS, 103; fish, 34.

EGG, THE, 16: custards, 20 ff.; omelets, 18 ff., 258; POACHED, 17; scrambled, 17; in MERINGUES, 24; in SMALL CHOW FOR CURRY, 250; -whites in SNOW CAKE, 182.
Eggplant: IMAM BAYÏLDÏ, 132; KARNI YARÏK, 239; MOUSSAKA, 242.
ELDER-FLOWER PANCAKES, 164.
ENDIVE AMANDINE, BRAISED, 216.

FENNEL, BRAISED, 217.
FILLING FOR POPPY SEED CAKE, 247.
Fish, 94 ff.: cold, cooked, 95; (CARP IN ASPIC), 161; (CARP CHINOIS), 162; -dumplings, 34; poached, 95; SPREAD, 186; to bone, 137; with chocolate sauce, 81. See also SQUID and shellfish.
Floating Island, 22.
FONDANT GRAPES, 266.
Fritters, 26.
FROSTING (for POPPY SEED CAKE), 247.

GALANTINE OF CHICKEN, 256.
GARLIC: mayonnaise, 264; NUTS, 186.
Garnishes, 188.

GINGER: fresh, for CURRY, 251; JELLY, WILD, 181.
GNOCCHI, SEMOLINA, 30.
GOOSE: DUTCH, 138; SAUERKRAUT-STUFFED, 134.
GOUGÈRE, 36.
GRAPE: -LEAF DOLMAS, 157; LEAVES, TO PRESERVE, 157.
GRAPES, FONDANT, 266.
GREENS: DANDELION, 151; LAMBS' QUARTERS, 153; purslane, 153.
GUACAMOLE, 233.

Ham: PIES, FOR PICNICS, COLD, 234; steamed, 92; huff crust for, 222; in BUBBLE AND SQUEAK, 112.
Hamburger, 197.
HASH, 109: BEEF, 126; PEPPER, 122; PINEAPPLE-STRAWBERRY, 123.
HOLLANDAISE SAUCE, 77.
HONEY CRISPS, 227.
HORSERADISH SAUCE, 100.
Huff crust, 222.

JAMS AND JELLIES: dogwood, 170; MARMALADA, 179; MARROW, 171; PEACH AND MAYAPPLE, 166; PLUM CONSERVE, 126; RHUBARB AND ANGELICA, 154; ROSE HIP, PURÉED, 170; WILD GINGER, 181.
JOHNNY CAKE, RHODE ISLAND, 29.

KIDNEYS IN WHITE WINE SAUCE, 175.
KIEVSKI CUTLETS, 140.

LAMB: curry, 250; KIDNEYS IN WHITE WINE SAUCE, 175; loaf, 114-115; roast, 88; in meat balls, 115; in MOUSSAKA, 242; in Steak and Kidney Pie, 105; in STUFFED QUINCES, 143; with eggplant, 115, 239, 242; with okra, 239.
LAMBS' QUARTERS, 153.
LARDY JACKS, 47.
LEMON BREAD PUDDING, 183.

LEMON BUTTER (CHEESE OR CURD), 83.
Liver-pâté, 117; HOT PÂTÉ, 194.
LOBSTER, 261.
LOMBO DE VITELA, 90.

MADEIRA SAUCE, 79.
MARMALADA, 179.
MARROW JAM, 171.
MAYONNAISE, 80: Green, 81.
MEAT, 86 ff.: balls, 115, 116; LOAF, 114; MINCE, 124; in BLANQUETTE DE VEAU, 102; in BUBBLE AND SQUEAK, 112; in CORDERO ASADO, 88; in DUTCH GOOSE, 138; in ETLI BAMYA, 239; in KARNI YARIK, 239; in LOMBO DE VITELA, 90; in MOJETE, 231; in MOUSSAKA, 242; in PIROZHKI, 259; in POLENTA, 235; in STUFFED QUINCES, 143; in SUKIYAKI, 110; in TOAD-IN-THE-HOLE. 25.
MEDIATRICE, LA, 233.
MERINGUES, 24: shell, 213; topping for pies, etc., 24.
MONT BLANC (Monte Bianco), 83.
MORELS, 150.
MOUSSAKA, 242.
Mousse, 121.
MUSHROOM: PICKLED, 214; PILAV STUFFING, 165; STROGANOV, 174; TURKEY WITH, 272.
Mushrooms: Agaricus campestris, 174; Amanita muscaria, 243; BEEFSTEAK, 173; Boletus, 245; Cantharellus cibarius (chanterelles), 165; Collybia velutipes, 165; Coprinus atramentarius, 165, 173; Coprinus micaceus IN BUTTER, 149; Coprinus comatus, 173; drying, 165; Fistulina hepatica, 173; Hypomyces lactifluorum, 243; Marasmius oreades, 165, 172; Morchella esculenta (MORELS), 150; Sparassis crispa, 173; PICKLED, 214; -PILAV STUFFING, 165; PUFFBALLS (Cal-

vatia maxima), 97, 169; -STRO-
GANOV, 191; TURKEY WITH, 272.
MUSTARD, 223: for Curry, 251;
-greens, 151.

NASTURTIUM PODS: PICKLED, 180;
STUFFED, 130.
NOODLES: BUTTERED, 217; PLAIN, 98.
NUTS: for curry, 250; GARLIC, 186;
PISTACHIO, FLAMBÉ, 263; -SMACKS,
232.

OKRA: gumbo, 253; meat with,
239.
OLIVES IN OIL, 185.
Omelet, 17 ff.: BAKED, 19; fried,
18; GIANT RUM, 258; rolled, 19,
258.
ONION STUFFING, 220.
OYSTERS: CORN, 26; in LA MEDI-
ATRICE, 233; in steak and kidney
pie, 105.

PAELLA À LA VALENCIANA, 264.
PAIN PERDU, 244.
PANCAKES: BUCKWHEAT, 58; ELDER
FLOWER, 164; (KING CRAB CRÊPES),
195; OVEN-BAKED, 60; POTATO, 62;
SNOW, 26; spinach, 61.
PASTE: CHOUX, 32; PUFF, 48 ff.
Pastry (*see* PIE), 45 ff.: crust for
roasts, 222; PUFF, 48 ff.
PÂTÉ: HOT, 194; liver, 117.
PEACH AND MAY APPLE JAM, 166;
PEPPER: HASH, 122; steak, 192.
Pickles and relishes: ARTICHOKES
IN OIL, 214, 255; COLD CATSUP,
122; MUSTARD, 223; MUSHROOMS,
214; NASTURTIUM PODS, 180;
OLIVES IN OIL, 185; PEPPER HASH
(SAUCE), 122; tomato, 122;
tomato soy, 191; SAUERKRAUT,
133
PIE, 45 ff.: APPLESAUCE, 212; beef-
steak and kidney, 105; CORN-
VEAL, 106; crumb crust, 201, 212;

HAM, FOR PICNICS, 234; LARDY
JACKS, 47; meringue shell, 213;
OSGOOD, 241; SOUR CREAM AND
RAISIN, 240; SUGAR, 241.
PIG'S STOMACH, STUFFED, 138.
PILAV: BAKED BULGUR, 271; MUSH-
ROOM, STUFFING, 165; WEDDING,
93.
PINEAPPLE-STRAWBETTY HASH, 123.
PINK LEMONADE, 167.
PISTACHIO NUTS FLAMBÉ, 263.
PIROZHKI, 259.
PLUM CONSERVE, 126.
POLENTA, 235.
POPPY SEED: CAKE, 246; -WAFERS,
269.
PORK (*See also* Ham): (DUTCH
GOOSE), 138; ROAST LOIN OF, WITH
BEANS, 91; -SAUSAGE in TOAD-IN-
THE-HOLE, 25; (SUCKING PIG),
219; in meat balls, 116.
Potatoes: canned, 208; mashed
with egg, 209; mashed with
garlic, 209; PANCAKES, 62.
Poultry (*See* Chicken, Goose,
Turkey).
Pousse café, 224.
PROFITEROLES, 33.
Puddings, 28 ff.: (AÇORDA), 29;
BREAD, 183; CORN, 31; plum, 218;
(TOAD-IN-THE-HOLE), 25; YORK-
SHIRE, 61.
PUFFBALLS, 97, 169.

QUAIL, BAKED, 176.
QUENELLES DE POISSON, 34.
QUINCE: (MARMALADA), 179;
STUFFED, 143.

RAVIOLI, 142.
REDBUD PODS, 154.
RHUBARB AND ANGELICA JAM, 154.
RICE: (MUSHROOM PILAV STUFFING),
165; (PAELLA À LA VALENCIANA),
264; PLAIN, 89; (WEDDING PILAV),
93; wild, 220; with GUMBO, 255.
ROSE HIP JAM, PURÉED, 170.

Rum: cherries, 168; in BISCUIT COCONUT, 262; in GIANT OMELET, 258.

SAFFRON BREAD OR CAKE, 57.
Salads, 189, 212: avocado as, 224, 262.
Sandwiches, 226.
SAUCES, 69 ff.: AVGOLIMONO, 159; (for BASIL SPAGHETTI), 84; BÉARNAISE, 77; BÉCHAMEL, 71; BOILED DRESSING, 152; BREAD, 80; BROWN, 75; CARAMEL, 85; CREAM, 73; chocolate, 81, 83; CHOCOLATE, 34; CUMBERLAND, 207; CURRY, 249; dessert, 82; DILL, 99; hard, 83, 218; HOLLANDAISE, 77; HORSE-RADISH, 100; LEMON BUTTER, 83; MADEIRA, 79; MAYONNAISE, 80; pear, 220; PEPPER, 122; THICK-ENED VELOUTÉ, 73; TOMATO, 143; VELOUTÉ, 72; VERTE, 81; white, 70; WHITE WINE, 175; (ZABAG-LIONE), 21, 200.
SAUERKRAUT, 133; -STUFFED GOOSE, 134.
Sassafras, 160, 253.
SESAME SEED WAFERS, 226.
SCONES, 230.
SCOTCH: SHORTBREAD, 221; -SNOW CAKE, 182.
Shellfish: clams, 244, 265; crab, 195; LOBSTER, 261; mussels, 119, 265; oysters, 105, 233; SHRIMP, 59, 96, 193, 250, 254, 265.
SHORTBREAD, 221.
SHORTCAKE, 156: meringue topping for, 24.
SHRIMP: AND PEAS, 193; curry, 250; GUMBO, 254; phoenix-tail, 59; SAUTÉED, 96; in PAELLA, 264.
SMALL CHOW FOR CURRY, 250.
SNOW: CAKE, 182; PANCAKES, 26.
SOUFFLÉ, BASIC, 27.
Soup, 177: course and garnishes, 188; "GREEN TURTLE," 163; IN-STANT BORSCHT, 189; TRIPE AND

ONIONS, 105; WATERCRESS, 260.
SOUR CREAM AND RAISIN PIE, 240.
SPAGHETTI, 84.
SPINACH: CREAMED, 210; -pancakes, 61; -puff, 210.
SQUASH: BLOSSOMS, BATTER-FRIED, 168; CREAMED BUTTERNUT, 208.
SQUID: SCALOPPINI, 96; SEPTEMBER, 97.
Steak and kidney pie, 105.
STRAWBERRY: SHORTCAKE, 156; -PINEAPPLE HASH, 123.
STUFFED CUCUMBERS, 130; eggplant, 132; GOOSE, SAUERKRAUT-, 134; grape leaves, 157; mussels, 119; NASTURTIUMS, 130; PIG'S STOM-ACH, 138; QUINCES, 143; vege-tables, 131; (SUCKING PIG), 219.
STUFFED (AND BONING:), 129; bread, 206; ONION, 220.
SUCKING PIG, 219.
SUGAR PIE, 241.
SUKIYAKI, 110.
Sumac (PINK LEMONADE), 167.

TOAD-IN-THE-HOLE, 25.
TOMATO: ASPIC, 263; broiled, 197; dolmas, 132; SAUCE, 143; SOY, 191; STEWED, 211.
TONGUE WITH DILL SAUCE, 99; veal, with white wine sauce, 177.
TORTILLAS, 42.
TRIFLE, 156.
TRIPE AND ONIONS, 105.
TURKEY, 203 ff.: OVERNIGHT, 205; stuffings, 205 ff.; WITH MUSH-ROOMS, 272.
Turkish dishes: CIRCASSIAN CHICK-EN, 117, 119; CIZBIZ KÖFTE, 115; döner kebab, 88; DOLMAS, 131; ETLI BAMYA, 239; Fasulya, 199; IMAM BAYILDI, 132; KARNI YARIK, 239; MIDYE DOLMASI, 119; PIDEH, 55; PILAV, 93; PISTACHIO NUTS FLAMBÉ, 263; STUFFED QUINCES, 143; YALANCI DOLMAS, 157; yoghurt, 187, 251.

Turnips, creamed, 199, 221.
TURTLE SOUP, 163.

Veal: (BLANQUETTE DE VEAU), 102; (CORN-VEAL PIE), 106; loaf, 114; (LOMBO DE VITELA), 90; tongues, 176.
VELOUTÉ SAUCE, 72.
VINEGAR CAKE, 39.

Waffles, 62.

WATERCRESS SOUP, 260.
WATERMELON ICE, 238.
Whale, 111.

YALANCI DOLMAS, 157.
YEAST BREAD, 52.
Yoghurt: for curry, 251; for dessert, 251; for dips, 187.
YORKSHIRE PUDDING, 61.

ZABAGLIONE, 21, 200.